# Materials and Techniques
# of Twentieth-Century Music

# Materials and Techniques of Twentieth-Century Music

## THIRD EDITION

### Stefan Kostka

*University of Texas at Austin*

PEARSON

Prentice
Hall

Upper Saddle River, New Jersey 07458

Library of Congress Cataloging-in-Publication Data

Kostka, Stefan M.
    Materials and techniques of twentieth-century music / Stefan Kostka.—3rd ed.
        p.     cm.
    Includes bibliographical references and index.
    ISBN 0-13-193080-X
    1. Composition (Music)   I. Title.

  MT40.K8 2006
  781.3'09'04—dc22    2005047615

**President, Humanities/Social Sciences:** Yolanda de Rooy
**AVP/Director of Production and Manufacturing:** Barbara Kittle
**Editor-in-Chief:** Sarah Touborg
**Acquisitions Editor:** Christopher T. Johnson
**Editorial Assistant:** Evette Dickerson
**Marketing Manager:** Sheryl Adams
**Marketing Assistant:** Cherron Gardner
**Managing Editor:** Lisa Iarkowski
**Production Editor:** Laura A. Lawrie
**Production Liaison:** Joe Scordato
**Manufacturing Manager:** Nick Sklitsis
**Manufacturing Buyer:** Benjamin Smith
**Cover Art Director:** Jayne Conte
**Cover Design:** Kiwi Design
**Composition:** Preparé

Credits and acknowledgments borrowed from other sources and reproduced,
with permission, in this textbook appear on appropriate page within text.

This book was set in 10/12 Times Roman by Preparé/Emilcomp and printed
by R. R. Donnelley & Sons, Inc. The cover was printed by R. R. Donnelley & Sons, Inc.

Pearson Education LTD.
Pearson Education Singapore, Pte. Ltd
Pearson Education, Canada, Ltd
Pearson Education–Japan

Pearson Education Australia PTY, Limited
Pearson Education North Asia Ltd
Pearson Educatión de Mexico, S.A. de C.V.
Pearson Education Malaysia, Pte. Ltd

10 9 8 7 6 5 4 3 2

ISBN 0-13-193080-X

*For my mother and father*

# Contents

## 3    THE VERTICAL DIMENSION: CHORDS AND SIMULTANEITIES    46

## 4    THE HORIZONTAL DIMENSION: MELODY AND VOICE LEADING    74

# 10 CLASSICAL SERIALISM    198

# 11 TIMBRE AND TEXTURE: ACOUSTIC   222

## 12   TIMBRE AND TEXTURE: ELECTRONIC                          245

## 13   SERIALISM AFTER 1945                                    264

# Preface

Instruction in music theory at the college level has for many years been concerned primarily with the music of the tonal era, spanning roughly some 300 years and including the Baroque, Classical, and Romantic periods. The reasons for this are not hard to imagine. After all, most of the masterworks that are our steady diet as concertgoers and performers were composed during that time, some significant exceptions such as concert-band music notwithstanding. And probably no one who has studied the tonal system in depth has failed to be impressed with what must surely rank as one of the greatest of humanity's artistic achievements.

But the achievements of the twentieth century have also been of great significance, and theorists in recent years have shown interest in devoting more instructional time to the music of that century. One problem, however, has been the lack of appropriate instructional materials. While there are several fine books available on twentieth-century music, few of them deal with the topic in a way that seems appropriate for the general music student, and it is this need that the present text is intended to meet.

*Materials and Techniques of Twentieth-Century Music* is organized primarily by compositional technique and only partly chronologically. Most chapters deal with some aspect of music (rhythm, for instance) throughout the twentieth century, but there is a quasi-chronological method in the ordering of the chapters. No attempt is made in the text to teach music history per se or to explore in detail the styles of individual composers. Instead, the emphasis is on musical materials and compositional techniques. Each chapter includes an introduction, several subheaded sections, and a summary. The discussions are illustrated by a large number of musical examples drawn from the music literature of this century. With few exceptions, the examples are currently available on recording, and as many of them as possible should be listened to. The last part of each chapter consists of exercise material that in most cases is divided into four subsections: Fundamentals, Analysis, Composition, and Further Reading. (See the Bibliography for complete bibliographical references for notes and Further Reading assignments.) Most teachers will find that there are more exercises than they can make use of profitably.

*Materials and Techniques of Twentieth-Century Music* is appropriate for a twentieth-century unit as short as several weeks or as long as a year. In the former case, I suggest omitting some of the chapters that are less vital for a short overview—perhaps Chapters 1, 7, 8, 11, 13, and 15, for example, depending on the interests of the instructor and students. A short course would also have to omit most of the exercise material, but the usefulness of these exercises for class drills and discussion should not be overlooked. Few teaching situations would allow the thorough study of every chapter and the completion of all of the exercises. Some of the Further Reading exercises, in particular, are appropriate only for the more advanced and highly motivated student. Another point to keep in mind is that some chapters (9 and 10, for instance) require more time than the average to complete successfully, while others (such as 8 and 15) require less.

To a certain extent, the chapters in this book are freestanding because they do not follow a chronological sequence, but there are exceptions. Chapter 9, 10, and 13 should be taken up in that order, although other chapters may be interspersed in between them. Also, some instructors assign Chapter 9 very early in the sequence so that students can have longer to practice with the concepts that it presents. Finally, Chapters 2 through 6 form the core foundation for many of the chapters to follow, so it would not be advisable to omit any of them.

## NEW TO THE THIRD EDITION

All of the chapters have been revised to a degree, but six of them received special attention. Chapter 2 (Scale Formations in Twentieth-Century Music) now introduces the augmented (hexatonic) scale. Chapter 9 (Nonserial Atonality) has been revised and expanded to include information on Forte labels and subsets, and the method of determining the best normal order has been modified. In addition, an appendix that contains a listing of set classes, Forte names, and interval-class vectors appears at the end of the book. The serial terminology in Chapters 10 and 13 has been brought into conformity with current practice. Chapter 12 (Timbre and Texture: Electronic) has been extensively rewritten and updated, and Chapter 15 (Minimalism and Beyond) has been revised to include developments since 1995.

The Further Readings lists at the end each chapter have been revised and updated. In addition, there are several new musical examples in this edition, most of them from works by female composers.

## ACKNOWLEDGMENTS

I benefited substantially in the development of this book from the critiques provided by my students at the University of Texas at Austin, and I am grateful for their sympathetic and helpful evaluations. David Rains was generous in sharing his expertise in the area of electronic music, while Mary Blackman applied her considerable organizational skills to the task of obtaining permissions. Thanks go as well to the staff of the Fine Arts Library of the University of Texas, and especially to Olga Buth and Karl Miller, for their expertise and assistance.

Many of the changes found in the second edition were suggested by my friend and colleague, Kent Kennan, whose close reading of the text was most valuable. Other helpful ideas came from James Bennighof of Baylor University, Joseph DiStephano of East Carolina University, William Dougherty of Drake University, and James O'Donnell of Indiana State University. The revision of Chapter 12 was done with a great deal of assistance from Charles Menoche, also of the University of Texas at Austin and a true authority on music technology. The enormous job of obtaining permissions was carried out with great efficiency by Laura Lawrie. Finally, I would like to express my gratitude to my wife, Mary Robertson, for her encouragement and for her inspiring love of music.

A number of people made helpful suggestions that were incorporated into the third edition, and I am grateful to them all but especially to Robert Fleisher of Northern Illinois University, Timothy McKinney of Baylor University, and Kip Wile of the Peabody Conservatory. The revision of Chapter 12 was largely done by Keith Kothman of Ball State Univesity, whose expertise was most appreciated. Other helpful ideas came from William Lake, Bowling Green Univesity, Per F. Broman, Bowling Green University, and Robert Maggio, West Chester University.

Stefan Kostka
*Professor Emeritus*
*University of Texas at Austin*

# ONE

# The Twilight of the Tonal System

## INTRODUCTION

Before beginning our study of the materials of twentieth-century music, we should first look back at what happened to the system of triadic tonality, the primary organizing force in the music of the preceding three centuries. Tonal music and the principles that govern it did not develop overnight, of course, nor did they decline overnight. In fact, tonal music still thrives today in music for television and film, commercials, jazz, and some popular music, and it even began a limited revival in the "serious" music of some postmodern composers toward the end of the twentieth century. Nevertheless, it is safe to say that by around 1900 the tonal system had become so strained by chromaticism and by the desire for originality that further development of the system seemed impossible. The situation was not unlike the one that prevailed around 1600, when the intervallic modal system of the Renaissance had run its course and was giving way to a new emphasis on harmony and what eventually emerged as triadic major/minor tonality. At both points in music history lively debates occurred in print and in person, and at both times there were composers who faithfully held to the older style while others rushed to develop the new. The cause of this crisis at the beginning of the modern era—the decline of the tonal system as an organizing force—is the subject of this chapter.

## DIATONIC TONAL MUSIC

Almost all of the music of the seventeenth and eighteenth centuries is essentially diatonic on all levels.[1] Diatonic tonal music does not, of course, lack accidentals or altered tones; after all, there exists hardly any tonal music of any length that does not contain altered tones. But in diatonic tonal music the difference between diatonic and altered tones is always clear, and seldom do we lose our tonal bearings, our sense of key and scale, and our immediate understanding of the function of the altered tones.

Diatonic relationships also prevail at the background levels of a diatonic tonal composition. Think of the keys that Bach is apt to reach in the course of a fugue, or the traditional key schemes for sonata forms and rondos. All represent diatonic relationships because in all cases the secondary tonalities are closely related to the primary tonality of the movement. Remember that the keys closely related to some primary key are those keys represented by the unaltered major and minor triads in the primary key. In a major key, ii, iii, IV, V, and vi are closely related tonics; in a minor key, III, iv, v, VI, and VII are closely related tonics.

Even at the highest level—key relationships between movements—diatonicism prevails. For example, all of the movements of a Baroque suite will be in a single key (the ultimate in diatonicism). More interesting in terms of the present discussion are the key relationships found in multimovement works of the Classical period. In such works, the first and last movements are *always* in the same tonality (although sometimes in a different mode), and this is considered the key of the composition as a whole. This is a fundamental characteristic of any multimovement tonal composition. In the music of the Classical period, the tendency is for one (and only one) of the inner movements to be in some contrasting but closely related key. Some examples are shown in the list below.

Only two of these works, the first of the Haydn symphonies and the third of the Beethoven quartets, exhibit a nondiatonic relationship between the key of an inner movement and the key of the piece. Both of the exceptions involve a chromatic mediant relationship (to be discussed later).

| *Mozart 8 Piano Sonatas K. 330–333, 457, 545 570, 576 (1778–89)* | *Haydn: 6 Symphonies, Nos. 99–104 (1793–95)* | *Beethoven: 6 String Quartets, Op. 18 (1800)* |
|---|---|---|
| I–IV–I | I–III–I–I | I–vi–I–I |
| I–I–I | I–IV–I–I | I–IV–I–I |
| I–IV–I | I–IV–I–I | I–♭VI–I–I |
| I–IV–I | I–V–I–I | i–I–i–i |
| i–III–i | I–vi–I–I | I–I–IV–I |
| I–V–I | I–IV–I–I | I–IV–I–I |
| I–IV–I | | |
| I–V–I | | |

## CHROMATIC TONAL MUSIC

The point at which tonal music becomes chromatic instead of diatonic is not an absolute one. Much of the harmony of chromatic tonal music can be analyzed by using the same vocabulary for altered chords, modulations, chromatic nonchord tones, and so forth, that we use in the analysis of diatonic music. It is partly a matter of emphasis. Instead of a texture with diatonic tones predominating over nondiatonic tones, both in number and in significance, we are dealing here with music that is so saturated with chromaticism that the diatonic basis of the music is no longer apparent to the listener. One writer refers to this style as "ultrachromaticism," which "results from the prevalent use—both harmonically and melodically—of the twelve tones of the chromatic scale."[2] Another puts it this way: "The critical distinction between the two styles lies in the transformation of the diatonic scalar material of the classical tonal system into the equally-tempered twelve note chromatic complex of the chromatic tonal system."[3] Using these broad definitions as a starting point, we will examine some of the details of nineteenth-century chromatic harmony. In one chapter our discussion cannot be as detailed as those found in several admirable books on this subject,[4] but it should be sufficient to suggest some analytical approaches to the style.

## CHROMATIC HARMONY

Two fundamental root movements in diatonic tonal harmony involve (1) the circle-of-5ths progression, as in vi–ii–V–I; and (2) the diatonic mediant progression, as in I–vi–IV–ii. Though these progressions by no means disappear in chromatic harmony, another relationship, the **chromatic mediant relationship,** finds a popularity that it did not have in earlier styles. Two triads or keys are in a chromatic mediant relationship if they are of the same quality (major or minor) and their roots are a major 3rd or minor 3rd apart. These relationships are illustrated in Example 1–1 (lowercase indicates minor). For some reason, the major-mode chromatic mediants (top staff of Example 1–1) seem to have been used more often than the minor-mode versions. Notice that in each case the two triads share exactly one pitch class.[5] Third-related triads of opposite quality (major and minor) sharing no pitch classes at all are said to be in a **doubly chromatic mediant relationship** (e.g., C major and E♭ minor). Chromatic and doubly chromatic mediants are more difficult to recognize if one of the chords is enharmonically spelled. For instance, the first pair of chords in Example 1–1 would still be in a chromatic mediant relationship if the second chord were spelled as C♭ major instead of B major.

EXAMPLE 1–1    Chromatic mediant relationships

Two examples from Liszt's *Les Préludes* illustrate the effective use of chromatic mediants. In the first (Example 1–2), the relationship is not between chords, but between the keys of C major and E major. Notice that this is a **direct modulation** (one that does not make use of a common chord between the two keys), but the modulation is smoothed over by the common tone (A♭/G♯) between the F minor and E major triads at the double bar.

EXAMPLE 1–2   Liszt: *Les Préludes* (1854), mm. 51–54

Chromatic mediant relationships between triads in a nonmodulating passage contribute to the color and excitement of Example 1–3. The excerpt is clearly in C major, and it uses the following progression:

C–a–F–d–B♭–G–C–A♭–F–C

Certainly both the circle-of-5ths and diatonic mediant progressions are important here, but the three chromatic mediant relationships (indicated by the "<m>" symbols in the example) add a certain freshness and unpredictability to the harmony of the passage. Incidentally, this simplified piano reduction gives only a hint of what this music is really like; try to listen to a recording with the full score.

EXAMPLE 1–3    Liszt: *Les Préludes* (1854), mm. 35–42 (simplified texture)

Example 1–4 provides a further illustration of chromatic mediants, and several other things besides. Chord roots, inversions, and qualities are indicated below the example. The progression contains two circle-of-5ths progressions (D–G and C–f) and three chromatic mediants. It also contains two **tritone relationships** (indicated by the "<t>" symbols in

the example), a root movement commonly found in earlier music in only a few progressions (IV–vii° in major, VI–ii° in minor, and N6–V). A listener could interpret Example 1–4 as a IV6–N6–V–I6 progression in G, followed by an identical progression in F, ending on a minor tonic. Except for the last chord, the excerpt illustrates a **real sequence,** a sequence in which the pattern is transposed exactly, as opposed to a diatonic sequence, where only the notes of a single diatonic scale are used, thus reproducing the pattern only approximately. A real sequence has the effect of quickly throwing the music out of one key and into another, even if only for the duration of a few chords. Real sequences contribute a good deal to the **brief tonicizations** that are typical of much chromatic harmony.

**EXAMPLE 1–4**   Wagner: *Siegfried* (1871), Act II, Scene I

WANDERER

C $^6$ <m> A♭ $^6$ <t> D    G $^6$ <m>B♭ $^6$ <m> G♭ $^6$ <t>  C          f

A real sequence begins Example 1–5 (mm. 1–4), using only dominant 7th chords (the last one enharmonically spelled) from the keys of D♭, B♭, E, and D♭ again. The root movements involve two chromatic mediant relationships and one tritone. Notice that in each case the dominant 7th chords share exactly two pitch classes. This is true only of dominant 7ths whose roots are separated by a minor 3rd or a tritone. Example 1–5 illustrates two more characteristics of chromatic harmony—**suspended tonality** and **enharmonicism.** The first term is used to refer to passages that are tonally ambiguous. The dominant 7th chords in Example 1–5 do little to establish any key, because they are both unexpected and unresolved, and the A♭7–C–A♭ progression that ends the excerpt is of little help. Presumably Liszt had the tonality of A♭ in mind, since the piece ends similarly to mm. 5–6. Play through the example, and see what you think. The enharmonicism involves the chord in m. 4. We hear all of the chords in mm. 1–4 as dominant 7th chords, but the chord in m. 4 is spelled as a German augmented-6th chord in C, resolving to a I6 instead of to the conventional tonic $^6_4$. Another kind of enharmonicism makes use of the ambiguous nature of the diminished-7th chord; an example would be to lead the listener to think a chord will resolve as a b°$^7$ chord but to resolve it as a g♯°$^7$ chord instead.

**EXAMPLE 1–5**  Liszt: "Blume and Duft" ("Flower and Fragrance") (1862), mm. 1–6

**Parallel voice leading,** keeping the chord type constant, is seldom found in diatonic tonal music, but it is a favored device of chromaticism. Probably the first sonority to be used in this fashion was the **diminished-7th chord,** as in Example 1–6. Here, in a passage modulating from C minor to E♭ major, four diminished-7th chords move in parallel motion down by half-steps in mm. 40–45. Notice that the spelling of the diminished-7th chords suggests that Beethoven was thinking of a circle-of-5ths progression, even though the listener might not perceive it that way:

*Circle of 5ths, Using*
*Dominant 7th Chords*

*Circle of 5ths, Substituting*
*Diminished-7th Chords*

D7–G7–C7–F7

f♯°7–b°7–e°7–a°7

EXAMPLE 1–6   Beethoven: *Coriolan Overture*, Op. 62 (1807), mm. 36–46
(simplified texture)

But no such functional analysis is possible in the next example. Here Wagner portrays ravens in flight by means of parallel half-diminished-7th chords, some of them enharmonically spelled. The effect is not one of a progression of chords toward a harmonic goal, but more like a line painted with a broad brush instead of drawn with a pen. Obviously, none of these chords function in the ways that half-diminished-7th chords do in diatonic harmony. The chords in Example 1–7 form a **nonfunctional chord succession,** which does not imply that it is useless, but rather that the chords do not "progress" in any of the ways found in diatonic tonal harmony.

EXAMPLE 1–7   Wagner: *Götterdämmerung* (1874), Act III, Scene 2

Nonfunctional chord successions are often the result of what we shall call **voice-leading chords**. Such chords are the result of goal-directed motion in the various voices, rather than an attempt to express some traditional harmonic progression. (Voice-leading chords such as the augmented-6th chord and the so-called omnibus progression[6] also may be found on occasion in tonal harmony.) This goal-directed motion is usually stepwise, often chromatic, sometimes in similar motion and sometimes not. The resulting verticalities are usually tertian (triads and 7th chords), but the chords form nonfunctional successions or brief tonicizations. For instance, play through Example 1–8. The essential elements are a chromatic descent from B4 to E4 in the top voice and B2 to E2 in the bass to make a convincing cadence.[7] The soprano and alto move in parallel major thirds until the last two beats, the alto stopping its descent upon reaching the leading tone, which eventually resolves. The tenor enters on a C4 and moves in parallel motion with the upper voices for three beats, stops momentarily on Bb/A♯3, and then moves to the 7th of the dominant chord before resolving to G3. The bass enters last, doubling the soprano momentarily before moving into its cadential figure. On a higher level, the progression in this excerpt is simply tonic–dominant–tonic, beginning with the incomplete tonic triad at the opening of the phrase. But on the surface, the chords created by the various voices, beginning with beat 2 of the first measure, are as follows (the c°7 and the F7 are enharmonically spelled):

F–E–Eb–c°7–F7–B7 (b5)–e

Although there is a IV6–ii°7–V$_3^4$ progression in Bb here, it is doubtful that anyone would hear it that way. The only traditional harmonic progression in the excerpt is the final authentic cadence (with a lowered 5th in the dominant 7th creating a French 6th sonority). The music preceding the cadence makes use of voice-leading chords and creates a nonfunctional chord succession.

**EXAMPLE 1–8**  Grieg: "Gone," Op. 71, No. 6 (1901), mm. 1–2 (*From Edition Peters.*)

The voice-leading chords in Example 1–8 were created primarily by parallel or similar motion. Three independent gestures combine to produce the voice-leading chords in Example 1–9. The first gesture is a chromatic ascent in the melody from F♯4 to G5 (doubled at the octave above). The second element is an augmented triad in the inner voices (beginning in the third measure of the excerpt), which moves, more slowly than the soprano, chromatically downward through a minor 3rd. The final element is the ostinato in the bass, swaying back and forth from B♭2 to A2, finally settling on A. The nonfunctional voice-leading chords created by the combination of these three gestures are sometimes tertian and sometimes not; some of them are highly dissonant (mm. 38–39, for example). Suspended tonality is the result, even at the end, where the final sonority does little to confirm the presumed tonality of G.

**EXAMPLE I–9**   Liszt: "Gray Clouds" ("Nuages gris") (1881), mm. 33–48   *(© Copyright 1952 Schott & Co., Ltd., London. Copyright renewed. All rights reserved. Used by permission of European American Music Distributors Corporation, sole U.S. and Canadian agent for Schott & Co., Ltd., London)*

**Unresolved dissonances,** as in the Liszt example, are typical of some late nineteenth-century music. In many cases they come about through the juxtaposition of apparently independent musical ideas (melodies, sequences, and so on) with no attempt being made to put those dissonances into any traditional context, and they often contribute to a feeling of suspended tonality.

Augmented triads and diminished-7th chords are both examples of **equal division of the octave.** Real sequences also frequently divide the octave into equal parts, usually by transposing the pattern by a minor 3rd or a major 3rd. Traditional division of the octave had been asymmetrical, as in the perfect 5th and perfect 4th of the tonic-dominant relationship and the major and minor 2nds that make up the major scale.

The music of Example 1–10 is less radical tonally than the previous example, but the voice leading is much more complex. All of the voices of the predominantly four-part texture in the piano tend to move by step, often chromatically, but there is no preconceived pattern to be discovered. The **nonfunctional bass line** does little to help us get our tonal bearings, except at the end, where a V7–I cadence in G major is apparent. Often in the excerpt the distinction between chord tones and embellishments is unclear, making chord labeling difficult. Nevertheless, if you play through the example slowly, you will notice the following:

> D major tonic (m. 7)
> Tonicization of A minor (E7–F in mm. 7–8 sounds like a: V7–VI)
> Tonicization of B♭ major (F7–B♭ in m. 9)
> Tonicization of C minor (G7–c in m. 10)
> Modulation to G major (iv6–Ger+6–$I_4^6$–V7–I in mm. 10–12)

A truly thorough analysis would have to consider the function, harmonic or otherwise, of all of the notes in the passage, but it will often serve the purposes of the performer or student just as well to identify the broader harmonic motions, as we have done in this case.

## CHROMATICISM AND MUSICAL FORM

The diatonic tonal relationships typically found within single movements in the Classical period (typically I–V or i–III) are gradually replaced in the nineteenth century with chromatic tonal relationships. While there are still many works from the nineteenth century that employ the traditional key schemes, a good number of others explore other relationships. A famous early example is the first movement of Beethoven's "Waldstein" Sonata, Op. 53, where the two keys of the exposition are C major and E major.

More destructive to the tonal system is the notion of beginning a movement in one key and ending it in another.[8] "Wrong key" beginnings, in which the listener is deliberately led astray for a few bars, constituted the first step. Examples include Beethoven's Symphony No. 1 (1799), beginning with a V7/IV, and the last movement of Mendelssohn's Piano Concerto No. 1 (1831), which begins with a short section in the supertonic key.

Still more experimental are the numerous works that seem to be in two keys. Two types can be identified. In the first, the piece contains two distinct parts, each in its own key. Examples include Schubert's Waltzes, Op. 50, Nos. 7, 24, and 31 (1825), and Chopin's Ballade No. 2, Op. 38 (1839). In the second type, the tonality of the work alternates more than once between a major key and its relative minor. Examples include Schubert's German Dance, Op. 33, No. 15, and Schumann's Davidsbündlertanz, Op. 6, No. 11 (1837).

EXAMPLE I–10   Hugo Wolf: "Anacreon's Grave" ("Anakreons Grab") (1888), mm. 7–12

The final stage is reached with those works that proceed through several keys, with none of them seeming to govern the tonality of the piece as a whole. Such works simply cannot be considered "tonal" in the traditional sense of the term. Examples include Liszt's symphonic poem *Orpheus* (1854) and the first movement of Saint-Saëns's Symphony No. 3 (1886).

There was also experimentation in the nineteenth century with unusual key schemes among the various movements of multimovement works. The greatest challenge to the tonal tradition came from those works in which the first and last movements are not in the same key. For instance, the three movements of Mendelssohn's Symphony No. 2 (1840) are in B♭ major, G minor, and D major. With Mahler the practice is almost a mannerism: Symphonies Nos. 2, 3, 4, 5, 7, and 9 (1894–1909) all belong to this category.

## SUSPENDED TONALITY AND ATONALITY

Earlier in this chapter we used the term "suspended tonality" to describe a passage with a momentarily unclear or ambiguous tonality. This term is appropriate only when used in the context of a tonal composition. It is not the same as **atonality,** a term that will appear frequently in this text, and which needs to be defined at this point.[9]

In a very general way, atonality means music without a tonal center. More specifically, it refers to the systematic avoidance of most of those musical materials and devices that traditionally have been used to define a tonal center. Those materials and devices would include, among others, the following:

Diatonic pitch material

Tertian harmonies

Dominant–tonic harmonic progressions

Dominant–tonic bass lines

Resolution of leading tones to tonics

Resolution of dissonant sonorities to more consonant ones

Pedal points

Although chromaticism led historically to atonality, chromatic tonal music is not the same as atonal music. A more thorough study of atonality will have to be postponed until later chapters, although the term will come up from time to time throughout this text.

*SUMMARY*

The decline of the tonal system as the primary organizing force in music coincided with and was largely due to the ascendancy of chromaticism. Diatonic tonal music is essentially diatonic on all levels, whereas chromatic tonal music is based to a much greater extent on the chromatic scale. Some of the characteristics of chromatic tonal harmony are the following (listed in the order in which they are introduced in the chapter):

    Chromatic mediant relationships
    Direct modulations
    Tritone relationships
    Real sequences
    Brief tonicizations
    Suspended tonality
    Enharmonicism
    Parallel voice leading
    Diminished-7th chords
    Nonfunctional chord successions
    Voice-leading chords
    Augmented triads
    Unresolved dissonances
    Equal division of the octave
    Nonfunctional bass lines
    Unclear distinction between chord tones and embellishments

Chromaticism is also a factor in musical forms in the nineteenth century, both within and between movements. At times, tonality lost its control over the tonal structure of individual movements and of multimovement works as well.

Atonality is not a characteristic of music of the nineteenth century. Atonal music avoids the use of most of those musical materials and devices that traditionally have been used to define a tonal center.

*NOTES*

1. "Diatonic" here simply means "in a given key." The notes and chords diatonic to C major are all drawn from the scale C–D–E–F–G–A–B–C.
2. Greg A. Steinke, *Bridge to 20th Century Music*, p. 79.
3. Gregory Proctor, "Technical Bases of Nineteenth-Century Chromatic Harmony: A Study in Chromaticism," p. 131.

4. See, for example, notes 2 and 3.

5. The term "pitch class" is used to group together all pitches that have an identical sound or that are identical except for the octave or octaves that separate them. For example, all B♯'s, C's, and D♭♭'s belong to the same pitch class, no matter in what octave they are found.

6. The omnibus progression is discussed in Benward/Saker, pp. 227–228, Gauldin, pp. 599–602, and Kostka/Payne, pp. 455–457.

7. Octave registers in this book follow the convention that names the octave starting with middle C as octave no. 4, the one below it as octave no. 3, and so on.

8. Much of the discussion that follows is based on: Sarah Reid, "Tonality's Changing Role: A Survey of Non-Concentric Instrumental Works of the Nineteenth Century."

9. There are various well-founded objections to this term. Nevertheless, it has by now attained a permanent place in our theoretical vocabulary, whereas possible improvements, such as "pantonality," have not. Also, though "atonal" is used by some writers only in reference to the preserial works of the second Viennese school, it is used in this book in its broader meaning of "not tonal."

## EXERCISES

### Part A: Fundamentals

1. For each triad below, list the four triads that are in a chromatic mediant relationship to it.

    B♭ major      C minor      F major      D minor      E major

2. Name several traditional chord progressions in tonal harmony that make use of chromatic mediant relationships. Use Roman numerals.

    Example: IV–V/V

3. Which of the following progressions involves dominant 7th chords that share two pitch classes?

    V7–V7/vi      V7/ii–V7/V      V7/IV–V7/V

4. For each dominant 7th chord below, list the three dominant 7th chords that share two pitch classes with it.

    E♭7      G7      F7      C♯7

## Part B: Analysis

1. Fauré: Barcarolle No. 6, Op. 70 (1896), mm. 24–28

   (a) This passage begins and ends in B major, but chords 4 and 5 imply some other key, although one of them is spelled enharmonically. What key is it, and what is its relationship to B major?

   (b) The raised 5th in chord 6 results in how many common pitch classes between chords 5 and 6?

   (c) Provide Roman numerals for all of the chords.

2. Berlioz: Requiem (1837), mm. 66–78.
   This passage modulates from B♭ major to G minor.

   (a) Are the keys of B♭ major and G minor in a chromatic mediant relationship?

   (b) Still another tonality is implied in mm. 71–74. What is it, and what is the relationship between that key and G minor?

   (c) Explain the construction of mm. 66–68.

   (d) Provide a Roman-numeral analysis in G minor of mm. 68–70 and mm. 75–78.

3. Grieg: "Summer's Eve," Op. 71, No. 2 (1901), mm. 9–19

   (a) Label the root and chord type of each of the numbered chords (e.g., "G7," "f♯," etc.).

   (b) List the tonalities implied by these chords.

   (c) Which of those tonalities is confirmed by a tonic triad?

   (d) The sixteenth-note figures use pitches from what tonalities?

   (e) What single tonality is the most important in this passage?

   (f) How many pitch classes are shared by chords 9 and 11? chords 12 and 14? chords 15 and 16?

   (g) Do these shared pitch classes appear in the same register?

   (h) Discuss the use of sequence in this passage.

4. Brahms: "Der Tod, das ist die kühle Nacht," Op. 96, No. 1 (1884), mm. 7–10.

   (a) Analyze the first and last chords in the key of C.

   (b) Label the roots and qualities of all of the other chords.

   (c) Assuming that second-inversion triads tend to be heard as tonic $^6_4$ chords, list all of the keys implied by dominant 7th chords or $^6_4$ chords.

   (d) The tonalities other than C are weakly implied, at best. Explain in your own words what is really going on in this passage.

5. Wagner: *Siegfried*, Act I, Scene 1

   (a) Explain this passage as best you can in your own words, following the approaches used in the previous exercises and in the chapter text. Incidentally, would there be any justification for hearing the B♭ in chord no. 7 as an A♯?

Stahl     nicht     hart     und     fest?

## Part C: Composition

1. Continue this example, using chromatic mediants above the asterisks and employing conventional voice leading.

C     *     G     *     C     *     F     D$^7$     G

2. Wagner: *Siegfried*, Act I, Scene 2
   Use the first two measures of this accompaniment as the first part of a three-part real sequence, moving down a minor 2nd each time. Place a <m> between each pair of chords in a chromatic mediant relationship.

e - wig ge - hor - chen sie   al  -  le       des  Spree  -  -  -  res

3. Using only augmented triads in a four-voice texture, see if you can combine a chromatically ascending soprano line with a circle-of-5ths sequence in the bass. Continue for several chords.

4. Compose a passage similar to Example 1–9, using a chromatically descending melody with chromatically ascending half-diminished-7th chords as an accompaniment. The accompaniment chords should be in second inversion and should ascend faster than the melody descends. Let the dissonances fall where they may.

5. Compose an example in four-part texture using a conventional harmonic progression and employing mostly stepwise motion in all of the voices. Then elaborate with a generous application of stepwise nonchord tones, especially chromatic passing tones, neighbors, and suspensions. The added tones, in most cases, should not create sharp dissonances (minor 2nds, major 7ths) with the chord tones or with each other. Be sure to do this work at a piano! The excerpt below can serve as an example.

## FURTHER READING

The suggested reading assignments are intended to help you get a broader exposure to the subject of this chapter. The approach and terminology used in the texts will probably differ from each other as well as from this text. Complete bibliographical information is provided in the Bibliography at the end of this book.

ALDWELL, EDWARD, AND CARL SCHACHTER. *Harmony and Voice Leading.* See Chapter 31, Chromatic Voice-Leading Techniques, and Chapter 32, Chromaticism in Larger Contexts.

BENWARD, BRUCE, AND MARILYN SAKER. *Music in Theory and Practice*, Vol. 2. See Chapter 12, Chromatic Mediants.

KOSTKA, STEFAN, AND DOROTHY PAYNE. *Tonal Harmony with an Introduction to Twentieth-Century Music.* See Chapter 27, Tonal Harmony in the Late Nineteenth Century.

SAMSON, JIM. *Music in Transition.* See Chapter 1, The Nineteenth-Century Background.

SIMMS, BRYAN R. *Music of the Twentieth Century.* See Chapter 1, Tonality in Transition.

STEINKE, GREG A. *Bridge to 20th Century Music.* See Chapter 4, Expanded Tonality, Chapter 5, Ultrachromaticism I, Chapter 6, Ultrachromaticism II, and Chapter 7, Denial of Harmonic Function.

# TWO

# Scale Formations in Twentieth-Century Music

## INTRODUCTION

The music of the Baroque, Classical, and Romantic periods was based almost exclusively on the major and minor scales with which we are all familiar. Though these scales have not been discarded altogether, composers in this century have also made use of a large number of other scale formations. Not all of these scale formations are new—in fact, some of them had been used long before the tonal era and had since fallen out of fashion. But new or old, these scales were all unfamiliar to audiences accustomed to major/minor tonality, and so they helped composers to distance themselves from the older style.

It is unusual in the twentieth century to find an entire piece that uses only a single scale (with the exception of chromatic and microtonal scales). Instead, one typically finds that only a few measures will use a particular scale, or the melody may conform to the scale while the accompaniment does not, or the music may include only a few notes that seem to imply the scale.

The organization of this chapter is based on the number of notes in the scale; that is, five-note scales first, then six-note, and so on. (In counting the number of notes, we do not include the octave, so the major scale, for instance, is a seven-note scale.) Examples have been chosen to illustrate clearly the scales being discussed, but the reader should be aware that in much music it would be difficult to say with certainty what scale formation is the basis of a given passage.

## FIVE-NOTE SCALES

"Pentatonic" is a generic term for all five-note scales, but when one refers to *the* pentatonic scale, the scale in Example 2–1 is usually the one that is meant. Notice that it uses only major seconds and minor thirds. Because this version of the pentatonic scale contains no half steps, it is sometimes called the **anhemitonic pentatonic scale.** The pentatonic scale is often used to give an oriental flavor to a passage, but it certainly occurs often enough outside of the Orient, particularly in folk melodies and children's songs.

EXAMPLE 2–1    The Pentatonic Scale

Any member of the pentatonic scale can serve as tonic; thus, five "modes," or rotations, are available.

EXAMPLE 2–2    Modes of the Pentatonic Scale

And, of course, the pentatonic scale can be transposed.

EXAMPLE 2–3    Transpositions of the Pentatonic Scale

The pentatonic scale is obviously a limited source of melodic pitch material, and it is also limited in its tertian harmonies. The only tertian chords that could be constructed from Example 2–1 are triads on C and A and a minor 7th chord on A. This means that the accompaniment to a pentatonic melody will probably be either nontertian or nonpentatonic or both. In Example 2–4 Bartók harmonizes a pentatonic melody (top line in the example) with major triads, using the melody note as the root of the triad in each case. The accompaniment here uses no particular scale, although the tonality is certainly C. A few measures later, the same melody is harmonized again with major triads, but this time each melody note is the 5th of its triad. The last melody note is changed to a D, resulting in a "half-cadence" on a G chord.

EXAMPLE 2–4    Bartók: *Bluebeard's Castle* (1911) (piano reduction)    *(© Copyright 1921, 1925 in the USA by Boosey & Hawkes, Inc. Copyright renewed. Reprinted by permission.)*

Other versions of the pentatonic scale are possible—versions employing minor 2nds and major 3rds—but they occur less often in Western music. One example is the scale sometimes known as the **Hirajoshi pentatonic**—as in A–B–C–E–F—which occurs in the closing section of George Rochberg's *Slow Fires of Autumn* (1979) and in the second movement of Janice Giteck's *Om Shanti* (1986); another, sometimes called the **Kumoi pentatonic**—as in D–E–F–A–B—was used by Ralph Vaughan Williams for the opening theme of his Concerto for Bass Tuba (1954) and by Jonathan Kramer in his *Moving Music* (1976).

## SIX-NOTE SCALES

The only six-note scale to see much use in the twentieth century is the **whole-tone scale.** It is constructed entirely from major 2nds (although one of them has to be notated as a diminished 3rd). In terms of pitch-class content, only two whole-tone scales are possible; any other transposition or "mode" will simply duplicate the pitch-class content of one of the scales in Example 2–5. The actual spelling of the scale is usually irrelevant; for instance, the first scale in the example could have used G♭–A♭–B♭ instead of F♯–G♯–A♯. The scales in Example 2–5 are labeled according to a convention that identifies the whole-tone scale that contains a C as WT–0 and the scale that does not as WT–1.

EXAMPLE 2–5    Whole-Tone Scales

The whole-tone scale is often associated with Impressionism, and especially with Debussy, but it is also found in the music of many other composers. Interestingly, it is even more limited than the pentatonic scale, both melodically and harmonically. No triads other than augmented ones are possible, and the only complete seventh chords available are the dominant seventh with the fifth lowered (the traditional French augmented-sixth sonority) or raised.

Example 2–6 begins with three measures using WT–0 followed by two measures using WT–1. The tonality or tonalities of the passage would be open to some interpretation.

**EXAMPLE 2–6**  Paul Dukas: *Ariadne and Bluebeard* (1906), Act III

A more recent use of the whole-tone scale is seen in Example 2–7. Here the whole-tone scale (WT–0) is in the vocal duet, except for the A at the end of Toni's melody. Notice that the pitch class G♯/A♭ is spelled one way in Hilda's part in m. 984 and another way in m. 986. The tonal center of this excerpt, if there is one, would be difficult to determine. The accompaniment will be discussed in more detail later in this chapter.

EXAMPLE 2–7   Hans Werner Henze: *Elegy for Young Lovers* (1961), Act I, Scene 12, mm. 984–986

The **augmented scale** (sometimes called the "hexatonic scale"), which also saw some use in both concert music and jazz in the twentieth century, consists of alternating half steps and minor 3rds. Two related instances are seen in Example 2–8, in both of which four-note sonorities are transposed down a minor 6th to create an augmented scale. Notice that the pitch-class content of the two scales is the same: C–C♯–E–F–A♭–A.

EXAMPLE 2–8    Ellen Taaffe Zwilich: Piano Trio (1987), III (piano only)    *(© Theodore Presser Co.)*

## SEVEN-NOTE SCALES: THE DIATONIC MODES

Modal scales had been largely out of favor with composers since the beginning of the Baroque, although interesting exceptions, such as the Phrygian opening of Chopin's Mazurka in C♯ minor, Op. 41, No. 1 (1839), do occur. But modality was enthusiastically rediscovered by a number of early twentieth-century composers. Though the modal theory of the Renaissance recognized both authentic and plagal modes, the distinction is not important in modern usage. One way to present the modes is to notate them using the pitches of the C major scale.

EXAMPLE 2–9    The Diatonic Modes

The Ionian mode is the same as the major scale, although some writers find it useful to use "Ionian" to refer to major-mode passages that do not employ traditional harmonic progressions. The Locrian mode has rarely been used, probably because it lacks a consonant tonic triad. An unusually clear use of the Locrian mode occurs in the opening of Shostakovich's String Quartet No. 10, Op. 118 (1964), second movement.

It is most efficient to learn the modes in relation to the major and natural-minor scale patterns. The following information should be memorized:

*Major Modal Patterns*

Lydian: same as major with raised $\hat{4}$.*

Mixolydian: same as major with lowered $\hat{7}$.

*Minor Modal Patterns*

Aeolian: same as natural minor.

Dorian: same as natural minor with raised $\hat{6}$.

Phrygian: same as natural minor with lowered $\hat{2}$.

Locrian: same as natural minor with lowered $\hat{2}$ and lowered $\hat{5}$.

You will not always be able to identify the scale being used just by determining the tonic and looking at the key signature because not all composers use modal key signatures. Instead, a composer might use the conventional major or minor key signature and add the accidentals necessary to produce the modal scale desired. This is the case in Example 2–10, where we see a G minor key signature used for a G Phrygian theme. Notice the leading-tone F♯ in the viola. Such nonscale tones are as common in modal music as they are in major/minor music, and we should not let them confuse us in our analysis.

EXAMPLE 2–10  Debussy: String Quartet, Op. 10 (1893), I, mm. 1–3

Animé et très décidé

*The caret over a number indicates scale degree.

There is no key signature at all for Example 2–11, the opening theme of a movement in A. The accompaniment to this Lydian tune consists only of A major triads in second inversion.

EXAMPLE 2–11    Bartók: *Music for String Instruments, Percussion, and Celesta* (1936), IV, mm. 5–9
(melody only)    *(© Copyright 1937 in the USA by Boosey & Hawkes, Inc. Copyright renewed. Reprinted by permission.)*

In Example 2–12 the music drifts easily from D Aeolian (mm. 1–4) into D Dorian (mm. 5–7). A change in modal flavor such as we find here is a frequently encountered device. Note that this is *not* a modulation, because the tonal center is unchanged.

EXAMPLE 2–12    Debussy: *Preludes, Book I* (1910), No. 6, "Footprints in the Snow"
("Des pas sur la neige"), mm. 1–7

## OTHER SEVEN-NOTE SCALES

Many other seven-note scales are possible, although none of them have been used as frequently as the diatonic modes. Fourteen modes can be derived from the scales shown in Example 2–13. All of them use major and minor 2nds exclusively, yet none of them is identical to any of the diatonic modes. These two scale systems, along with our familiar diatonic modal system, exhaust the possibilities for seven-note scales using only major and minor 2nds.

EXAMPLE 2–13   Two Seven-Note Scale Systems

You may expect to encounter these scale formations occasionally in twentieth-century music. The first scale in Example 2–13 (a mode of the melodic minor scale) was used several times by Bartók, and it has acquired the name Lydian-Mixolydian because of its combination of raised 4th and lowered 7th scale degrees. Debussy makes momentary use of this scale on C in the first three measures of Example 2–14. Then the G and A are replaced by A♭ in m. 148, resulting in the WT–0 whole-tone scale.

EXAMPLE 2–14   Debussy: *The Joyous Isle (L'isle joyeuse)* (1904), mm. 145–151

Some seven-note scales make use of one or more augmented seconds. A familiar example is the harmonic minor scale. Example 2–15 would seem to be constructed from a G Aeolian scale with a raised fourth scale degree.

EXAMPLE 2–15   Grieg: "Shepherd Boy," Op. 54, No. 1 (1891), mm. 1–8   *(From Edition Peters.)*

To list all of the possibilities would be impractical.[1] It is enough to be aware that a particular passage must be approached on its own terms, not with the assumption that only certain scales are allowed.

## EIGHT-NOTE SCALES

**Octatonic**, like pentatonic, is a generic term that has nevertheless come to refer to a specific scale. This scale, illustrated in Example 2–16, consists of alternating whole and half steps, so another name for this scale is the **whole-step-half-step scale**. Yet another name for it is the **diminished scale**, which refers to the fact that any two nonenharmonic diminished-7th chords combined will produce an octatonic scale (in Example 2–16a they are $f\#^{o7}$ and $g\#^{o7}$). There are only two modes to this scale—one beginning with a whole step (Example 2–16a) and one beginning with a half step (Example 2–16b). In addition, there are only three possible transpositions: the two shown here and one that combines a $d^{o7}$ and an $e^{o7}$ (or their enharmonic equivalents). Any other transposition or mode will simply duplicate the pitch-class content of one of these three octatonic scales. The actual spelling of an octatonic scale is optional; for instance, the F♯ and G♯ in Example 2–16a could have been written as G♭ and A♭.

EXAMPLE 2–16   The Octatonic Scale

The octatonic scale is a rich source of melodic and harmonic material. It contains all of the intervals, from minor 2nd up to major 7th. All of the tertian triads except for the augmented triad can be extracted from this scale, as can four of the five common 7th-chord types (the major-7th chord cannot). If it has a weakness, it is its symmetrical construction, a characteristic it shares with the whole-tone scale, which can make establishment of a tonal center more difficult.

Certain nineteenth-century Russian composers, notably Rimsky-Korsakov, were among the first to make use of the octatonic scale. An excerpt from a twentieth-century Russian work appears as Example 2–17. In this passage Scriabin uses the octatonic scale formed by diminished-7th chords on A and A♯ (or C and C♯, etc.—the spellings are arbitrary). The tonality here, if there is one, would seem to be E♭.

**EXAMPLE 2–17**   Alexander Scriabin: Prelude, Op. 74, No. 5 (1914), mm. 14–17   *(Excerpted from the International Music Co. edition, New York, NY 10018.)*

Another Russian-born composer whose name is associated with the octatonic scale is Stravinsky.[2] Diminished-7th chords on B and C♯ account for all of the pitch material in the first 6½ measures of Example 2–18. The C♮ in the bassoon begins a transition back to a diatonic pitch material. The horns are in F in this excerpt.

**EXAMPLE 2–18   Stravinsky:** *Oedipus Rex* **(1927), rehearsal no. 158**

While the use of whole-tone and modal scales declined as the twentieth century progressed, the opposite seems to have been true of the octatonic scale, which made frequent appearances even in music of the 1990s. The octatonic scale has also found a home in contemporary jazz, where it is especially useful in improvisation over diminished-7th chords and altered dominants.

## THE CHROMATIC SCALE

Many musical passages in the twentieth century avail themselves of all or nearly all of the tones of the chromatic scale. In some cases it is only the harmony or only the melody that is chromatic, while in other cases both are. In Example 2–19 Hindemith omits only the pitch class D in the course of an eighteen-note melody. Hindemith's melody is obviously a tonal one, beginning strongly on F and ending with a convincing melodic cadence on A. We could even "explain" the chromaticism in terms of diatonic scales—F major (notes 1–6), Gb major (notes 7–14), and A minor (notes 14–18)—but such explanations of chromatic passages are not always helpful. Turn back to Example 2–7 and consider the accompaniment. The voices, you will recall, are confined almost entirely to a whole-tone scale, but the accompaniment uses the chromatic scale as its pitch source. All twelve notes of the chromatic scale are used in the first 1½ measures of the accompaniment, and though there are some conventional sonorities (an A major triad in m. 984 and a Db major triad in m. 986), it makes no sense to attempt to discuss the accompaniment in terms of any scale other than the chromatic.

EXAMPLE 2–19   Paul Hindemith: Sonata for Trombone and Piano (1941), I, mm. 1–5
(trombone only)   *(©Schott & Co., Ltd., London, 1942. Renewed. Assigned to B. Schott's Soehne, Mainz. All rights reserved. Used by permission by European American Music Distributors Corporation, sole U.S. and Canadian agent for B. Schott's Soehne, Mainz.)*

## MICROTONAL SCALES

In modern usage, *microtone* means any interval smaller than a minor second. While we might assume that microtones are a very recent discovery, they actually were used in the music of ancient Greece and were mathematically defined by the theorists of that time. Nevertheless, microtones, like the diatonic modes, were rediscovered in the twentieth century by composers who have used them in new and varied ways.[3] Though in most cases the microtones employed have been quarter-tones—that is, an interval half the size of a minor 2nd—other microtonal intervals have been used as well.

A number of methods have been derived for specifying microtones in musical notation. In his Chamber Concerto (1925), Alban Berg notated quarter-tones by placing a "Z" (for "Zwischenton") on the stem. The "Z" means the performer must raise the tone if the musical line is ascending chromatically and lower it if it is descending. Julián Carrillo, in his *Bosquejos for String Quartet* (1926), used a slanted line after the notehead to indicate a quarter-tone alteration up or down, while Bartók used ascending and descending arrows above the notes in his Violin Concerto No. 2 (1937).

Other methods have typically involved variants of the traditional system of accidentals. György Ligeti uses microtones of various sizes in his String Quartet No. 2 (1968). In his system, an arrow is attached to a flat, sharp, or natural sign, pointing up or down. The resulting intervals are no larger than quarter-tones and may be smaller, the precise size being determined partly by context and partly by the choice of the performer. Krzysztof Penderecki in several works uses variants of the traditional sharp sign to indicate tones a quarter-tone and three quarter-tones higher, and variants of the flat for a quarter-tone and three quarter-tones lower. Traditional accidentals are used for half-step intervals.

A method used by Witold Lutoslawski is seen in Example 2–20. In this work he employs four special accidentals:

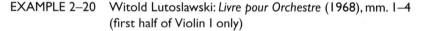

    ↲ = lower the note by a quarter-tone

    ↓ = lower the note by three quarter-tones

    † = raise the note by a quarter-tone

    ‡ = raise the note by three quarter-tones

In each of these two phrases Lutoslawski fills in the quarter-tone chromatic space between A4 and E5, cadencing first on C, then on D♭. The midpoint, of course, would be the quarter-tone between these two pitches.

EXAMPLE 2–20    Witold Lutoslawski: *Livre pour Orchestre* (1968), mm. 1–4
                        (first half of Violin I only)

Microtones smaller than a quarter-tone have been used on occasion. One example by Ligeti was mentioned above; another is Ben Johnston's String Quartet No. 2 (1964), employing a scale with 53 tones to the octave. Harry Partch advocated microtones of various sizes, especially a 43-tone scale using unequal intervals, and he designed instruments to play them.[4] Julián Carrillo founded an ensemble, the Orquesta Sonida 13, that specialized in playing in microtones. In his own music, Carrillo experimented with intervals as small as sixteenth-tones—one-eighth of a minor 2nd.

Stringed instruments would seem to be the most suited of all traditional instruments for playing microtones, pianos and organs the least. Nevertheless, microtonal works for specially tuned pianos have been composed. Examples include *Three Quarter-Tone Pieces for Two Pianos* (1923–24) by Charles Ives, Henri Pousseur's *Prospections* (1952) for three pianos, using sixth-tones, and Johnston's *Sonata for Microtonal Piano* (1965). The most natural environment of all for microtones is the electronic medium, where the entire pitch spectrum can be precisely partitioned into intervals of any size or combination of sizes; however, a discussion of electronic music will have to be postponed until a later chapter.

## OTHER POSSIBILITIES

It would not be correct to assume that everything there is to know about scales in twentieth-century music has been discussed in this chapter. There are always other possibilities. Olivier Messiaen, for example, has been interested in what he calls "modes of limited transposition." These are scales of from six to ten notes that have fewer than twelve transpositions without duplication of pitch-class content.[5] He has identified seven such scales, including the whole-tone and diminished (octatonic) scales, and used them in various compositions. (This quality, known as "transpositional symmetry," is discussed in more detail in Chapter 9.)

Another possibility is the simultaneous use of more than one scale type. We have already seen this in connection with Example 2–7, where a whole-tone vocal duet was provided with a chromatic accompaniment. In Example 2–21 an E Phrygian melody is set over an E major ostinato.

EXAMPLE 2–21    Bartók: *Mikrokosmos* (1926–37), No. 148, Six Dances in Bulgarian Rhythm, No. I, mm. 4–8    *(© Copyright 1940 by Hawkes & Son (London) Ltd. Copyright renewed. Reprinted by permission of Boosey & Hawkes, Inc.)*

Be sure not to confuse the simultaneous use of different scales with "polytonality," a term for the simultaneous use of different tonal centers. This will be discussed in a later chapter.

---

### SUMMARY

Though the major and minor scales of the tonal era have by no means become extinct in the twentieth century, they have to some extent been supplanted by a variety of other scales, some of them quite old, others recently devised, using from five to dozens of notes within the octave. The scales most often encountered in twentieth-century music are included in this chapter, but you should not be surprised to encounter still others, some of which may not even have names.[6] The scales discussed in this chapter include the following:

Pentatonic scale (with modes and variants)

Whole-tone scale

Augmented scale

Diatonic modes

Other seven-note scales using only major and minor 2nds

Seven-note scales using augmented 2nds

Octatonic (diminished) scale

Chromatic scale

Microtonal scales

Modes of limited transposition

The distinctive character of a particular phrase or melodic figure may often be explained by reference to some scale type that is only hinted at. For instance, Example 2–12 was seen to conform entirely to the Aeolian and Dorian modes. But Debussy chose to begin the melody in a manner that reminds us of yet another scale, the whole-tone scale: B♭–C–D–E–D–C–B♭.

---

### NOTES

1. Vincent Persichetti illustrates and names several on p. 44 of his *Twentieth-Century Harmony*.
2. Pieter C. van den Toorn, in *The Music of Igor Stravinsky*, finds the octatonic "collection" in much of Stravinsky's music.

3. Joseph Yasser, in *A Theory of Evolving Tonality*, attempted to show that a nineteen-tone scale would be the logical historical successor to the chromatic scale.

4. Harry Partch, *Genesis of a Music*.

5. Olivier Messiaen, *The Technique of My Musical Language*, pp. 58–62.

6. Several dozen scales are named and defined by Robert Fink and Robert Ricci in *The Language of Twentieth Century Music;* see especially the list on p. 114.

## *EXERCISES*

### *Part A: Fundamentals*

1. Taking the pattern C–D–E–G–A as the model, notate pentatonic scales starting on the following notes:

    G      F♯      B      E♭

2. Notate whole-tone scales starting on the following notes:

    E      C♯      A♭      F

3. Notate the following modal scales:

    –(a)  Dorian on F           – (e)  Phrygian on A           (i)  Lydian on D♭
    – (b)  Mixolydian on E          (f)  Aeolian on A♭          (j)  Dorian on C
    –(c)  Lydian on E♭          –(g)  Aeolian on G          (k)  Phrygian on B
    (d)  Mixolydian on D          –(h)  Locrian on F♯          – (l)  Ionian on B♭

4. Notate the following octatonic (diminished) scales:

    – (a)  One beginning F♯–G          (d)  One combining a°7 with b°7
    – (b)  One beginning A♭–B♭          (e)  One combining d♯°7 with e°7
    (c)  One beginning D–E♭          (f)  One combining a♯°7 with e♯°7

5. Notate and label every major, minor, augmented, or diminished triad available in the following scales:

    (a)  Pentatonic on A          (d)  Mixolydian on A♭
    (b)  Whole-tone on B          (e)  Octatonic beginning E–F
    (c)  Phrygian on C♯

## Part B: Analysis

1. Respighi: *The Pines of Rome* (1924), "Pines near a Catacomb," mm. 6–9 (piano reduction)

   (a) The tonal center in this excerpt is E♭. Name the scale.

2. Debussy: *Six Antique Epigraphs* (1914), I, mm. 4–7

   (a) Name the scale found in the melody.

   (b) The melody at the beginning of the excerpt suggests G as a tonal center. If it is, the melody combined with its accompaniment uses what G scale?

   (c) The cadence at the end of the excerpt suggests C as a tonal center. In that case, the melody combined with its accompaniment uses what C scale?

3.  Anton Webern: Symphony, Op. 21 (1928), I, mm. 1–14

    (a)  This is a "concert score"—all of the instruments sound as notated. What scale is being used?

4. Alfredo Casella: *Eleven Children's Pieces* (1920), "Siciliana," mm. 1–19
   This excerpt suggests several scales, all with D as a tonal center. Be sure to consider the accompaniment when answering the following questions.

   (a) Which scale is used in mm. 1–9?

   (b) And in mm. 9–11?

   (c) What scale is hinted at in m. 12?

   (d) And what scale is used in mm. 13–17?

   (e) There are eight pitch classes in mm. 18–19. Do they form a diminished scale?

Allegretto dolcemente mosso

*(il ritmo sempre molto preciso)*

*p* espressivo, semplice, come una melodia popolare

*pp* dolcissimo

5.  Joan Tower: *Island Prelude* (1988), m. 135 (oboe cadenza)
    This excerpt is derived from a single scale, with the exception of the predominant B's in the second system. (These may be intended to help prepare the final cadence in m. 145, which is on an E chord with a B in the oboe.) What scale is used here?

6.  Debussy: Preludes, Book I, "Sails" ("Voiles"), mm. 38–44

   (a)  Two scales are used in this excerpt. The first is in mm. 38–41. What is it?

   (b)  The second scale is found in mm. 42–44. Name it.

## Part C: Composition

1.  Compose short melodies illustrating the pentatonic, whole-tone, octatonic, and chromatic scales.
2.  Compose short melodies illustrating the Dorian, Phrygian, Lydian, Mixolydian, and Aeolian modes. In each melody, try to emphasize the tonic note as well as those notes that are especially characteristic of that scale.

3. Continue this example, using the G Mixolydian mode.

4. Continue this example, using the F Dorian mode.

5. Compose an example that makes use of several different scales, using the Casella excerpt (Example 2–B–4) as a model. Label each scale you use.
6. Compose an example of two-voice counterpoint using the octatonic scale. Start with a slow, rather simple tune, unaccompanied, and bring in the second voice after a measure or two. Continue to a cadence on an octave. Compose for instruments in your class, or be able to play it at the piano.

## FURTHER READING

DALLIN, LEON. *Techniques of Twentieth Century Composition.* See Chapter 3, Modal Melodic Resources, the section titled "Additional Scale Resources" in Chapter 4, and Chapter 16, Microtones.

KOSTKA, STEFAN, AND DOROTHY PAYNE. *Tonal Harmony with an Introduction to Twentieth-Century Music.* See the section titled "Scales" in Chapter 28.

PERSICHETTI, VINCENT. *Twentieth-Century Harmony.* See Chapter 2, Scale Materials.

PISTON, WALTER. *Harmony.* See the section titled "Modal Scales and Modal Harmony" in Chapter 30 and the sections titled "The Pentatonic Scale," "The Whole-Tone Scale," and "Artificial Scales" in Chapter 31.

STEINKE, GREG A. *Bridge to 20th Century Music.* See Chapters 9 and 10, Enlarged Scale Resources I and II.

VINCENT, JOHN. *The Diatonic Modes in Modern Music.* See Chapter 30, The Modes in the Contemporary Period.

# THREE

# The Vertical Dimension: Chords and Simultaneities

## INTRODUCTION

The music of the tonal era is almost exclusively tertian in its harmonic orientation. That is, its harmonies can generally be thought of as being constructed of stacked 3rds, the only exceptions being "voice-leading chords" such as the family of augmented-6th chords and the chords produced by the omnibus progression. That tonal music used tertian harmony was not the result of a conscious decision on anyone's part but instead was the result of classifications of consonance and dissonance and the development over centuries of various voice-leading procedures. The fact that the underlying harmonies in the tonal style are known to be tertian makes the labeling of chords and the identification of nonchord tones in tonal music a relatively simple task.

Much of the music of the twentieth century is also basically tertian, but there is in addition a good deal of music using chords built from 2nds, from 4ths, and from combinations of various intervals. Even the tertian music frequently uses new kinds of tertian sonorities, as we shall see. One result of this unlimited array of harmonic material is that the distinction between chord tones and nonchord tones is often difficult or impossible to make. Also, chords sometimes seem to result more or less accidentally from the combination of harmonically independent lines. For these reasons, many writers prefer at times to use terms such as "verticality," "simultaneity," "sonority," or "note complex" instead of "chord." In this text, however, "chord" will be used freely along with the other terms to refer to any vertical collection of pitches, no matter how it originates.

The present chapter surveys in an organized way the chords found in twentieth-century music. The *contexts* in which these chords are used is a subject that involves both voice leading and harmonic progression. These topics will be taken up in Chapters 4 and 5.

## CONVENTIONAL TERTIAN SONORITIES

Tertian triads and 7th chords are an important, if less preponderant, part of the harmonic vocabulary of twentieth-century music. Certain composers make more use of these sounds than others do. Some of the works by composers such as Sergei Rachmaninoff, Gian Carlo Menotti, and Aaron Copland, for example, might be expected to contain a high proportion of triads and 7th chords, whereas other composers, such as Paul Hindemith, tend to reserve the pure sound of a triad for important cadences or even for the end of a movement. Still other composers rarely make use of these more traditional sounds. Examples of the use of triads and 7th chords will be found in later chapters, where voice leading and harmonic progression are discussed.

Tertian sonorities "taller" than the 7th chord—9th chords, 11th chords, and 13th chords—are not an important part of the harmonic vocabulary before the late nineteenth or early twentieth century. In theory, any diatonic triad can be extended to a 13th chord before its root is duplicated (see Example 3–1). In practice, however, it is the dominant and secondary dominant chords, and to a lesser extent the supertonic and submediant chords, that tend to be singled out for this treatment. Chromatic alterations, especially of chords with a dominant function, are often used. Example 3–2 illustrates some of the possibilities.

EXAMPLE 3–1   Diatonic 13th chords

C:   $I^{13}$      $ii^{13}$      $iii^{13}$  *(etc.)*

EXAMPLE 3–2   Altered Dominants

C:   $V^9_+$      $V9\flat$      $V11\sharp$ *(etc.)*

Chords taller than a 7th are frequently incomplete, posing certain problems in analysis. In Example 3–3, for instance, the first chord would probably best be analyzed as an incomplete supertonic 11th chord because of the $\hat{2}$–$\hat{5}$–$\hat{1}$ bass line, but one could also argue that it is a $V^4_3$. And is the second chord an incomplete dominant 9th or an incomplete dominant 13th? The answer depends on whether one hears the C5 in the melody as a chord tone or as an appoggiatura, and either reading is defensible. The final chord is a tonic triad, the F3 in the tenor being an ornamented suspension.

**EXAMPLE 3–3**   Debussy: Preludes, Book II (1913), "Heaths" ("Bruyères"), mm. 1–5

$A\flat$:                                                                                                           ii$^{11}$        V$^{9?}$           I

Ninths and other tall chords can be inverted, of course, but inversions can be problematical, as we just saw with the ii$^{11}$ chord in Example 3–3. Referring back to Example 3–1, notice that the pitch-class content of every diatonic 13th chord is identical, meaning that every diatonic 13th chord could be analyzed as an inversion of every other diatonic 13th chord. The situation is only slightly less ambiguous with 9th and 11th chords, as Example 3–4 illustrates.

**EXAMPLE 3–4**   Inverted 9th and 11th chords

C$^{13?}$       C$^{13?}$
F$^{9?}$        D$^{11?}$

A typically ambiguous example is seen in Example 3–5. The excerpt begins with a tonic triad in D major, but the next chord is open to some interpretation (remember to include the flute part in your analysis). The pitch classes, in alphabetical order, are A, C, D, E$\flat$, F$\sharp$, G. Bass notes usually want to be roots, if they can, and the high D in the flute on the fourth beat reinforces the notion that this might be some sort of G chord. On the other hand, the G could be the 11th of a complete D 11th chord: D–F$\sharp$–A–C–E$\flat$–G, and the A5 to D6 in the flute seems to support that. Or perhaps it should be analyzed as a D 9th chord presented simultaneously with G, its note of resolution. The uncertainty is not resolved by the B$\flat$ major 7th chord that follows, since neither G–B$\flat$ nor D–B$\flat$ seems particularly compelling as a progression. The remainder of the excerpt is more straightforward: A minor 7th to D minor 7th in m. 3, both slightly ornamented, to a more lavishly ornamented G major triad in m. 4.

**EXAMPLE 3–5**    Prokofiev: Sonata for Flute and Piano, Op. 94 (1943), I, mm. 1–4

*(Music by Sergei Prokofiev. Edited by Jean-Pierre Rampal. Copyright © 1986 International Music Co.*
*Copyright renewed. International copyright secured. All rights reserved. Used by permission.)*

## TERTIAN CHORDS WITH ADDED NOTES

Though the possibility of a triad's having a note added a 6th above the root was recognized by theorists as early as the eighteenth century, chords with added notes (sometimes called *chords of addition*) did not become an accepted part of the harmonic vocabulary until the twentieth century. The basic chords are usually triads, and the added notes (always figured above the root) are usually 2nds or 6ths, less frequently 4ths. Any triad with an added 6th could also be analyzed as a 7th chord, but the context will usually settle the issue, as Example 3–6 illustrates. Similarly, a triad with an added 2nd or 4th could be interpreted as an

**EXAMPLE 3–6**    Added 6th and Inverted 7th Chords

incomplete 9th or 11th chord, especially if voiced with the added note above the triad. Since the root is the same in either case, the distinction is not a crucial one. For all practical purposes, a chord with an added 2nd or 4th can be considered the same as one with an added 9th or 11th. See Example 3–7.

EXAMPLE 3–7   Chords with Added 2nds and 4ths

F:    I add2    I add9    I add4    I add11

The situation is unambiguous in Example 3–8, where the cadential chords are the dominant 7th and the tonic with added 6th in G♭ Major. And in Example 3–9, the final chord is clearly a C triad with an added 9th. But Example 3–10 is more involved. In the first phrase (mm. 1–2) a double pedal point on G4 and B4 (in the middle of the texture) adds

EXAMPLE 3–8   Debussy: Preludes, Book I (1910), "The Girl with the Flaxen Hair" ("La fille aux cheveux de lin"), mm. 23–24

G♭:    IV V    vi V ——→V⁷    I add6

EXAMPLE 3–9   Debussy: Preludes, Book II (1913), "Canope," mm. 29–33

C:         iv    I add9

bite to a conventional progression. Though several of the sonorities could be analyzed as added-note chords, the pedal-point analysis is just as good, explaining all the dissonances except the added 4th in the passing tonic $^6_4$. The second phrase (mm. 3–4) keeps the B as a pedal point, shifting it down an octave in m. 4. Again, the pedal point accounts for most of the dissonances, but the tonic triads are probably best analyzed as added-note chords.

EXAMPLE 3–10   Stravinsky: Suite Italienne (1932), "Introduction," mm. 1–4   *(© Copyright 1934 by Boosey & Hawkes (London) Ltd. Copyright renewed. Reprinted by permission of Boosey & Hawkes, Inc.)*

Added notes are a feature of what is sometimes called "wrong-note style," in which the listener's conventional expectations are almost met, but not quite. This was the case in Example 3–10, where Stravinsky is *almost* quoting Pergolesi, an early eighteenth-century composer. The result is often humorous, as in Example 3–11, where the melody heads toward a G4 but lands a half-step too high (m. 41), then a half-step too low (m. 42), before finally succeeding (m. 43).

EXAMPLE 3–11   Gian Carlo Menotti: *The Telephone* (1946), mm. 41–43 (piano vocal score)
*(© Copyright 1947 (Renewed) by G. Schirmer, Inc. (ASCAP) International copyright secured. All rights Reserved. Reprinted by permission)*

## TERTIAN CHORDS WITH SPLIT CHORD MEMBERS

A special kind of added-note chord features one or more chord members that are "split" by adding a note a minor 2nd away. Common examples are triads and 7th chords with split 3rds, but split roots, 5ths, and 7ths also occur. Some of the possibilities are shown in Example 3–12. There is no standard analytical symbol for split chord members. In this text an exclamation point will be used, as in the example. The dominant 7th chord with split 3rd is a traditional "blues" chord, where it is analyzed as a dominant 7th with an augmented 9th. Debussy uses a D♭7 (3!) in Example 3–13 to achieve a Spanish flavor. The split 3rd (F♭) is spelled here as an augmented 9th (E♮). Either analysis is acceptable.

**EXAMPLE 3–12**   Chords with Split Chord Members

F (3!)    F (1!)    F⁷ (7!)    F⁷ (3!)

**EXAMPLE 3–13**   Debussy: Preludes, Book II (1913), "La Puerta del Vino," mm. 9–15

In Example 3–14 Ravel uses a series of major triads with split roots. The effect is not as dissonant as you might expect because of the speed at which the chords are played.

EXAMPLE 3–14    Ravel: *Mirrors* (1905), "Sorrowful Birds," m. 15

Aaron Copland uses split-3rd chords on C and E in Example 3–15. The effect is intensified by the strings, which play E's that are a quarter-tone flat and G's that are a quarter-tone sharp. Notice the notation that Copland uses here for the quarter-tones, a system used also by Alois Hàba, among others.

EXAMPLE 3–15   Copland: *Vitebsk* (1929), mm. 1–2   *(© Copyright 1934 by the Aaron Copland Fund for Music, Inc. Copyright renewed. Reprinted by permission of Boosey & Hawkes, Inc. Sole licensee.)*

A more complex example was contained in Example 2–7 (p. 26). The accompaniment in m. 984 clearly contains an A major triad on beat 3, accented. Below and above it are C♮s (a split 3rd), the higher C leaping up to an F (a split 5th), while an inner voice sustains an E♭ (another split 5th). Meanwhile, the singers produce B♭ (split root) and G♯ (adding a major 7th to the chord). The listener cannot follow all of this, of course; the aural effect is one of extreme dissonance competing with the sound of a pure triad.[1]

## OPEN-5TH CHORDS

While a large number of added-note chords are possible, there is only one important "chord of omission"—that is, a traditional sonority that is transformed into something unusual by leaving out a note—and this is the triad without a 3rd. Omitting the root or the 5th, or omitting anything from a 7th chord, only results in yet another traditional sonority. But the sound of an open 5th had been out of style for centuries, except for its occasional use in two-part counterpoint.

The sound of open 5ths rapidly becomes tiresome, so extended passages based on this chord are rare. Typically they are used to create an impression of the Orient or of the distant past. In Example 3–16 open 5ths on G and A are used to introduce a chant melody in the chorus. The notation of the time signatures in Example 3–16 is a very practical one that a number of twentieth-century composers have adopted.

EXAMPLE 3–16    Carl Orff: *Carmina Burana* (1936), "Veris leta facies," mm. 4–6    *(Copyright 1937*

## QUARTAL AND QUINTAL CHORDS

Composers of the twentieth century have not restricted themselves to tertian sonorities—that is, to chordal formations based on stacked 3rds. There are essentially only four possibilities:

Chords built from 2nds (7ths)
Chords built from 3rds (6ths)
Chords built from 4ths (5ths)
Chords built from mixed intervals

In this section we will explore quartal and quintal chords—those built from 4ths and 5ths. Later sections will deal with chords constructed from 2nds and with mixed-interval chords.

A *quartal chord* can have as few as three pitch classes (as in Example 3–17a) or it can have several (Example 3–17b). It is sometimes possible to omit a member of a quartal or quintal chord (the E4 in Example 3–17b, for instance) without losing its character. Various voicings and octave duplications are also used (as in Example 3–17c), but some arrangements could destroy the quartal character of the sonority. *Quintal chords* work the same way (as in Example 3–17d), but they have a more open and stable sound and, of course, occupy more vertical space per chord member. Surely a near-record for range must be held by the ten-note quintal chord that occurs near the end of György Ligeti's *Melodies for Orchestra* (1971), spanning a range of more than five octaves, from A♭1 to B6.

**EXAMPLE 3–17**   Quartal and Quintal Chords

A convenient way to describe quartal and quintal chords is to use, for example, "3 × 4 on B" to mean a three-pitch-class quartal chord with B as the bottom pitch class, as in Example 3–17a. Example 3–17b would be a "7 × 4 on C♯." All of the chords in Example 3–17c would be "4 × 4 on E," and "5 × 5 on G" would describe Example 3–17d. A static 6 × 4 chord on A is the basis for Example 3–18.

**EXAMPLE 3–18**   Howard Hanson: Symphony No. 2, Op. 30 (1930), I, rehearsal J (strings only)

The chords in Example 3–19 are almost exclusively quartal, but the analysis is complicated by arpeggiations and voicings. One possibility is to analyze the harmony as four quartal chords, as marked on the score.

a = 5 × 4 on F♯

b = 3 × 4 on D ("inverted")

c = 5 × 4 on B♭

d = 4 × 4 on D♭

**EXAMPLE 3–19**  Copland: Piano Fantasy (1957), mm. 20–24  *(© Copyright 1957 by the Aaron Copland Fund for Music, Inc.; copyright renewed. Used by permission of Boosey & Hawkes, Inc., sole licensee.)*

A second approach (and still others are possible) would be to combine a and b into a single 7 × 4 chord on F♯ and to combine c and d into a single 7 × 4 chord on B♭. Both of these analyses are supported by the pedal markings. Notice that the a/b chord contains all of the pitch classes of the G major scale, whereas the pitch classes from C♭ major make up the c/d chord. Notice also the oversize time signatures Copland employs here. Presumably these are seen more readily than are the traditional time signatures, certainly when used in a conductor's score, as in Example 3–20.

The last 21 measures of the movement from which Example 3–20 is taken are static harmonically, consisting for the most part of embellishments of a quintal chord on D♭. At the very end, shown here, the chord turns out to be a 5 × 5 chord on D♭.

EXAMPLE 3–20   Percy Grainger: *Lincolnshire Posy* (1937), III, "Rufford Park Poachers," mm. 99–103

Quartal and quintal chords are most often made up of perfect intervals, but augmented and diminished 4ths and 5ths may be included. In Example 3–21 each of the arpeggiated triplet chords, as well as the eighth-note chords beneath them, is a 3 × 4 chord, with the lower 4th augmented.

EXAMPLE 3–21  Debussy, Preludes, Book II (1913), "Ondine," mm. 4–7

The use of diminished 4ths and augmented 5ths in quartal and quintal chords can lead to perplexing questions, since these intervals sound like 3rds and 6ths. An example is Alexander Scriabin's "mystic chord," a sonority that flavors much of his music, although he seldom uses it in literal fashion. The "mystic chord" is found in at least the two forms shown in Example 3–22. Example 3–22a contains one °4, while Example 3–22b contains two of them. As long as the voicing is predominantly quartal, as it is here, it is probably correct to analyze both chords as altered 6 × 4 chords, but other voicings might lead to other analyses. The diminished scale can serve as the source for the chord in Example 3–22b. If you turn back to Example 2–17, you will see that this chord is strongly suggested in various transpositions and voicings in that excerpt.

EXAMPLE 3–22  Scriabin's Mystic Chord

## SECUNDAL CHORDS

The third possibility for chord construction is the secundal chord, a sonority built from major or minor 2nds or from a combination of the two. Such chords may be voiced as 7ths rather than as 2nds, but this is the exception. More often the notes of a secundal chord are placed adjacent to each other, an arrangement sometimes referred to by the terms "cluster" and "tone cluster."

The secundal chord in the second measure of Example 3–21 is voiced as a cluster, but the arpeggiations obscure this somewhat (the chord is F♯–G–A–B–C♯). Example 3–23 provides a clearer illustration of clusters.

EXAMPLE 3–23   Charles Ives: Piano Sonata No. 2 *(Concord)* (1915), II   *(Copyright © 1951 (Renewed) by Associated Music Publishers, Inc. (BMI) International copyright secured. All rights reserved. Reprinted by permission.)*

(faster and faster)

In some keyboard works, special notation is used to indicate whether or not the black keys are to be included in the cluster. Others require that the cluster be performed with the forearm or with a board. In Example 3–24, the pianist plays black keys with the left hand and white keys with the right, resulting in nearly chromatic clusters of eight or nine pitches each.

EXAMPLE 3–24   Sofia Gubaidulina: Lamento for Tuba and Piano (1977)
*(© 1991 by Musikverlag Hans Sikorski, Hamburg.)*

In Example 3–25a, the composer suggests two ways of playing a "lateral tremolo" between white and black keys, shown in Example 3–25b.

**EXAMPLE 3–25**   William Bolcom, No. 5 from *12 New Etudes for Piano* (1986), m. 11
*(© 1988 by Edward B. Marks Music Company.)*

a.     b.

The chords that accompany the first violin in Example 3–26 might be explained as secundal chords, the first one containing the pitch classes G♭, A♭, B♭, C, and D, and the other chords being transpositions of the first one. The voicing of the chords, however, is not as clusters, but as alternating major 3rds and tritones, resulting in the sound of an incomplete B♭ 13th chord:

G♭4
⎫ tritone
C4
⎫ major 3rd
A♭3
⎫ tritone
D3
⎫ major 3rd
B♭2

EXAMPLE 3–26  Paul Hindemith: String Quartet No. 3, Op. 22 (1921), V, mm. 64–66

## MIXED-INTERVAL CHORDS

A **mixed-interval chord** is one that did not originate as a series of 2nds, 3rds, or 4ths,[2] but instead combines two or more of those interval types (with their inversions and compounds, of course) to form a more complex sonority. The possibilities are numerous.

Most mixed-interval chords are subjects to other interpretations—that is, they could, on closer inspection, be arranged to look like secundal, tertian, or quartal chords. The mixed-interval chord in Example 3–27 will be used to illustrate this. It could be arranged, although incorrectly, as:

| | |
|---|---|
| a secundal chord | D–E–F–G♯–A♯–B |
| a tertian chord | E–G♯–B–D–F–A♯ |
| a quartal chord | F–B–E–A♯–D–G♯ |

EXAMPLE 3–27  George Walker: Piano Sonata No. 4 (1985), II, m. 58

In most cases the context will suggest the best analytical approach. For instance, the sonata from which Example 3–27 comes is an atonal work with few, if any secundal, tertian, or quartal chords, so it is appropriate to call this a mixed-interval chord, even if that term is too broad to be very descriptive.

This brings us to the question of just how one goes about analyzing and labeling these sonorities, a complicated problem that has been tackled by various composers and theorists—notably Paul Hindemith, Howard Hanson, and Allen Forte. Because so many combinations of intervals are possible, a completely new system of chord classification had to be devised, and this system is the subject of much of Chapter 9.

## WHOLE-TONE CHORDS

Any chord whose members could be obtained from a single whole-tone scale is a **whole-tone chord**.[3] A number of such chords are possible, of course. A few of them are illustrated in Example 3–28. Such sonorities for the most part appeared rarely in classical tonal harmony, but some whole-tone chords, including those in Example 3–28, are at least reminiscent of traditional chords. Example 3–28b, for instance, is an incomplete dominant 7th chord, and Example 3–28d is a French augmented-6th chord, but Examples 3–28c and e would have to be explained as altered versions of simpler chords.

EXAMPLE 3–28    Whole-Tone Chords

   (a)       (b)       (c)       (d)       (e)

Whole-tone chords will naturally occur in any music that is based on the whole-tone scale. For an illustration, turn back to Example 2–6 (p. 25), a whole-tone excerpt by Dukas. The first measure uses a French augmented-6th sonority (B♯–E–F♯–A♯). When the B♯ moves to E in the next measure, we are left with only the notes of an incomplete dominant 7th chord (E–F♯–A♯). Neither of these chords is used in a traditional manner. The last two measures are based on a different whole-tone scale, and the whole-tone chords, though present, are more difficult to characterize.

More interesting, perhaps, is the use of whole-tone chords in passages that are not based primarily upon the whole-tone scale, because here they provide an unexpected harmonic color. Again an earlier example, Example 2–10 (p. 28), can provide an illustration. In this case the pitch environment is Phrygian, except for the last chord of the second measure (A♭–F♯–C–D). The altered tone, F♯, produces a whole-tone chord that could be explained as a French augmented-6th chord moving directly to the tonic G, or as a second-inversion dominant 7th in G with a flatted 5th (A♭). More whole-tone chords are seen in Example 3–29, the first phrase of a work that is atonal until a suggestion of a G♭ tonal center in the final cadence. In this phrase the measures alternate between WT–1 and WT–0, although each measure includes a passing tone that is out of the scale.

**EXAMPLE 3–29    Scriabin: Etude, Op. 56, No. 4 (1907), mm. 1–4**

Finally, look once more at the Hindemith excerpt, Example 3–26. We have analyzed the chords in this excerpt as secundal chords, as mixed-interval chords, and as 13th chords; we can see now that they are also whole-tone chords, each one being derived from one of the two whole-tone scales.

## POLYCHORDS

A **polychord** combines two or more chords into a more complex sonority, but it is crucial that the listener be able to perceive that separate harmonic entities are being juxtaposed if the result is to be a true polychord. Any 11th or 13th chord could be explained as a combination of two simpler sonorities, but this would be an incorrect analysis if we do not hear them that way.

**EXAMPLE 3–30    Apparent Polychords**

In order to be heard as a polychord, the individual sonorities that make up the polychord must be separated by some means such as register or timbre. In Example 3–31 the first and last chords could easily be heard as 11th chords, but in the rest of the phrase the different registers and the pervading contrary motion between the two chordal units result in an unambiguous polychordal texture. Persichetti concludes another of his works, the Symphony for Band, Op. 69 (1956), with a spectacular polychord that combines four registrally distinct sonorities: B♭ major, A major 7th, B major 7th, and F major with an added 9th. The resulting polychord contains all twelve pitch classes.

**EXAMPLE 3–31** Vincent Persichetti: *Little Piano Book,* Op. 60 (1953), "Prologue," mm. 1–4

*(© 1954 Elkan-Vogel, Inc. Used by permission of the publisher.)*

Adagio pesante

Stravinsky's famous "Petrushka chord" combines two triads a tritone apart: C major and F♯ major. This polychord is seen in Example 3–32, along with another polychord: F♯ major/G major. In the orchestral version, the ascending figures are played on a piano, the descending ones on clarinets.

**EXAMPLE 3–32** Stravinsky: *Petrushka* (1911), Second Tableau     *(© Copyright 1912 by Hawkes & Son (London) Ltd. Copyright renewed. Reprinted by permission of Boosey & Hawkes, Inc.)*

The constituents of polychords are usually tertian triads or 7th chords, but all of the other kinds of sonorities discussed in this chapter could also conceivably be susceptible to polychordal treatment. For instance, near the end of Example 2–7 (p. 26) there is a 3 × 4 chord on E in the upper staff of the accompaniment and a D♭ major triad in the lower staff. The only requirement for a polychord is that the listener be able to perceive the chords as separate entities. There will inevitably be ambiguous cases, however, where one listener hears a polychord and another hears a single complex sonority.

The use of a polychord does not necessarily indicate that a passage is polytonal. Polytonality will be discussed in more detail in Chapter 5.

## SUMMARY

The harmonies of tonal music were limited for the most part to tertian triads and 7th chords. In contrast, composers of the twentieth century have felt free to make use of any conceivable combination of pitches. In the most simple terms, there are four possibilities for chord construction:

> Secundal chords (also tone clusters)
> Tertian chords (including 9ths, etc.)
> Quartal chords (also quintal chords)
> Mixed-interval chords

Tertian chords, the most traditional of the four types, have been subjected to some new variations:

> Added notes
> Split chord members
> Open 5ths

One special case, especially important in the early part of the century:

> Whole-tone chords

And finally, the possibility of juxtaposing two or more aurally distinguishable sonorities:

> Polychords

It is frequently the case that a particular sonority is open to more than one interpretation. This is particularly true with mixed-interval chords, many of which can be arranged to resemble secundal, tertian, or quartal chords. The student must be sensitive to the context and the voicing in attempting to choose the best analytical approach. The three chords in Example 3–33, though containing the same pitch classes, obviously must be analyzed differently.

EXAMPLE 3–33   Three Different Chords Containing the Same Pitch Classes

## NOTES

1. Another approach to chords with added notes and split chord members is taken by Bryan Simms in *Music of the Twentieth Century*, pp. 55–58. He identifies nine pairs of "triadic tetrachords"—that is, four-note chords that contain a major or minor triad. The first chord of each pair is a major triad plus one of the other nine notes of the chromatic scale, while the second chord of each pair is the mirror inversion of the first.
2. Some writers use the term *compound chord*.
3. Some theorists use the term *whole-tone dominant* for whole-tone chords that have a traditional dominant function.

## EXERCISES

### Part A: Fundamentals

1. Review the nine chord types in the Summary section. Then find one example of each type in the example below.

2. Make up one example of each of the nine chord types and notate them on staff paper. Try not to duplicate any of those found in the text. Label each chord.
3. Find the doubly chromatic mediant relationship in Example 3–9.
4. Name the scales used in the following excerpts:

    (a) Example 3–3, treble-clef melody
    (b) Example 3–9, last four measures (without the E♭; C is tonic)
    (c) Example 3–15
    (d) Example 3–21
    (e) Example 3–26, cello only (missing an A)
    (f) Example 3–27

### Part B: Analysis

1. Two different types of tetrachords are used in Example 2–8 (p. 27), one in 8a and one in 8b. Identify these chord types.
2. Debussy: Preludes, Book I, "The Engulfed Cathedral," m. 1–5
   There are three planes to the texture of this excerpt. One is the static three-note chord

in the highest register, another is the quarter-note chords, and the third is the three-note chords in the lowest register. What kind of chord do all three planes make use of? To what scale do the quarter-note chords belong?

Profondément calme  (Dans une brume doucement sonore)

3. Stravinsky: *The Rake's Progress* (1951), III
   What kind of sonority predominates in this passage?

*(© Copyright 1951 by Hawkes & Son (London) Ltd. Copyright renewed. Reprinted by permission of Boosey & Hawkes, Inc.)*

4. Debussy: *The Joyous Isle* (1904), mm. 152–55
   And in this one?

5. Ravel: "Minuet on the Name of Haydn" (1909), mm. 50–54
   The chords here are tertian. Label the six bracketed chords with Roman numerals.

6. Ravel: Sonatina (1905), I, mm. 79–84
   This excerpt contains several sonorities that could be analyzed as added-note chords.
   Find them, as well as an unconventional German augmented-6th chord.

7. Charles Ives: Violin Sonata No. 4 (1915), II
   Explain or discuss each of the five labeled chords.

8. Alban Berg: "Warm Is the Air" ("Warm die Lüfte"), Op. 2, No. 4 (1910), mm. 20–25
   This is a complicated and intriguing excerpt from early in Berg's compositional output. Our analysis will be concerned only with the piano part, while recognizing that the relationship between the voice and the accompaniment would have to be considered in a complete analysis.

   (a) There are at least two ways to approach chords a–f analytically. One is to understand how they are "generated"—that is, how they come about. What sort of pattern does the bass line under chords a–f follow?

   (b) Meanwhile, the right hand in chords a–f moves a three-note chord down chromatically. How would you classify that chord?

   (c) The second way of dealing with chords a–f is to analyze each individually. The last of them could be analyzed as a dominant 7th with split 3rd: B7(3!). The others appear to be mixed-interval chords, but closer inspection reveals that they could also be analyzed as tertian chords. Which chords out of a–e could be analyzed as incomplete dominant 7th chords with split 3rds?

(d) And which could be analyzed as incomplete 13th chords?

(e) Of the remaining chords (g–l), list any that are identical to or are transpositions of one of the earlier chords (a–f).

(f) What single category would best describe chords g, i, and k?

(g) What pattern seems to emerge in chords g and i?

(h) Considering your answer to the preceding question, what note seems to be missing from chord k?

(Reprinted by permission of the original publisher, Robert Lienau, Berlin.)

## FURTHER READING

DALLIN, LEON. *Techniques of Twentieth Century Composition.* See Chapter 6, Chord Structure.

KOSTKA, STEFAN, AND DOROTHY PAYNE. *Tonal Harmony with an Introduction to Twentieth-Century Music.* See pp. 482–491.

PERSICHETTI, VINCENT. *Twentieth-Century Harmony.* See Chapter 3, Chords by Thirds; Chapter 4, Chords by Fourths; Chapter 5, Added-Note Chords; Chapter 6, Chords by Seconds; Chapter 7, Polychords; and Chapter 8, Compound and Mirror Harmony.

PISTON, WALTER. *Harmony.* See pp. 499–507 in Chapter 31, Scalar and Chordal Types.

REISBERG, HORACE. "The Vertical Dimension in Twentieth-Century Music," in Gary Wittlich, ed., *Aspects of Twentieth-Century Music.* See pp. 322–372.

SIMMS, BRYAN R. *Music of the Twentieth Century.* See the section titled "Triads and Triadic Extensions" in Chapter 3.

STEINKE, GREG A. *Bridge to 20th Century Music.* See Chapters 11 and 12, Expanded Chord Vocabulary I and II.

# FOUR

# The Horizontal Dimension: Melody and Voice Leading

## INTRODUCTION

Voice leading—how chords are created by the motion of individual voices—is one of the main concerns of conventional tonal theory.[1] Even today the voice-leading conventions followed by composers of the tonal era occupy an important part of the course of study in colleges and universities around the world. But a glance at the table of contents of this book will reveal that voice-leading conventions are not a central issue in much of the music of the twentieth century. In fact, as we shall see later in this chapter, one of the most hallowed principles of voice leading was an early casualty of the assault on musical conventions made by a number of composers around the turn of the century.

Melody, on the other hand, is usually slighted in courses in music theory, perhaps because we tend to think of such courses as dealing with tonal *harmony* rather than with tonal *music*. Nevertheless, all of us probably have a pretty good notion of what conventional tonal melodies are like, even if we have never actually tried to analyze one. The first part of this chapter will examine some of the new melodic techniques that have been used by composers in the twentieth century. But before looking at some twentieth-century examples, it might be worthwhile to spend a little time with a familiar tonal melody.

## TONAL MELODY

The last movement of Mozart's Piano Sonata in D Major, K. 284, is a set of variations on an original theme (that is, on a theme composed by Mozart himself and not borrowed from someone else). Of course, the theme consists of not just the melody, but also the accompaniment, texture, harmony, dynamics, register, articulation, and so forth; in this discussion, however, we will concentrate on the melody, given in Example 4–1. Like many fine melodies, this tune is deceptively simple. Its four phrases begin in mm. 1, 5, 9, and 14, each phrase preceded by an anacrusis. In every case the anacrusis consists of two A's, but in the pickup to m. 9 the A's are ornamented with G♯ neighbors. In every case but m. 9, the pickups are followed by a strong half-note D on the downbeat. Not only do all the phrases begin the same, but they also end the same, with a two-note stepwise descent beginning on the strong beat of the fourth measure of the phrase. Again the third phrase offers some contrast, this time by augmenting the rhythm of the cadential figure (m. 12), followed by an unexpected 3½ beats of silence that Mozart has much fun with in the variations. Finally, each phrase reaches its highest pitch—the climax or focal point—in the second or third measure of the phrase, giving them a certain similarity of basic contour.

The unity that is provided by the consistent beginnings and endings of the phrases and by their contours is complemented by an interesting motivic organization within and between the phrases. The interior of phrase 1 uses two motives, marked "a" and "b" in the example. Motive "a" is used in contrary motion (or inversion) in m. 2, and motive "b" is used in sequence in m. 3. Phrase 2 begins after the pickup figure with inversions of both "a" (m. 5) and "b" (m. 6) and introduces a new figure, "c," which is used twice in m. 7. The third phrase offers more contrast motivically just as it did in its use of the anacrusis and cadence figures. The figures in m. 9 are heard as variants of "c," but just as apparent to the

**EXAMPLE 4–1** Mozart: Piano Sonata, K. 284 (1775), III, mm. 1–17 (melody only)

listener is the chromatic descent in the same measure: A–G♯–G–F♯, possibly a compressed version of "a" in contrary motion. Motive "a" is heard sequentially three times in mm. 10–11, the last time in rhythmic augmentation. Another interesting way to hear m. 11 is as a sequential continuation of the stepwise descent from m. 9, with m. 10 serving as a *forte* interruption. Finally, phrase 4 begins with a literal return of mm. 1–2 (except for the dynamics), followed by a literal transposition of mm. 7–8! That is, phrase 4 joins the first half of phrase 1 to the second half of phrase 2 to effect a shortened return of the opening period.

Slightly over half of the melodic intervals in Mozart's melody are major or minor 2nds, and 2nds and 3rds together account for seven-eighths of the intervals. All but two of the thirteen leaps larger than a 3rd are followed by motion contrary to the direction of the leap. One thing accomplished by the 3rds and the larger intervals is clarification of the harmonic structure. In mm. 16–17, for example, the implied harmonies are obviously I–IV (or ii)–I–V7–I. Though the harmonies are not always so unambiguous, the basic harmonic structure implied by the melody is usually clear.

To summarize:

1. The melody exhibits a high degree of motivic unity, brought about through such devices as repetition, return, sequence, and inversion.

2. Each phrase has a single high point somewhere near the middle of the phrase.

3. The melody moves primarily in 2nds and 3rds, with larger leaps usually being followed by a change of direction.

4. The basic harmonic structure is implied by the melody.

It would certainly be incorrect to assume that the basic characteristics of Mozart's melody have been discarded by all composers in the twentieth century. With the exception of the fourth item in our list above, it would be safe to say that a great many twentieth-century melodies make use of the same compositional devices employed by Mozart. Nevertheless, we will frequently encounter differences that will help us to understand what it is that gives twentieth-century melody its characteristic sound.

## SOME NEW STYLISTIC FEATURES OF TWENTIETH-CENTURY MELODY

To illustrate this part of the discussion we will begin with a famous theme by Richard Strauss, a theme that belongs more to the late Romantic era than to the twentieth century, but one that exemplifies how melody had developed since Mozart's time.

One of the first things that one notices about this melody is its wide range—from E♭2 to D5, just short of three octaves—with most of this span occurring in the first measure. While stepwise motion accounts for about half of the intervals, large leaps (larger than a 3rd) are much more prevalent than in Classical style. The rhythm, too, offers a contrast to Mozart's melody, the rhythmic variety, for example, being much greater in the Strauss excerpt. Certain other features of this melody, including motivic organization, are similar to Mozart's.

EXAMPLE 4–2    Strauss: *Ein Heldenleben* (A Hero's Life), Op. 40 (1898), mm. 1–13 (melody only)

Large leaps occur still more frequently in the Hindemith theme discussed in Chapter 2 (Example 2–18, p. 33). Notice that in this theme there are no 3rds at all, whereas about half of the intervals are perfect 4ths or perfect 5ths. Though the range of this melody is not wide in comparison with Mozart's, the effect when it is played on the trombone is of a wider range than is actually the case. The chromatic scale that is the source of the pitch material in this melody is, of course, only one of the new scale resources available to the composer.

It would be misleading to imply that all twentieth-century melodies span a wide range and use a large number of leaps. Though this would be true of many melodies, others do just the opposite. The range of the melody in Example 4–3 is only a perfect 5th, and the largest interval is a minor 3rd. One aspect that gives this melody its twentieth-century sound is its chromaticism. Each phrase (if we take each slurred segment as a phrase) spans some segment of the chromatic scale:

| | | |
|---|---|---|
| Phrase 1 | M3 | (A–C♯) |
| Phrase 2 | tt | (A–E♭) |
| Phrase 3 | P4 | (B–E) |
| Phrase 4 | P4 | (B♭–E♭) |

In each case, the second part of the phrase fills in chromatic notes missing from the first part. Another feature of this melody is its unconventional rhythm. While details of twentieth-century rhythm are the topic of a later chapter, we can observe here that, in spite of the carefully notated changes in time signature, the listener perceives only an unpredictable mixture of eighths and quarters, with stressed notes coming at irregular intervals.

**EXAMPLE 4–3**    Bartók: *Music for String Instruments, Percussion, and Celesta* (1936), I, mm. 1–4

*(© Copyright 1937 in the USA by Boosey & Hawkes, Inc. Copyright renewed. Reprinted by permission.)*

The examples discussed so far have been instrumental melodies, but the developments in the vocal idiom have been similar. Turn back to the Berg excerpt, Example 3–B–8 (p. 72), and you will notice the same tendency toward more and wider leaps, the comparatively wide range, especially for such a short excerpt, and its use of the chromatic scale. The rhythm, while perhaps not unconventional, is more varied than in the Mozart theme. Observe also that the melody does not imply the harmonic structure, in that you could not predict the chords that Berg would choose to harmonize this melody; in fact, about half of the vocal pitches are not contained in the chords that accompany them. The same proportion of notes might be nonchord tones in a tonal song, but in the Berg many of the "nonchord tones," such as the first and last notes of the excerpt, are left unresolved.

Two points made so far can be reviewed with the help of Example 4–4. Beginning with the flute part (the flute in G sounds a perfect 4th lower than written), notice the extreme range of almost three octaves, with most of that occurring within m. 2 alone, and the overwhelming preponderance of leaps, especially wide ones, over stepwise motion. The vocal range is not so extreme, but the voice part is equally disjunct and difficult to perform. Both parts draw their pitch material from the chromatic scale and employ unconventional rhythmic techniques. Both parts also use more expression marks (dynamics, articulation) than was customary in earlier styles, which, while not strictly a melodic phenomenon, certainly contributes to the effect.

**EXAMPLE 4–4**  Pierre Boulez: *Le marteau sans maître (The Hammer without a Master)*, (1955), III,
mm. 1–15   *(Copyright 1954 by Universal Edition (London) Ltd., London. Final version © copyright 1957
by Universal Edition (London) Ltd., London. Poems de Rene Char © copyright 1964 by Jose Corte, Editeur,
Paris. Copyright renewed. All rights reserved. Used by permission of European American Music Distributors
Corporation, sole U.S. and Canadian agent for Universal Edition (London) Ltd., London.)*

The Boulez excerpt is an example of an important trend among some twentieth-century composers to write what many would call less lyrical melodies—that is, melodies that seem inherently less vocal, less flowing, more angular, and frequently more fragmented than we might expect from a tonal melody. Other composers—Gershwin, Hanson, Sibelius, and many others—have kept more faithfully to the lyrical tradition of melody writing. A fine twentieth-century example of a long, flowing melody in the lyrical tradition is the opening theme of William Walton's Violin Concerto (see Example 4–5). This melody contains the numerous leaps so characteristic of many twentieth-century melodies, but its implied tertian harmonies, its straightforward tonality (with some modal flavor), and above all its mode of expression are obviously more Romantic than modern in conception. Some composers in more recent years have shown a renewed interest in melodicism in the traditional sense, either through the quotation of melodies from earlier times or through the composition of new, more lyrical melodies. Both of these aspects will be discussed in later chapters.

**EXAMPLE 4–5**   William Walton: Violin Concerto (1939), I, mm. 1–18 (solo violin only)
*(© 1939 by Oxford University Press. Reproduced with permission.)*

Finally, we might observe that music of the twentieth century seems to be less concerned with melody in general. While much of tonal music is essentially homophonic—melody with accompaniment—the tendency in the twentieth century has been to put more emphasis on other aspects of music, such as rhythm, texture, and timbre.

## SOME ASPECTS OF MELODIC ORGANIZATION

The motivic devices such as those seen in Mozart's melody—repetition, return, sequence, inversion—occur also in twentieth-century melodies. Surely the melodies in this chapter by Strauss, Bartók, and Walton could be discussed in those terms. Repetition and sequence were also seen in previous examples by Lutoslawski (Example 2–20, p. 35), Debussy (Example 3–21, p. 59), Hindemith (Example 3–26, p. 62), and Scriabin (Example 3–29, p. 64). Other melodic devices peculiar to the twentieth century have also come into use. Study Example 4–6, paying special attention to the three phrase marks. The three segments that occur under the phrase marks, though not related in traditional ways, are related nevertheless. The segments are:

1. A–C–C♯
2. D♯–F♯–D
3. C♯–B♭–D–C♯

Each of these segments contains three pitch classes. If we rearrange them, we see that each segment spans a major 3rd and the interval content of each segment is identical:

1. A–C–C♯ = m3 + m2
2. D–D♯–F♯ = m2 + m3 (same intervals in reverse order)
3. B♭–C♯–D = m3 + m2

EXAMPLE 4–6    Anton Webern: Five Canons, Op. 16 (1924), I, mm. 2–5 (voice only)

This kind of motive, really a collection of intervals that can be rearranged and inverted, is often called a **pitch-class cell.** The use of cells, usually of three or four notes each, is an important unifying factor in some twentieth-century music, so important that a special terminology has been developed to deal with it. This terminology will be introduced in Chapter 9.

Another significant factor in the organization of melody has been the development of twelve-tone melody. This term does not refer to just any melody employing the whole chromatic scale, but instead to a melody in which each and every pitch class is used once and only once (tremolo figures and immediate repetitions are allowed). The horn melody in Example 4–7 is such a melody. Once the twelve pitch classes have been presented, another series of twelve pitch classes, related to the first one, can begin. This procedure is discussed in more detail in Chapter 10.

**EXAMPLE 4–7**   Arnold Schoenberg: Wind Quintet, Op. 26 (1924), III, mm. 1–7

*(Used by permission of Belmont Music Publishers.)*

Two points about the notation of Example 4–7 should be made here. One is that this is a "C score," meaning that all of the instruments sound where written, a development that has no doubt met with the approval of students of music everywhere. The second point concerns the boldface "H" and "N" that appear at the beginning of the excerpt. Schoenberg and others used these letters to designate the *Hauptstimme* (primary voice) and the *Nebenstimme* (secondary voice). The end of the *Nebenstimme* in Example 4–7 is marked in the bassoon at the end of m. 7. In a more complex texture, the *Hauptstimme* and the *Nebenstimme* would be the two most important parts, and it would be up to the conductor and performers to bring them out.

Many melodies are arranged so that there is a single high point in each phrase or in the melody as a whole, an approach that has been followed more or less faithfully for centuries. If you look back at the melodies presented in this chapter so far, you will find that this holds true for every one of them.

In more general terms, one could say that melodic organization in the twentieth century tends to be less apparent at the surface level, and the progress of twentieth-century melodies is less predictable than that of tonal melodies. The phrases are less often equal in length, and the clear period forms of the Classical era are the exception. Repetition and sequence, while still found, are often abandoned in favor of other techniques.

## VOICE LEADING IN TWENTIETH-CENTURY MUSIC

In the traditional study of tonal harmony, a great deal of attention is paid to the subject of voice leading, or part-writing, and with good reason. Throughout the tonal era and for centuries prior to its beginning, there were voice-leading conventions that were followed by all composers and that did much to contribute to the homogeneity of their styles. This homogeneity was most pronounced among composers who lived during the same period, such as Haydn and Mozart, but some elements are shared by all composers of the tonal era.

Some of the "rules" that we learn in harmony courses are not actually all that general, even when they are tested against tonal music. These include those procedures gleaned from the study of the works of a particular composer (usually Bach) or that are really valid only for a particular medium (usually choral). We learn them in order to begin the study of tonal composition in a controlled and uncomplicated environment. Two conventions that do seem to be applicable throughout the tonal era, however, are the following:

1. Parallel 5ths and octaves, especially the former, should be avoided.[2]
2. Any chord 7th should resolve down by step.

It is, of course, possible to find passages of twentieth-century music that still adhere to these conventions. This seems to be the case in Example 4–8, from a work that may be more familiar to you under the title "Adagio for Strings." The harmonic vocabulary here is tertian, simplifying the task of sorting out the nonchord tones, but there are several places where more than one interpretation is possible. A suggested chordal analysis is included in the example. There are four 7th chords in the excerpt, with the 7th in each case resolving down by step into the next chord; the voice leading in the other instruments follows for the most part the traditional preference for smooth chord connection. While Example 4–8 exhibits smooth voice leading, very disjunct voice leading is a characteristic of much twentieth-century music. Examples of disjunct voice leading from earlier in this text include Example 2–7 (p. 26) and Example 2–B–3 (p. 40).

Closer examination of Example 4–8 reveals two sets of parallel 5ths and the same number of parallel octaves. One of the sets of 5ths involves a nonchord tone (mm. 3–4, violin II and cello), so it might conceivably be allowed, and both sets of octaves involve temporary octave doubling between an ornamented melody and its slower-moving accompaniment (mm. 4–5 and 7–8), also possibly acceptable. But the parallel 5ths between violin I and cello in mm. 5–6 cannot be explained at all satisfactorily in traditional terms. This, of course, is not an error on the part of the composer, but instead indicates that one of the most sacred rules of counterpoint no longer has the validity that it once had.

**EXAMPLE 4–8**   Samuel Barber: String Quartet No. I, Op. 11 (1936), II, mm. 1–8

Molto Adagio

Parallel 5ths and octaves may occur incidentally in an otherwise traditional texture, as in Example 4–8, but they frequently play a more significant role. For instance, in Example 3–B–6 (p. 70) Ravel makes consistent use of parallel 5ths in the lowest register. Parallel 5ths also occur in **chordal parallelism,** a very important development in twentieth-century music. In tonal music the use of first-inversion triads moving in parallel motion was an accepted compositional device, serving in many cases as a connection between two more important chords and in others as a means of thickening a melodic line. The use of a three-part texture resulted in parallel 3rds, 4ths, and 6ths, but no parallel 5ths or octaves occurred. Other uses of harmonic parallelism included parallel °7 chords and, less frequently, parallel ᵩ7 chords. Though parallel 5ths might occur on rare occasion, as in one of the Wagner examples (Example 1–7, p. 8), their use was exceptional.

One reason for the traditional avoidance of parallel 5ths and octaves was that these intervals, more than any other consonant interval, when used in parallel motion imply a breakdown of counterpoint—that is, of relatively independent musical lines. We tend to think of counterpoint as something found in fugues, but counterpoint of some kind was the basis of most tonal music, which in fact evolved the way it did largely because of contrapuntal procedures. In the twentieth century, however, composers have been unrestrained in their use of harmonic parallelism and have shown no aversion to the use of parallel intervals of all kinds. This has led to a redefining of some aspects of counterpoint and to new developments in texture. If we can compare a single melodic line to a line drawn on a canvas with a pen, then the analogy used earlier comparing harmonic parallelism to painting with a broad brush may prove helpful. In Example 4–9, for instance, ascending scales in both hands of the piano part are broadened into root-position triads wih roots doubled, resulting in parallel 5ths and octaves.

**EXAMPLE 4–9**  Bartók Piano Concerto No. 2 (1931), I, mm. 295–304   *(© Copyright 1933 by Hawkes & Son (London) Ltd. Copyright renewed. Reprinted by permission of Boosey & Hawkes, Inc.)*

Harmonic parallelism, so typical of much twentieth-century music, is often referred to as **planing.**[3] Parallelism may be **diatonic,** meaning that it uses only the white keys of the piano or some transposition of them (see Example 4–9), **real,** meaning that the sonority is exactly transposed (see the piano in mm. 1–2 of Example 4–10), or **mixed,** meaning that the parallelism is not consistently diatonic or real (see the cellos in m. 4 of Example 4–10). Though there are lots of "parts" sounding in Example 4–10, it is really an example of three-part counterpoint, twentieth-century style. The three parts are:

1. Violins and violas. Use of diatonic planing in m. 1 and real planing in mm. 2–4.

2. Cellos and piano. Real planing until m. 4, where two minor triads are employed. The planing in this measure is mixed.

3. Basses.

Notice that the three parts have their own contours and, to some extent, their own rhythms, fulfilling the essential requirements of counterpoint.

**EXAMPLE 4–10** Roger Sessions: Symphony No. 2 (1946), IV, mm. 1–4 (piano and strings only)

Mixed parallelism, as in m. 4 of Example 4–10, is not unusual. Most of the planing in the first two measures of Example 4–11 is diatonic, but Debussy uses an E♮ in one chord, presumably to avoid the sound of a diminished triad at this point. In the last two measures of the example the planing is clearly mixed, although the roots of the chords all belong to A♭ major.

**EXAMPLE 4–11** Debussy: Preludes, Book I (1910), "Dancers of Delphi," mm. 11–14

Triads are not the only sonorities that can be planed. Example 4–12 begins with five inverted 9th chords, followed by five inverted 7th chords, then by five 7th chords in root position, and, finally, by four root-position triads. Real planing is employed within each group. The progression from complex sounds to simple ones is aurally obvious and effective.

**EXAMPLE 4–12**   Roy Harris: Symphony No. 7 (1952) (strings only)

Nontertian sonorities are frequently planed as well. Real planing of quartal chords occurs in Example 3–21 (p. 59), and there is diatonic planing of clusters in Example 3–23 (p. 60).

We have seen that the tradition that forbade certain parallels is no longer followed in much music of the twentieth century, but what about the other convention that we discussed, the one about dissonance treatment? In tonal music we sometimes use the term "essential dissonance" to refer to dissonances between members of the same chord (such as between the root and 7th) as opposed to "nonessential dissonances" involving ornamentation (passing tones and so forth). It is usually not difficult when analyzing tonal music to separate the essential dissonances from the ornaments, and the essential dissonances generally resolve in predictable fashion. Neither of these is necessarily true in twentieth-century music. For instance, turn back to Example 4–7 and play it on a piano or listen to a recording. At the beginning, the E♭ in the horn is sustained against G–A–B–C♯ in the bassoon, after which the C♯ is sustained against E♭–C–B♭ in the horn. In neither case is it possible to distinguish essential from nonessential dissonances, since there is no way of identifying the "chords," and the dissonances appear to be approached and left freely.

This free treatment of dissonance, called "emancipation of the dissonance" by Schoenberg,[4] is the norm in a large proportion of twentieth-century works. Many of the examples already used in this text also illustrate free treatment of dissonance, including those listed below. In some of these excerpts the chords are not difficult to identify, but in none of them are dissonances consistently handled in a traditional fashion.

| | |
|---|---|
| Example 2–7 (Henze, p. 26) | Example 3–21 (Debussy, p. 59) |
| Example 2–12 (Debussy, p. 29) | Example 3–23 (Ives, p. 60) |
| Example 2–17 (Scriabin, p. 32) | Example 3–26 (Hindemith, p. 62) |
| Example 2–21 (Bartók, p. 36) | Example 3–31 (Persichetti, p. 65) |
| Example 3–10 (Stravinsky, p. 51) | Example 3–32 (Stravinsky, p. 65) |
| Example 3–14 (Ravel, p. 53) | Example 4–4 (Boulez, p. 79) |
| Example 3–15 (Copland, p. 54) | Example 4–10 (Sessions, p. 87) |
| Example 3–19 (Copland, p. 57) | Example 4–12 (Harris, p. 90) |

This "emancipation of the dissonance" has led some to suggest that the whole notion of dissonance should be reevaluated, since a dissonance by some definitions means a sound that requires resolution to a consonance. If sounds need not resolve, are there perhaps no longer any dissonances? This makes very good sense, but we still need a term to label the effect produced by certain combinations of sounds, and "dissonance" remains the most popular choice.

In spite of the repeal of the rules governing parallels and dissonance treatment, there are probably certain basic truths about voice leading that are independent of style. One of them is that counterpoint is threatened whenever voices move in parallel motion, and this is especially true when the intervals between the voices are exactly maintained. For example, parallel major 3rds would tend to destroy a two-voice contrapuntal texture faster than a mixture of major and minor 3rds. Another principle is that the smoothest effect when moving from one chord to another is gained if common tones are maintained where possible and all voices move by the smallest available interval. Finally, the effect of a dissonance can be softened by smooth motion—common tones or steps—into and out of the dissonance.

In the twentieth century these truths are no longer conventions to be followed, but instead are merely tools or approaches that are among those available to the composer. So what conventions remain to guide the composer, if the rules concerning parallels and dissonances no longer hold? None, really, which is what Stravinsky meant when he wrote of the "abyss of freedom" and of the "terror" he felt when faced with this multiplicity of choices. He went on to say that he defined a new set of compositional rules (Stravinsky referred to them as "limitations" and "obstacles") for each work.[5] The task of the composer is to create a work that is consistent, that is stylistically unified within its own self-defined universe. The task of the student is to try to understand what that universe is and how the different aspects of the composition fit into it.

## SUMMARY

The traditional approaches to composing melodies are still available to the composer, and certainly there are twentieth-century melodies that exhibit many of them. What interests us here is not so much the traditional aspects of twentieth-century melodies as those aspects that set them apart from the music of the past. Though the fragmentation of styles in the twentieth century makes any generalization difficult, a list of the tendencies seen in twentieth-century melody would include the following:

Wider range

More leaps

More chromaticism

Less lyricism

Unconventional rhythm

More expression marks

Avoidance of traditional harmonic implications

Less regular phrase structure

Motivic use of pitch-class cells

Twelve-tone melody

Less emphasis on melody in general

Voice-leading procedures in the twentieth century are as varied as the multiplicity of musical styles would suggest. The traditional procedures are still available and have not been discarded entirely, but some important conventions of tonal harmony must now be considered as options rather than rules. As a result, parallel motion of all kinds is acceptable, including harmonic planing, while dissonances have been freed from conventional resolutions, and even from any requirement for resolution at all.

## NOTES

1. Throughout this chapter and much of the remainder of this book, "tonal" is used to refer to the system of functional harmonic tonality employed in Western art music from around 1600 to around 1900. This use of the term admittedly can be misleading, since it implies that all other music is atonal. The author hopes that this disclaimer will head off any such misconceptions.

2. Parallel octaves were allowed when one part merely doubled another consistently at the interval of an octave. The same cannot be said of 5ths.

3. Some prefer to use the term "organum" for harmonic parallelism in the twentieth century, especially when it involves root-position triads.

4. Arnold Schoenberg, *Style and Idea*, pp. 216–17.

5. Igor Stravinsky, *Poetics of Music*, pp. 63–65.

## EXERCISES

### Part A: Fundamentals

The Fundamentals exercises in this chapter provide a review of material from earlier chapters.

1. Find a doubly chromatic mediant relationship between two adjacent chords in some example in this chapter.

2. Notate the following scales:

   (a) Pentatonic on A♭

   (b) Whole-tone on G

   (c) Phrygian on F

   (d) Dorian on G♯

   (e) Octatonic (diminished) beginning D–E

3. Review the summary at the end of Chapter 3. Of the nine chord types listed there, which term best describes:

   (a) the chords in mm. 3–4 of Example 4–10?

   (b) the chords in Example 4–12?

### Part B: Analysis

1. Alban Berg: Violin Concerto (1935), I, mm. 84–93 (solo violin only)
   Discuss this melody, including the following points:

   (a) What elements are especially typical of twentieth-century melody?

   (b) Is any part of this melody a twelve-tone melody?

   (c) Does this melody make use of pitch-class cells?

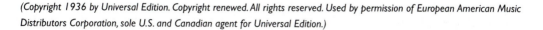

2. Edgard Varèse: *Density 21.5* (1936, 1946), mm. 1–17
   Discuss this melody, including the following points:

   (a) Which of its elements are especially typical of twentieth-century melody?

   (b) Is any part of this melody a twelve-tone melody?

   (c) List those portions of the melody that could be analyzed as octatonic.

   (d) How is the melody organized in terms of motives? Other aspects?

3. Karl Korte: *Aspects of Love* (1965), I, mm. 1–3
   Write out the bass line of this excerpt, and under each bass note label the root and

quality of the chord (except for the open 5ths, where the quality cannot be determined). Some of the chords are spelled enharmonically. Then answer the following questions.

(a) In what ways does the voice leading in this excerpt depart from conventional practice, especially in terms of "forbidden" parallels and dissonance treatment? List specific instances.

(b) Toward the end of the excerpt the composer employs enharmonic spellings. Why not just use sharps or flats in all voices?

*(Used by permission of E. C. Schirmer Music Company. A division of ECS Publishing.)*

4. Review the discussion of Example 4–10. Then briefly discuss the texture of Example 4–11, using a similar approach.
5. Study the voice leading in the following examples.

Example 2–4 (p. 24)    Example 3–10 (p. 51)    Example 3–23 (p. 60)

Example 2–10 (p. 28)    Example 3–20 (p. 58)    Example 3–29 (p. 64)

Example 2–11 (p. 29)    Example 3–21 (p. 59)    Example 3–B–8 (p. 72)

Then answer the questions below, using each example only once.

(a) Which one features two sets of parallel 5ths in imitation?

(b) Which one uses diatonic planing of triads?

(c) Which one uses real planing of triads?

(d) Which two use real planing of nontertian sonorities?

(e) Which one features clusters in parallel motion?

(f) Which one features unresolved dissonances?

(g) Which one adheres most closely to traditional voice leading?

## Part C: Composition

1. Compose a melody exhibiting several of the characteristics of twentieth-century melody discussed in the Summary (but not including pitch-class cells or twelve-tone melody), and list those characteristics. Try not to let your melody sound too random, and see that every phrase includes a single high point.

2. Compose a melody following the preceding instructions, but using the cell E–G–G♯ and its mirror inversion E–C♯–C as a unifying factor. The cell and its inversion may be used in any transposition and in any octave, and the notes of the cell may be used in any order. Label each appearance of the cell with brackets.

3. Compose an adagio melody in the same style as the horn melody in Example 4–7, using the pitch classes from that melody, but in reverse order.

4. Compose a short example in which a Phrygian melody is accompanied by planed triads (diatonic planing).

5. Continue the following example, using real planing throughout.

6. Compose an excerpt similar in style to Example 4–B–3, following these guidelines:

(a) Use triads, 7th chords, and open 5ths only. Label each chord.

(b) Approach each 7th by step or common tone, and leave it by step up or leap down.

(c) Include some parallel fifths.

(d) Be sure that each part is easy to sing.

## FURTHER READING

DALLIN, LEON. *Techniques of Twentieth Century Composition*. See Chapter 4, Twentieth Century Melodic Practices, and the section titled Parallelism in Chapter 7.

KLIEWER, VERNON L. "Melody: Linear Aspects of Twentieth-Century Music," Chapter 4 in Gary Wittlich, ed., *Aspects of Twentieth Century Music*.

PERSICHETTI, VINCENT. *Twentieth-Century Harmony*. Much of Chapters 3–7 is devoted to details of voice leading.

# FIVE

# Harmonic Progression and Tonality

## INTRODUCTION

The late nineteenth and early twentieth centuries saw the decline of the tonal system, which had been an important organizing factor in music since the early Baroque. In its place came not a new system but a splintering, a multiplicity of solutions to the problems of harmonic progression and tonality. At the most general level, music is either tonal or not tonal (usually termed atonal), but various approaches may be taken in both of those categories. As we shall see, even the tonal music of the twentieth century was of a new sort, one without a standardized vocabulary of harmonic progressions.

## TRADITIONAL APPROACHES TO HARMONIC PROGRESSION

The beginnings of triadic tonality can be found in music composed many years before the beginning of the tonal era. Through evolutionary processes (influenced by voice-leading conventions and the nature of musical acoustics), certain chord successions became standard cadential formulas long before tonal harmony came into being and even longer before the development of the theory of chord roots. Chief among these was the progression that would later be analyzed as a V–I cadence, but other cadences, such as IV–I, vii°6–I, and iv6–V, were also used. As the language of tonality developed, the V–I progression became the prototype of the normative harmonic progression, as seen in the diatonic circle-of-5ths progression:

I–IV–vii°–iii–vi–ii–V–I

  or

i–iv–VII–III–VI–ii°–V–i

All of the roots in these progressions move by descending diatonic 5th, either perfect or diminished. The same is true in the following progressions, which use some altered chords. Notice that leading-tone chords can substitute for dominant chords of equivalent function.

V7/V–V–I                              vii°7/vi–vi–vii°7/V

VI–N6–V                              V7/vi–vii°7/ii–V7/V

If the subdominant triad is allowed to substitute for the supertonic triad, putting ii–V and IV–V in the same category, and vii° is allowed to substitute for V, we find that most of the standard chord progressions of tonal music are circle-of-5ths types. Exceptions include those that involve "linear" chords, such as augmented-6th chords, and others used to extend the phrase, such as the "deceptive" progression (V–vi).

This system turned out to be extremely flexible. It allowed a broad range of expression and made possible the composition of long works organized over a background harmonic structure. But late in the nineteenth century and in the early decades of the twentieth, compositional assaults on the system became so insistent that traditional tonality and its associated harmonic progressions all but disappeared from the works of "serious" composers. The procedures that have been discussed in earlier chapters—the introduction of new scales and chord types and the redefinition of the fundamental principles of voice leading—had much to do with the decline of tonal harmony.

Conventional harmonic progressions still occur with some frequency, especially at cadences, in works from the early part of the twentieth century. Two such examples from earlier in this text are Example 3–3 (p. 48), by Debussy, and Example 3–B–5 (p. 69), by Ravel. Examples of conventional progressions from later in the century generally are found in works with a nationalistic or folk-music background, such as Copland's *Billy the Kid;* in the works by staunchly conservative composers such as Rachmaninoff; or in works of a lighter, more entertaining sort, like Menotti's *The Telephone* (see Example 3–11, p. 51). Since the 1970s, conventional tonal music has found new life in an important style called "neoromanticism," to be discussed in Chapter 15.

Perhaps the healthiest and most vital continuation of traditional harmony was in the "popular" music of the twentieth century, which includes everything from Broadway musicals to folk music to jazz to rock music. The harmonizations of most of this music can be analyzed using traditional approaches, but the analysis should concentrate on the composer's actual harmonization, not on the chord symbols that often appear in popular-music editions and which are frequently at odds with the original score. More recent rock music, especially since the introduction of electronic synthesizers, has shown an increasing tendency to leave behind its harmonic roots in the blues tradition and to concentrate on unconventional timbres and nonstandard progressions, while rap music is entirely rhythmic without any harmony or tonality at all.

## NEW APPROACHES TO HARMONIC PROGRESSION

We might expect that, as the older system declined, a new one would have developed to take its place, perhaps one built on root movements of a 3rd or on more-involved cycles of root movements. In fact this did not happen. There is no common harmonic language shared by all composers, although composers are free to devise and follow their own stylistic "rules" (recall the Stravinsky quote on p. 91).

Even twentieth-century modal music tends to avoid root movements by 5ths, as well as the voice-leading constraints of traditional major-minor music. But there are exceptions, as in Example 2–B–4 (p. 42), where a simple modal melody is accompanied by tertian chords. The harmonization of most of this excerpt is quite traditional, although the supertonic $^6_4$ chords in mm. 10 and 12 and the altered dominant in m. 18 are not. Nevertheless, this is a fairly close modal equivalent of a conventional tonal progression.

Composers who still make use of tertian sonorities generally do so in the context of unusual or unpredictable harmonic successions. In Example 3–9 (p. 50) Debussy ended a piece with the following progression:

Em–AM–Fm–CM$^{add9}$

This succession of chords is surely intended to be unpredictable to the listener, to delight and surprise rather than to perform the task of most tonal progressions, which is to satisfy expectations. It is of no help to the listener that a similar progression appeared earlier (mm. 4–5), because the similarity is one of gesture rather than of detail:

E♭M–A♭M–G♭M–Dm

Much of the element of surprise in these two passages is provided by doubly chromatic mediant relationships: A major–F minor and G♭ major–D minor.

Examples of such successions—one hesitates to call them progressions—abound in twentieth-century tertian music. Example 5–1 is simpler, the chords consisting of an A minor tonic triad and its B♭ minor neighbor. Notice the free use of nonchord tones in the bass melody.

**EXAMPLE 5–1**  Aram Khachaturian: Piano Concerto (1936), II, mm. 1–8 *(Copyright © 1947 UNIVERSAL MUSIC COPR. Copyright renewed. All Rights Reserved. Used by permission.)*

The subject of harmonic progression becomes even murkier when nontertian chords are considered, because the roots of such chords are not defined by any generally accepted theory or by the common agreement of listeners. The most successful attempt to develop a universal theory of chord roots was carried out by Paul Hindemith in his *Craft of Musical Composition*,[1] first published in 1937. Although his theory does account for all possible chords (with the exception of microtonal chords) and had a certain amount of influence in the middle of the century, it has since fallen into disfavor, largely because, as Hindemith himself wrote, "A true musician believes only in what he hears,"[2] and his fellow musicians remained unconvinced.

If it is no longer possible to create meaningful harmonic progressions based on chord roots, are there other possibilities? One would be to arrange a succession of chords according to some measurement of the tension, or dissonance, that each contains. Again, Hindemith was one of the few to attempt a systematic approach to harmonic tension that would account for all possible sonorities. He devised six chord groups, with six subgroups bringing the total number of classifications to twelve. To most of these was assigned a relative degree of harmonic tension, which, along with other aspects of his theory, allowed Hindemith to propose "progressions" of chords arranged according to their tension.[3] As with his theory of chord roots, this aspect of Hindemith's theory has not withstood the test of time. Nevertheless, it would be foolish to dismiss out of hand the considered opinions of an accomplished composer, and the interested reader is urged to study his theory in its entirety.[4]

Even without a universally accepted theory, a composer is, of course, free to attempt progressions of tension. Other possibilities might include progressions of register, chord type, density, numbers of pitch classes, and so forth. We are on unfamiliar ground here, as we often are in approaching twentieth-century works, and imagination and flexibility of approach are important analytical tools.

## NONHARMONIC MUSIC

In its broadest definition, harmony means the vertical aspect of music, and a harmony, or chord, is any collection of pitch classes sounded simultaneously. Such broad definitions are sometimes useful, but they may also distract us from the fact that a good deal of twentieth-century music is not harmonic in conception. Sometimes the "simultaneities" in a piece are just that—the more or less uncontrolled coming-together of very independent lines: Although Schoenberg was certainly not completely indifferent to the vertical dimension, it would appear that the primary emphasis in Example 5–2, for instance, is on lines, rather than the chords that they produce. (Remember that the bass clarinet will sound a major 9th lower than written.) The term **linear counterpoint** is often used for music of this sort, where the compositional method is evidently overwhelmingly linear. This approach is typical of much atonal music, but it occurs in other styles as well.

EXAMPLE 5–2    Schoenberg: *Pierrot Lunaire,* Op. 21 (1912), "Madonna," mm. 1–4

*(Used by permission of Belmont Music Publishers.)*

## ESTABLISHING A TONAL CENTER

Before examining how tonality is established in twentieth-century works, let us review how this was accomplished in traditional tonal harmony. One important element was a descending perfect-5th root movement to tonic combined with a half-step leading-tone motion, also to tonic. The tonicizing effect was often made more convincing by a harmonic tritone formed by scale degrees 7 and 4 resolving stepwise to 1 and 3. Other elements were important also, such as melodic emphasis on 1, 3, and 5, melodic skips between 1 and 5, and formal considerations.

All of these elements may be present to some degree in twentieth-century music that has a tonal center, but a traditional V7–I cadence would be exceptional. Instead, other ways have been devised to make the tonal center clear to the listener. Essentially, these methods establish **tonic by assertion**—that is, through the use of reiteration, return, pedal point, ostinato, accent, formal placement, register, and similar techniques to draw the listener's attention to a particular pitch class. When analyzing the tonality of a passage, it is important to pay attention to melodic aspects as well as harmonic ones, since melodic factors are often crucial in determining the tonality.

For instance, in Example 5–3 the tonality of D is clearly indicated by the motion from tonic to dominant in the voice and by the D pedal point. A three-chord harmonic progression continually circles around D by half-steps (C♯–E♭–D) until the Sonnet ends with the progression with which it began: D–C♯–E♭–C–D. While there is no V–I harmonic progression here, Britten does outline a V$^7$ chord in the bass until the arrival of the penultimate chord.

**EXAMPLE 5–3** Britten: Serenade for Tenor Solo, Horn, and Strings, Op. 31 (1943), "Sonnet," mm. 33–37 *(© Copyright 1944 by Hawkes & Son (London) Ltd. Copyright renewed. Reprinted by permission of Boosey & Hawkes, Inc.)*

Example 5–1 convinced us that A is the tonal center of the passage without the use of a pedal point. There is also no hint of dominant harmony or of any conventional scale on A, and the leading tone appears only once (in m. 7, as A♭); in addition, there are just as many measures of B♭ minor chords as there are of A minor chords. Yet we hear A as the tonal center because it was there first, before the melody began, and because A is important both melodically and harmonically at the beginning and end of the phrase. The B♭ minor triads, while interesting, do not distract our attention from the true tonal center.

Example 5–2, on the other hand, does little to establish any tonal center. Play through the individual lines to convince yourself of this (the effect is even stronger when the parts are performed simultaneously). We will return briefly to the subject of atonality later in this chapter.

We will use the term **pitch-centricity** in reference to music that is tonal but in which the tonal center is established through nontraditional means. Though not an ideal term, it will help us to distinguish between the tonal music of the seventeenth through nineteenth centuries and the pitch-centric music of the twentieth century.

## TERTIAN AND NONTERTIAN PITCH-CENTRICITY

As we examine additional pitch-centric examples, we will attempt to categorize them into one of two types: tertian pitch-centricity and nontertian pitch-centricity. As the terms imply, the first type uses primarily chords built from 3rds, whereas the second type usually avoids such sonorities, except perhaps at cadences. Many examples will be of a mixed type, displaying features of both.

Examples 5–1 and 5–3 are both examples of tertian pitch-centricity. Another example of tertian pitch-centricity is seen in Example 2–B–4 (p. 42), whose harmonic progression was discussed earlier in this chapter. In that excerpt, the tonality of D is clearly established, both melodically and harmonically. Melodically, D is established by formal placement (beginnings and ends of phrases), by agogic accent, and by the frequent reiteration of D. The harmonic aspects that establish D as the tonal center include formal placement, pedal point, reiteration, and (in mm. 18–19) a V–I root movement (although not a traditional V7–I progression).

Much of the composition in which Example 5–4 appears is in a tertian pitch-centric style, but the excerpt shown here is nontertian. Even though there is an open 5th on D at the end of the excerpt, suggesting a tertian harmony, the excerpt is basically nontertian, since there is little else about the harmony or melody that suggests tertian construction. The tonality of D in Example 5–4 is established by both melodic and harmonic factors. Notice that the first phrase in the flute begins on A and ends on D, while the second begins on F (E♯) and ends on A, which is followed by F♯ and D. All of these notes are members of major or minor triads on D. In the piano part the emphasis on the pitch classes D and A is obvious. Even though this music is basically nontertian, the traditional dominant-to-tonic relationship is employed to help establish the tonality.

**EXAMPLE 5–4**  Walter Piston: Flute Sonata (1930), I, last 6 measures  *(Copyright © 1933 (Renewed) by Associated Music Publishers, Inc. (BMI). International copyright secured. All rights reserved. Reprinted by permission.)*

Example 5–5 seems to have a mixture of tertian and nontertian elements. It begins with an F major triad, the third chord is an F minor triad, and the last sonority is an open 5th on F, but the other four chords in the excerpt sound more like quartal or mixed-interval chords. The tonality in Example 5–5 is established by several factors. The melody obviously centers around F, and the harmony of the phrase begins and ends on F, while in the inner voices there is a double pedal point on F and C. Another interesting feature is the duet between alto and bass, moving in parallel major 10ths until the last two chords, where contrary motion takes over.

EXAMPLE 5–5    Hindemith: *Ludus Tonalis* (1943), Interlude (No. IX), mm. 8–10

*(© Schott & Co., Ltd., London, 1943. Copyright renewed. All rights reserved. Used by permission of European American Music Distributors Corporation, sole U.S. and Canadian agent for Schott & Co., Ltd., London.)*

## POLYTONALITY

**Polytonality** is conceptually similar to the polychord, which was defined in Chapter 3 as a combination of two or more aurally distinguishable sonorities. Likewise, polytonality is the simultaneous use of two or more aurally distinguishable tonal centers, almost all examples consisting of two tonal centers rather than three or more. The term **bitonal** is sometimes used for polytonal music with two tonal centers. As a general rule, each tonal layer in a polytonal passage will be basically diatonic to its own scale.

The last section of Debussy's "Fireworks" (see Example 5–6) begins in D♭, over which is superimposed a C major melody (a reference to "La Marseillaise") and its counterpoint. Only in the last three measures is the polytonal conflict resolved, with the D♭ tonality winning out.

**EXAMPLE 5–6**  Debussy: Preludes, Book II (1913), "Fireworks" ("Feux d'artifice"), mm. 91–99

In Example 5–7 bitonality occurs in a modal setting. Here the first violin is in E♭ Dorian, while the cello is in D Dorian (notice the planed triads). Meanwhile, the other instruments are playing only D's and E♭'s. In both Example 5–6 and Example 5–7 the tonalities were a minor 2nd apart, but this is in no sense a "rule" of bitonality. Other relationships can and do occur.

EXAMPLE 5–7    Bartók: String Quartet No. 3 (1927), II

An interesting example of polytonality involving four tonal levels is found in the second movement of Henry Brant's *Angels and Devils* (1932, 1947), where a pair of piccolos and three pairs of flutes are notated in four different keys. It would take a sharp ear indeed to sort all of this out aurally, but most listeners are probably aware that some sort of polytonality is involved.

## ATONALITY

**Atonality** was a development even more radical than the various sorts of pitch-centricity in twentieth-century music. The ways in which atonality has been achieved and the analytical approaches that have been developed for atonal music are extensive and will be discussed in later chapters. For now it will suffice to define atonal music as music in which the listener perceives no tonal center. Since this is a subjective definition, listeners will not always agree as to whether a particular example is tonal or atonal, but the following examples from earlier in the text would probably be heard as atonal by most musicians.

> Example 2–7 (Henze, p. 26)
>
> Example 2–17 (Scriabin, p. 32)
>
> Example 2–B–3 (Webern, p. 40)
>
> Example 4–4 (Boulez, p. 79)
>
> Example 4–7 (Schoenberg, p. 82)
>
> Example 5–2 (Schoenberg, p. 102)

## PANDIATONICISM

Most atonal music, as well as a large proportion of other works composed in the twentieth or late nineteenth century, is based on the chromatic scale. Presumably as a reaction against such unremitting chromaticism, some composers have employed a style known as *pandiatonicism*. The term *pandiatonic* is used to describe a passage that uses only the tones of some diatonic scale but does not rely on traditional harmonic progressions and dissonance treatment. Some writers prefer to require a diatonic passage to be atonal before it can be defined as pandiatonic, while others do not. In this text we will follow the approach that pandiatonic passages may be tonal or atonal, tertian or nontertian. An earlier excerpt by Ives, Example 3–23 (p. 60), illustrates nontertian pandiatonicism. Most of the sonorities in the excerpt are clusters derived from the C major scale. The three altered notes that appear do not seem to destroy the basic pandiatonic sound. The tonality is not obvious, but it is probably G, which at the end is both the highest and the lowest pitch class.

The pandiatonic passage in Example 5–8 makes use of the C major scale. It is best classified as tertian, but the chords are sometimes difficult to identify with certainty. Later in the piece, the music "modulates" through several pandiatonic areas, including C♯, G♭, and F. Other famous pandiatonic passages occur in Stravinsky's *Petrushka* and Copland's *Appalachian Spring*.

**EXAMPLE 5–8**   Stravinsky: Serenade in A (1925), I, mm. 52–58   *(© Copyright 1926 by Hawkes & Son (London) Ltd. Copyright renewed. Reprinted by permission of Boosey & Hawkes, Inc.)*

### SUMMARY

Traditional tonal harmony and the circle-of-5ths progressions associated with it survived in various kinds of popular music as well as in a small proportion of "classical" music in the twentieth century. Otherwise, harmonic progression has to be regarded as a nonissue in an era without a common harmonic vocabulary and no generally accepted theory of chord roots. The declining interest in the vertical dimension is exemplified by linear counterpoint, in which the "chords" seem truly to be mere simultaneities created by the relatively uncontrolled relationships between independent lines.

For the most part, at least after the first few decades of the century, "serious" music has been either pitch-centric or atonal. Pitch-centric music, whether tertian or nontertian, has had to rely on methods other than the V7–I progression for establishing a tonality. These methods include such devices as pedal point and ostinato, accent (metric, agogic, or dynamic) and formal placement. Melodies play a larger role in determining the tonality than was the case in tonal music.

Other developments in twentieth-century tonality include polytonality, the employment of two or more tonal centers simultaneously; atonality, the avoidance of a tonal center; and pandiatonicism, the use of a diatonic scale in a nontraditional context.

## NOTES

1. Paul Hindemith, *Craft of Musical Composition*, Vol. I.
2. Hindemith, *Craft*, p. 156.
3. See especially pp. 158–60.
4. Other attempts have been made to compute the dissonance level of chords, but none has had the influence of Hindemith's. One example is in Wallace Berry, *Structural Functions in Music*, pp. 107–11.

## EXERCISES

### Part A: Fundamentals

Define each of the following terms.

1. Chromatic mediant relationship
2. Cluster
3. Mode of limited transposition
4. Pitch-centricity
5. Pandiatonicism
6. Pitch-class cell
7. Planing
8. Polychord
9. Real sequence

### Part B: Analysis

Each of the following excerpts for analysis is to be approached in the same way:

a. Assuming the excerpt is pitch-centric, what is the tonal center, and what melodic and harmonic factors contribute to establishing that tonality?
b. Is the pitch-centric style tertian, nontertian, or a mixture of the two?
c. Is the excerpt polytonal? If so, discuss.
d. Is the excerpt pandiatonic? If so, discuss.
e. Do you find any evidence of traditional harmonic progressions? Explain your answer.

1. Example 2–4, p. 24 (Bartók: *Bluebeard's Castle*)
2. Example 2–12, p. 29 (Debussy: "Footprints in the Snow")
3. Example 3–5, p. 49 (Prokofiev: Flute Sonata)

4. Example 3–B–6, p. 69 (Ravel: Sonatina)
5. Example 3–B–8, p. 72 (Alban Berg: "Warm Is the Air")
6. Copland: *El Salón México* (1936)

7. Darius Milhaud: *Saudades do Brasil* (1921), "Botafogo," mm. 1–10

## *Part C: Composition*

As an alternative to any of the following exercises, disregard the music that is provided and compose your own example, illustrating the specified techniques.

1. Continue in B♭, illustrating tertian pitch-centricity.

2. Continue in a mostly nontertian pitch-centric style. Try to convince the listener of a tonal center on D.

3. Compose an excerpt using polychords with A as a tonal center. End your example with the following cadence.

4. Continue, illustrating C major pandiatonicism and the use of an ostinato.

Brightly

5. Use bitonality (B and D) at the beginning of this example, resolving into a single tonality at the end.

Slowly

## FURTHER READING

Dallin, Leon. *Techniques of Twentieth Century Composition*. See Chapter 7, Harmonic Succession, Chapter 8, Tonality, and Chapter 9, Cadences.

Hindemith, Paul. *Craft of Musical Composition*, Vol. I. See especially the sections on interval roots (pp. 68–74, 79–89), chord roots (pp. 94–106), and harmonic tension (pp. 106–108, 158–164).

Persichetti, Vincent. *Twentieth-Century Harmony*. See the sections on "Progression" (pp. 182–188) and "Cadential Devices" (pp. 206–209), as well as pp. 248–261 in Chapter 12, Key Centers.

Reisberg, Horace. "The Vertical Dimension in Twentieth-Century Music," in Gary Wittlich, ed., *Aspects of 20th Century Music*. See the section titled "Negation of Harmony," pp. 372–385.

Steinke, Greg A. *Bridge to 20th Century Music*. See Chapter 1, which deals with melodic tonality.

Zieliński, Tadeusz A. "Harmony and Counterpoint," in John Vinton, ed., *Dictionary of Contemporary Music*.

# SIX

# Developments in Rhythm

## INTRODUCTION

One of the many features distinguishing the music of the twentieth century from that of the tonal era is its preoccupation with rhythm. Though rhythm is an important element of tonal music, perhaps in ways that are still not completely understood, the surface rhythm of most tonal pieces is relatively straightforward and easy to comprehend, so much so that analyses of such pieces often make little or no mention of the rhythmic dimension. In contrast, in many twentieth-century compositions the focus is on rhythm at least as much as on pitch, and the surface rhythms are frequently varied and complex. This chapter will explore some of the ways that these varieties and complexities are achieved, but first it will be useful to review some terminology.

> *Rhythm*—The organization of the time element in music.
> *Beat*—The basic pulse.
> *Simple beat*—Division of the beat into two equal parts.
> *Compound beat*—Division of the beat into three equal parts.
> *Meter*—The grouping of beats into larger units.
> *Duple meter*—The grouping of beats into twos.
> *Triple meter*—The grouping of beats into threes.
> *Quadruple meter*—The grouping of beats into fours.
> *Measure*—One full unit of the meter.

In simple beat, the beat note has traditionally been as large as a half-note and as small as a sixteenth-note. The customary time (meter) signatures for simple beat, then, have consisted of a 2, 3, or 4 over a 2, 4, 8, or 16. In compound beat, the custom has been for the top number of the meter signature to be the number of *divisions* of the beat that may occur in the measure; thus, the top number will always be 6, 9, or 12, for duple, triple, or quadruple meters, respectively. The bottom number specifies the duration of the division of the beat, traditionally a quarter-note, an eighth-note, or a sixteenth-note. The usual time signatures for compound beat, then, have consisted of a 6, 9, or 12 over a 4, 8, or 16.

|  | *Duple* | | | | *Triple* | | | | *Quadruple* | | | |
|---|---|---|---|---|---|---|---|---|---|---|---|---|
| Simple | $\frac{2}{2}$ | $\frac{2}{4}$ | $\frac{2}{8}$ | $\frac{2}{16}$ | $\frac{3}{2}$ | $\frac{3}{4}$ | $\frac{3}{8}$ | $\frac{3}{16}$ | $\frac{4}{2}$ | $\frac{4}{4}$ | $\frac{4}{8}$ | $\frac{4}{16}$ |
| Compound | $\frac{6}{4}$ | $\frac{6}{8}$ | $\frac{6}{16}$ | | $\frac{9}{4}$ | $\frac{9}{8}$ | $\frac{9}{16}$ | | $\frac{12}{4}$ | $\frac{12}{8}$ | $\frac{12}{16}$ | |

The listener perceives the beat type (simple or compound) by listening to the way the beat divides (into twos or threes); the meter is conveyed by the characteristic pattern of accents, although these are typically not explicitly notated in the music. The accents that express the meter are usually agogic ones, but subtle dynamic accents are also sometimes added by the performer. The traditional patterns of metric accents are shown below, with ">" indicating an accent, "(>)" indicating a weaker accent, and "–" indicating no accent.

```
Duple       1   2   |   1   2   |
            –   >       >   –

Triple      1   2   3   |   1   2   3   |
            >   –   –       >   –   –

Quadruple   1   2   3   4   |   1   2   3   4   |
            >   –   (>) –       >   –   (>) –
```

## SYNCOPATION

**Syncopation** is a term used either when a rhythmic event such as an accent occurs at an unexpected moment or when a rhythmic event fails to occur when expected. Syncopation is an important element of twentieth-century music, and one that is so familiar that it probably does not need much discussion here. An excerpt containing syncopation was seen in Example 5–8 (p. 109). In that example the syncopation comes about by denying an articulation on the fourth eighth-note of the melody in the first three measures of the excerpt as well as on the downbeat of the last measure.

Syncopation that follows any kind of perceptible pattern may indicate that some other rhythmic device is being employed. In the Stravinsky excerpt (Example 5–8), the melody in the first 3½ measures could be heard in a variety of meters, including $\frac{3}{4}$ and $\frac{4}{4}$, as well as the notated $\frac{6}{8}$. Even when syncopation does not follow a pattern, one listener may hear it as a change of meter while another hears it as a syncopation within a single meter. This brings us to one of the main difficulties of rhythmic analysis: the necessity of recognizing that what is perceived is often different from what is written.

## WRITTEN RHYTHM AND PERCEIVED RHYTHM

Of course, it is perfectly possible to compose music in such a way that the listener will not be able to perceive the notated beat type or meter type or both. The first of Chopin's Preludes, Op. 28, is heard in compound time, but it is notated in $\frac{2}{8}$, with most of the beats being divided into sixteenth-note triplets. Contradictions between the way rhythm is heard and the way it is written are especially common in twentieth-century music. An example similar to the Chopin prelude, but more complex, is the second movement of Webern's Variations for Piano, Op. 27 (1936). Although written in a very fast simple duple, it seems to most listeners to be in a slower compound meter, with occasional odd-length beats thrown in. The beginning of the piece is seen in Example 6–1, with the perceived rhythm notated below. (It could also be heard in $\frac{3}{8}$.) Notice the extra eighth-note rest in the second measure.

**EXAMPLE 6–1**   Webern: Variations for Piano, Op. 27, II, mm. 1–4   *(Copyright 1937 by Universal Edition. Copyright renewed. All rights reserved. Used by permission of European American Music Distributors Corporation, sole U.S. and Canadian agent for Universal Edition Vienna.)*

Often the conflict between written and perceived rhythms arises out of consideration for the performer. Example 6–2a shows an excerpt from the first edition of Kent Kennan's trumpet sonata, in which traditional $\frac{4}{4}$ and $\frac{3}{4}$ time signatures are used. By the time of the second edition, some thirty years later, performers had become so accustomed to untraditional time signatures that Kennan felt safe notating it as shown in Example 6–2b.

In many of the examples discussed in this chapter, it will be necessary to distinguish between rhythm as written and rhythm as perceived. In all cases we will take the perceived rhythm as the true rhythm.

EXAMPLE 6–2A    Kennan: Sonata for Trumpet and Piano (1956), I    *(© 1956, Remick Music Corporation.)*

EXAMPLE 6–2B    Kennan: Sonata for Trumpet and Piano (1986), I    *(© 1986 Warner Bros.)*

## CHANGING TIME SIGNATURES

Though changing from one time signature to another in the course of a movement is not a device exclusive to the twentieth century, it is certainly one that has seen more use in the twentieth century than in the tonal era. Terms for this technique include **changing meters**, **mixed meter**, **variable meter**, and **multimeter**. Changing meters can be implied by shifted accents or syncopations, or they can be explicitly notated by the composer. Several examples have already illustrated changing time signatures, among them the following:

Example 2–20 (p. 35):    $\frac{3}{4}$    $\frac{2}{4}$    $\frac{3}{4}$

Example 3–20 (p. 58):    $\frac{3}{4}$    $\frac{5}{8}$    $\frac{4}{8}$

Example 4–7 (p. 82):    $\frac{6}{4}$    $\frac{7}{4}$

Example 4–8 (p. 84):    $\frac{4}{2}$    $\frac{5}{2}$    $\frac{4}{2}$

Example 6–2b:    $\frac{9}{8}$    $\frac{7}{8}$    $\frac{2}{4}$    $\frac{8}{8}$    $\frac{5}{8}$    $\frac{8}{8}$    $\frac{5}{8}$    $\frac{6}{8}$    $\frac{5}{8}$    $\frac{7}{8}$

A more problematical example was Example 4–9 (p. 85), where the meter signatures fluctuated between $\frac{3}{8}$ and $\frac{2}{8}$, even though the perceived rhythm of the solo piano part remained steadfastly in $\frac{2}{8}$. A closer examination of the accompanying orchestral parts, however, reveals that the changing time signatures do reflect the rhythm of the accompaniment. This example will be discussed in more detail later.

## NONTRADITIONAL TIME SIGNATURES

The list of time signatures given at the beginning of this chapter has been considerably expanded by twentieth-century composers. Of greatest significance has been the use of values *other* than 2, 3, 4, 6, 9, or 12 for the top number of a time signature. While 5 and 7 have been especially favored (this is why some employ the term **asymmetric meter** for this device), others such as 1, 8, 10, and 11 have not been completely neglected.

The notated time signature in Example 4–12 (p. 90) is $\frac{4}{4}$, but it is obvious from the phrasing and accents that the *perceived* meter is $\frac{5}{4}$. Most examples of nontraditional meters can easily be heard as changing meters, and this is also true of Example 4–12, which sounds like $\frac{2}{4}$ alternating with $\frac{3}{4}$. However, Example 4–10 (p. 87), also in $\frac{5}{4}$, does not seem to divide clearly into 2 + 3 or 3 + 2. In Example 5–7 (p. 107), the divisions of the $\frac{5}{8}$ measures seem to imply 1 + 2 + 2, 2 + 2 + 1, and 2 + 3, with the first violin and the cello not always in agreement in any particular measure.

Example 6–2b illustrates several nontraditional time signatures: $\frac{5}{8}$, $\frac{7}{8}$, and $\frac{8}{8}$. Of course, $\frac{8}{8}$ contains the same number of eighth-notes as $\frac{4}{4}$; Kennan presumably used $\frac{8}{8}$ to call the performer's attention to the irregular division of the measures into 3 + 3 + 2 eighth-notes (instead of the customary 4 + 4). The term **additive rhythm** is sometimes used for passages such as this, where some short note value (here the eighth-note) remains constant but is used in groups of unpredictably varying lengths. Another instance of additive rhythm is seen in Example 5–B–6 (p. 111), employing time signatures of $\frac{5}{8}$, $\frac{8}{8}$, and $\frac{11}{8}$.

When a traditional time signature is transformed into a nontraditional one by the use of a nonstandard metric accent, one approach is to indicate the new metric accent with dotted lines, as in Example 5–B–6. Another way is to specify the new pattern of metric accents in the time signature itself, as Bartók did in the "Scherzo" of his String Quartet No. 5 (1934). There he transforms $\frac{9}{8}$ (traditionally 3 + 3 + 3) into a nontraditional 4 + 2 + 3 by use of a $\frac{4+2+3}{8}$ time signature, a type sometimes referred to as a **complex meter.** At a vivace tempo, the listener hears three beats of unequal length per measure, a variation on the traditional $\frac{3}{4}$ scherzo. The trio is in an unusual quadruple meter, predominantly $\frac{3+2+2+3}{8}$. Another approach to transforming traditional time signatures is to use the traditional signature, but to use accents and phrase marks to indicate the metric accent. This is the case in Example 6–3, where the two hands play groups of sixteenth-notes of varying length in notated $\frac{4}{4}$ and $\frac{3}{4}$ meters.

| | *m. 9* | *m. 10* | *m. 11* | *m. 12* |
|---|---|---|---|---|
| R.H.: | rest | 6 + 6 | 6 + 6 | 1 + 5 + 2 + 4 |
| L.H.: | 5 + 1 + 4 + 2 | 4 + 2 + 5 + 1 | 6 + 6 | rest |

**EXAMPLE 6–3** Milton Babbitt: *Three Compositions for Piano* (1947), No. 1, mm. 9–12

In "*. . . quasi una fantasia . . .*" (1988) György Kurtág employs an unusual method of defining nontraditional time signatures, such as these:

3/♩ + 1/♪.     4/♩ + 3/♪     2/♩ + 5/♪

The effect of the first two signatures is to create a measure of four or five beats with a short final beat. The last example creates a three-beat measure with a very long final beat.

The nontraditional time signature that is the most difficult for performers is probably the fractional time signature. In the third measure of Example 4–4 (p. 79) Boulez writes 4/3 over 2, meaning four beats, each of them the length of one-third of a half-note. Note also the use of $\frac{5}{8}$ and $\frac{7}{8}$ in the example, the latter apparently being divided into two $\frac{7}{16}$ segments. Although each note value maintains a nearly constant metronomic duration in this excerpt (the quarter-note, for example, equals mm. 104 or 105 throughout), the effect is of a fluid and constantly fluctuating tempo.

## POLYMETER

The metrical equivalent of polytonality is **polymeter,** the simultaneous use of two or more aurally distinguishable time signatures. There are three possibilities: same time signature, but displaced (Example 6–4a); different signatures, with barlines coinciding (Example 6–4b); and different signatures, with barlines not coinciding (Example 6–4c). Though all three of these combinations occur, the third is perhaps the most striking aurally and the most frequently employed. Remember that in each case we are referring to the aural effect, not necessarily to the actual notation.

EXAMPLE 6–4   Polymeter

In Example 6–5 the polymeter (type c) is explicitly notated in the viola and cello parts. It comes about through the canon at the octave, with the viola leading the cello by one measure. The fourth and fifth measures of the viola part are in $\frac{3}{4}$ and $\frac{2}{4}$, while beneath those measures the cello plays the third and fourth measures of the canon with time signatures of $\frac{2}{4}$ and $\frac{3}{4}$.

**EXAMPLE 6–5**   Bartók: String Quartet No. 3 (1927), II

Music with barlines that do not coincide, as in Example 6–5, may be troublesome for an ensemble or a conductor, so polymeter is often implied instead of explicitly notated. This is the case in Example 6–6, a few pages later in the same quartet—again a canonic example, this time between the two violins. Here the viola and cello are clearly in $\frac{3}{8}$, but the violins sound as if they are in a polymetric canon (type a) with each other, as well as being polymetric (type c) with the accompaniment. The rhythms might be rebarred as in Example 6–7.

EXAMPLE 6–6   Bartók: String Quartet No. 3 (1927), II   *(© Copyright 1929 in the USA by Boosey & Hawkes, Inc. Copyright renewed. Reprinted by permission.)*

EXAMPLE 6–7   Explicit Polymetric Notation

A less complicated example of implied polymeter was seen in Example 4–9 (p. 85), discussed above in connection with changing time signatures. In this instance the piano maintains a steady $\frac{2}{8}$ meter, although it is notated to conform with the changing meters of the brasses.

Polymeter with coinciding barlines (type b) is probably the least commonly used. Remember that the simultaneous use of $\frac{2}{4}$ and $\frac{6}{8}$, for instance, is not really polymeter but instead poly*division* of a single meter. One example of polymeter type b is seen in Example 6–8. Here the flutes and harps are continuing a $\frac{3}{4}$ waltz that was begun eight measures earlier. Meanwhile, beneath the waltz, the lower woodwinds and lower strings take up a $\frac{2}{4}$ melody that contrasts with the waltz in both meter and tonality.

**EXAMPLE 6–8** Stravinsky: *Petrushka* (1911), third tableau *(Excerpted from the Norton Critical Edition. Used by permission of W. W. Norton & Co., Inc., and Edwin F. Kalmus & Co., Inc.)*

## AMETRIC MUSIC

We recognize the beat and meter type of a passage by listening to the way that the beat divides and the way that beats group into larger units. Once we have grown used to devices such as changing meters and nontraditional meters, we are able to identify them aurally as well. Yet some music seems to exhibit no perceivable metric organization, a style we will refer to as **ametric.** Gregorian chant is a good example of ametric music, as is much electronic music.

Some writers use the term "arhythmic" for music in which rhythmic patterns and metric organization are not perceivable. But if we accept a very general definition of rhythm as covering "all aspects of musical movement as ordered in time,"[1] then music cannot be arhythmic, but only ametric.

Not all music written without a time signature is ametric. For instance, four of the five movements of Hindemith's String Quartet No. 3 (1921) have no meter signature at all, but the music is barred, and the implied time signatures are clear both to the eye and to the ear. At the same time, some music notated *with* a time signature is written in such a way as to sound ametric. A good example of this is the Boulez excerpt discussed earlier in this chapter (Example 4–4, p. 79), which, while precisely notated, sounds free and improvisionary to the listener.

Music without barlines may be metric or not, depending on the composer's intention and the listener's interpretation. Although Ives used no time signature and no barlines in Example 3–B–7 (p. 71), a listener still might hear a steady $\frac{2}{4}$ organization. But Example 3–23 (p. 60), also by Ives, is almost certainly ametric, as is the rest of the movement from which it is excerpted.

Luciano Berio's *Sequenza I* (1958) uses a short barline (see Example 6–9), and the "measure" itself is assigned a specific tempo—M.M. 70 at the beginning. This composition is definitely ametric, however, because the actual durations are specified only by the placement of the notes within the measure. In the first measure, for example, the G5 is to be given the longest duration, because it occupies the greatest portion of the measure. Notation of this sort is sometimes called *proportional notation*. Accidentals in this excerpt affect only the notes they precede.

**EXAMPLE 6–9**   Berio: *Sequenza I* (1958), first staff

Many techniques developed after 1960 result in ametric effects, often involving some degree of improvisation, as in Example 6–9 and in Example 6–10. In that example the temporal organization is determined by timed segments, with unmetered improvisation going on within them. These and other improvisatory techniques will be covered in more detail in Chapter 14.

**EXAMPLE 6–10**  Joseph Schwantner: *And the Mountains Rising Nowhere* (1977)

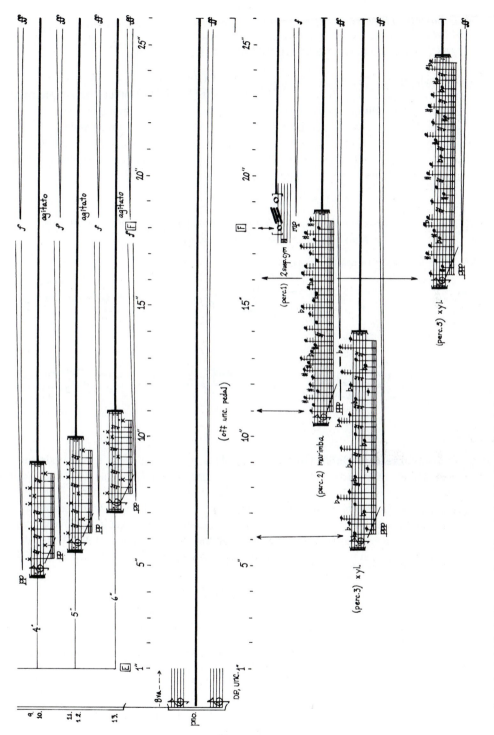

* whistle short "stacc." pitches (specific pitches not indicated, only general register)

127

## ADDED VALUES AND NONRETROGRADABLE RHYTHMS

Two techniques from the fertile imagination of Olivier Messiaen will be discussed here. The first one, called **added values,** involves complicating an otherwise simple rhythmic pattern by the addition of a short duration in the form of a dot, a note, or a rest. In Example 6–11 each added value is identified by a "+". The first three measures would clearly be in $\frac{4}{4}$ without the added values; with them, the effect is still of quadruple meter, but with one or two longer beats in each measure. The rest of the example is more complicated rhythmically and would probably be perceived as ametric.

EXAMPLE 6–11   Messiaen: *The Technique of My Musical Language,* Example 13, mm. 1–6

*(© Editions Alphonse Leduc. Used by permission of the publisher.)*

A **nonretrogradable rhythm** is simply a rhythmic pattern that sounds the same whether played forward or backward (in retrograde). A trivial example would be a group of four eighth-notes, but Messiaen is interested in more complicated patterns. The rhythm of each measure in Example 6–12 is nonretrogradable, and each measure also contains added values. Notice that the rhythmic activity builds gradually to a climax in the seventh measure, followed by an immediate relaxation through longer note values. Both of the Messiaen examples are drawn from the sixth movement of his *Quartet for the End of Time* (1941).

EXAMPLE 6–12   Messiaen: *The Technique of My Musical Language.*   *(© 1944 Editions Alphonse Leduc.*
*Used by permission of the publisher.)*

Another way to look at nonretrogradable rhythms is that each one contains some rhythmic pattern followed by its retrograde, resulting inevitably in a rhythmic *palindrome*, a term used for any structure in language or music that reads the same forward as it does backward. Therefore, any piece that makes use of rhythmic retrogrades on a larger scale could also be considered an example of nonretrogradable rhythms. For instance, the second movement of Webern's Symphony, Op. 21 (1928), begins with an eleven-measure theme that is a rhythmic palindrome, a technique that is found through much of the movement.

## TEMPO MODULATION AND POLYTEMPO

Elliott Carter is generally credited with being the first to use a particular method of changing tempos precisely by making some note value in the first tempo equal to a different note value (or at least to a different proportion of the beat) in the second tempo. For example, to "modulate" from ♩ = 80 to ♩ = 120, one could begin using eighth-note triplets in the first tempo. These triplet eighths have a duration of 240 per minute (three times the ♩ = 80 rate). This rate of 240 turns out to be the rate of the simple division of the beat (the eighth-note) at the new tempo of ♩ = 120. (See Example 6–13). This device has been called "metric modulation" because it usually involves changing time signatures; however, a change of tempo is the real objective, so we will use the term **tempo modulation.** This technique does bear a resemblance to the common chord modulation of tonal music, in that one or more measures will contain elements of both tempos.

EXAMPLE 6–13   A Simple Tempo Modulation

Carter evidently employed tempo modulation for the first time in his Cello Sonata (1948). A relatively simple example is found in Movement II, which begins in cut time at ♩ = 84. Later the meter changes to ⁶⁄₈ with the eighth-note remaining constant. The most reliable way to calculate the new tempo is to first compute the tempo of the common note value in the first tempo:

If ♩ = 84, then ♪ = 4 × 84 = 336

and then to figure out what that means in terms of the beat in the second tempo:

If ♪ = 336, and the new beat is the dotted quarter, then the new tempo is 336/3 = 112.

A more complex example occurs in the third movement, which begins in ³⁄₄ with ♪ = 70. The tempo modulation then follows these steps:

1. Change to $^6_{16}$, keeping the beat constant, so $♪. = 70$.

2. Change to $^{21}_{32}$, keeping the 32nd-note constant. This unusual time signature is *not* compound septuple, as one might expect. Instead, it is a *triple* meter, with each beat equaling a doubly dotted eighth-note. When $♪. = 70$ (above), $♪ = 420$ (because there are six 32nds in one dotted eighth). Since the 32nd remains constant, and there are seven 32nds in the new beat value ($♪..$), the new tempo is $420/7 = 60$.

3. Change to $^2_8$, keeping the beat constant, so $♪ = 60$.

Similar in concept to polymeter but much less often encountered is **polytempo,** the simultaneous use of two or more aurally distinguishable tempos.[2] One example of this is Ives's *The Unanswered Question* (1908), a work for four flutes, trumpet, and strings. The trumpet and strings maintain a steady tempo of $♩ = 50$, but the six statements by the flutes are heard at increasing tempos and dynamics, from *Adagio* and *p* to *Molto agitando* and *ffff*. A composer who has devoted much of his life to the problem of polytempo and other rhythmic concerns is Conlon Nancarrow, who worked for decades in relative obscurity in Mexico, composing music with extremely complex ratios of tempos and rhythms that were realized on player piano rolls, the only practical way such music could be performed before the advent of the computer. (In Study No. 36, for example, the ratios between the tempos are $17:18:19:20$.) Recordings of his music finally became generally available in the 1980s, and these were followed by a number of nonmechanical works that explore the same issues.

In his String Quartet No. 1, Carter solves the problem of polytempo in a different way—by explicit notation. Here all of the parts are notated in the same tempo, $♩ = 120$, but only the cello *sounds* as if it is playing at that tempo. Because of the way the music is notated, the aurally perceived tempos, in terms of beats per minute are:

| | |
|---|---|
| Violin I | 36 |
| Violin II | 96 |
| Viola | 180 |
| Cello | 120 |

Or, stated as ratios from top to bottom: $3:8:15:10$, meaning that the cello, for instance, will play 10 notes in the span of three notes in Violin I. All of this is part of a large-scale tempo modulation that will eventually settle into the tempo heard in the viola.

**EXAMPLE 6–14**  Carter: String Quartet No. 1 (1951), I, mm. 22–26   *(Copyright © 1955 (Renewed) by Associated Publishers, Inc. (BMI). International copyright secured. All rights reserved. Reprinted by permission.)*

## SERIALIZED RHYTHM AND ISORHYTHM

The term **serialized rhythm** is generally used in connection with pieces in which the rhythmic aspects are governed by some preconceived series of durations. This will be discussed in more detail in Chapter 13.

We will use the term *isorhythm* to refer to the use of a rhythmic pattern that repeats using different pitches. The pitches may or may not themselves form a repeating pattern, but if they do, it must be of a different length than the rhythmic pattern. If the rhythm and pitch patterns are the same length, we use the term **ostinato** rather than isorhythm.

Isorhythm is not a widely used device in twentieth-century music, but it can be very effective. Much of Act III, Scene 3 of *Wozzeck* is based on the rhythmic pattern seen in the first 3½-measures of the bottom staff in Example 6–15—in fact, all of the music in the example is derived directly from that pattern. The effect here is polymetric, the 3½-measure pattern in the low register rising inexorably over two whole-tone scales a major 7th apart, while Wozzeck tries desperately to explain to Margret how blood got onto his hand.

**EXAMPLE 6–15**   Berg: *Wozzeck* (1921), Act III, Scene 3, mm. 187–98   *(Copyright 1931 by Universal Edition A. G., Wien. Copyright renewed. All rights reserved. Used by permission of European American Music Distributors Corporation, sole U.S. and Canadian agent for Universal Edition, A. G., Wien.)*

## SUMMARY

One aspect of rhythm in twentieth-century music that must catch the attention of any performer is its difficulty. Certainly there was nothing in the rhythm of the tonal era to parallel the complexity of twentieth-century rhythms, and one might have to go back to the late fourteenth century to find a comparable preoccupation with complicated rhythms. While most musicians could perform the rhythms of a tonal work at sight, it is doubtful that they would be as successful with the works from which Example 4–4 (p. 79) and Example 6–12 are drawn.

Some of the specific techniques discussed in this chapter have included the following:

Syncopation

Changing time signatures

Nontraditional time signatures

Using 5, 7, etc., for the top value

Fractional top values

Complex meters such as $\frac{3+2+3}{8}$

Additive rhythm

Polymeter

Same signature, barlines not coinciding

Different signatures, barlines coinciding

Different signatures, barlines not coinciding

Ametric music

Proportional notation

Added values

Nonretrogradable rhythms

Tempo modulation

Polytempo

Serialized rhythm

Isorhythm

Certainly this chapter has not exhausted all of the details of rhythm in the twentieth century, but it has brought up some of the main points. One problem that you will discover if you do more reading in this area is that terminology relating to rhythm is not standardized. You will encounter terms such as "cross-rhythm" and "combined meters" that were not used in this chapter but refer to techniques discussed here using different terminology.

Finally, it is most important to remember that music is an aural experience, and you cannot always make an intelligent observation about the rhythm of a piece by a casual glance at the score. Such devices as polymeter and changing time signatures may be quite perceptible aurally, even though they are not explicitly notated. In all such cases, analyze the music by the way it sounds, not by the way it looks.

## NOTES

1. Harold S. Powers, "Rhythm," in *The New Harvard Dictionary of Music*.
2. As of this writing, a comprehensive list of examples of polytempo is available at <http://www.greschak.com/polytempo/ptbib.htm>.

## EXERCISES

### Part A: Fundamentals

1. Which example in this chapter was the best illustration of pandiatonicism?
2. On what scale is Example 6–1 based?
3. Which example best illustrates quintal chords?
4. The fourth movement of Corigliano's String Quartet (1995) is a fugue that features polytempo. Let's assume that the viola plays the fugue subject at a tempo of $\quarternote = 70$. When the second violin enters, it has four notes to every five in the viola. The next entrance is by the first violin, which plays three notes to every two played by the second violin. The final statement of the subject is in the cello, which plays three notes to every four in the first violin. What would be the tempo for each of the instruments?
5. The following questions dealing with tempo modulation are based on techniques used by George Perle in his String Quartet No. 5 (1960, 1967).

   (a) In the first movement, Tempo I is $\halfnote = 96$. In order to get to Tempo II, Perle specifies that the old triplet eighth-note (one-third of a quarter-note) be equal to the new sixteenth-note. What is the tempo of the quarter-note (not the half-note) in Tempo II? Show your work.

   (b) In the third movement, Tempo II is $\halfnote = 96$. In order to get back to Tempo I, Perle specifies that the old dotted half-note be equal to the new half-note tied to an eighth. What is the tempo of the quarter-note in Tempo I? Show your work.

   (c) Also in the third movement, Tempo III is $\halfnote = 120$. In order to get back to another tempo, Perle specifies that the old eighth-note be equal to one-fifth of the new half-note. Is the new tempo Tempo I or Tempo II? Show your work.

6. Be able to perform the rhythms of the following examples:

   (a) Example 2–21 (p. 36)—right hand only, with the eighth-note as the beat note.
   (b) Example 3–20 (p. 58)—top staff only.

(c) Example 3–32 (p. 65)—top staff, with the eighth-note as the beat note.

(d) Example 4–2 (p. 77).

(e) Example 4–3 (p. 78).

(f) Example 4–7 (p. 82)—top staff with the right hand, bottom with the left.

(g) Example 4–B–2 (p. 94).

(h) Example 5–7 (p. 107)—top staff with the right hand, bottom with the left.

(i) Example 5–B–6 (p. 111)—bottom staff, vivace.

(j) Example 6–2—both versions.

(k) Example 6–5—bottom two staves.

(l) Example 6–6—top two staves.

(m) Example 6–11.

(n) Example 6–12.

(o) Example 6–13.

(p) Example 6–14—Violin II and Cello.

(q) Example 6–15—Wozzeck's line and the bottom staff.

## Part B: Analysis

1. Example 2–21 (p. 36) has nine eighth-notes to the measure, but the time signature is not $\frac{9}{8}$. What do you think would be an appropriate time signature for this example?
2. Discuss the rhythm and meter of Example 4–3 (p. 78), concentrating on those aspects that are characteristic of twentieth-century music.
3. Analyze Example 6–3 in more detail. (Note: Each accidental affects only the note it precedes.) Do any measures share identical patterns of rhythms or accents? Are any the retrograde (reverse) of others? Are there any repeated or retrograded pitch patterns?
4. Analyze Example 6–12 in more detail. Can you find any relationship between the rhythms of successive or nonsuccessive measures? Is there any logic or pattern to the pitch choices?
5. Bartók: *Forty-four Violin Duets* (1931), No. 33, "Song of the Harvest," mm. 6–15 Discuss rhythmic and tonal aspects of this excerpt. To what scale does the combined pitch material of both staves conform?

6. Francis Poulenc: *Promenades* (1921), V, "En avion," systems 3 and 4
   Discuss rhythmic and pitch aspects of this excerpt, including consideration of chord types and tonality.

## Part C: Composition

1. Compose an example for clarinet or trumpet using several different nontraditional time signatures. All of the pitch material should be from a single diminished scale.
2. Compose a short polymetric passage for two violins in the Phrygian mode.
3. Compose a four-part clapping piece employing tempo modulation.
4. Compose and be able to perform a melody illustrating added values and nonretrogradable rhythms.
5. Compose an isorhythmic passage for three instruments in your class. Try to employ some of the techniques seen in Example 6–15.
6. Compose and perform an example that uses time signatures and strict tempos, yet sounds ametric to the listener.

## FURTHER READING

COPE, DAVID. *Techniques of the Contemporary Composer.* See Chapter 8, Rhythm and Meter.

DALLIN, LEON. *Techniques of Twentieth Century Composition.* See Chapter 5, Rhythm and Meter.

GANN, KYLE. *The Music of Conlon Nancarrow.*

KOSTKA, STEFAN, AND DOROTHY PAYNE. *Tonal Harmony with an Introduction to Twentieth-Century Music.* See the section titled "Rhythm and Meter" in Chapter 28.

LESTER, JOEL. *Analytic Approaches to Twentieth-Century Music.* See Chapter 2, Rhythm and Meter.

SIMMS, BRYAN R. *Music of the Twentieth Century.* See pp. 92–108 of Chapter 5, Rhythm and Meter.

SMITHER, HOWARD E. "The Rhythmic Aspect of 20th-Century Music." See pp. 71–84.

SMITHER, HOWARD E., AND FREDERIC RZEWSKI. "Rhythm," in John Vinton, ed., *Dictionary of Contemporary Music.*

WILLIAMS, J. KENT. *Theories and Analyses of Twentieth-Century Music.* See Chapter 7, Rhythm and Meter.

WINOLD, ALLEN. "Rhythm in Twentieth-Century Music," in Chapter 3 Gary Wittlich, ed., *Aspects of 20th Century Music.*

# *SEVEN*

# Form in Twentieth-Century Music

## INTRODUCTION

All of the formal structures and procedures found in the tonal era survived into the twentieth century. That is, in twentieth-century music we still encounter sonatas and rondos, canons and fugues, sectional and continuous variations, and binary and ternary forms. Not surprisingly, many works employing traditional formal structures date from the first few decades of the century or were composed by relatively conservative composers, but this is not always the case. Schoenberg, for instance, hardly considered by his contemporaries to be a conservative, often composed his serial works in classical forms.

Yet to many musicians some of the older forms seem strangely uncomfortable in twentieth-century garb. The reason for this may well lie in the weakening of tonal centricity in almost all music of the twentieth century, to the point of its total avoidance in atonal styles. The essence of sonata form, in particular, involved a dramatic conflict of tonalities—a large-scale tonal dissonance established in the exposition and resolved in the recapitulation. It can be argued that once that conflict of tonalities loses its impact, to the point that it seems to make little difference to the listener at what pitch level the piece ends, the drama of the sonata is lost.

Tonality is less of an issue in the traditional contrapuntal forms—canon and fugue, especially—which may explain in part their healthy survival in this century. The same could also be said of variations, whether sectional or continuous, and both have aged well. Ternary form, one of the most basic musical structures, has perhaps weathered the storm best of all, since its design—statement, contrast, return—can be applied to a wide variety of styles, from tonal to electronic.

We will survey in this chapter the survival of these and other forms from earlier periods, as well as the appearance of forms unique to the twentieth century. Because it is beyond the scope of this text to present long works or even extended excerpts, there are few musical examples in this chapter. However, all of the works referred to are readily available in both score and recording. In addition, a number of references will be made in the text and exercises to works found in four widely used anthologies. The abbreviations in parentheses will be used when referring to them.

BURKHART, CHARLES. *Anthology for Musical Analysis*, 6th ed. Belmont, Calif.: Schirmer, 2004 (BUR).

KOSTKA, STEFAN, AND ROGER GRAYBILL. *Anthology of Music for Analysis.* Upper Saddle River, N.J.: Prentice Hall, 2004 (K-G).

TUREK, RALPH. *Analytical Anthology of Music*, 2d ed. New York: McGraw-Hill, 1992 (TUR).

WENNERSTROM, MARY H. *Anthology of Twentieth-Century Music*, 2d ed. Englewood Cliffs, N.J.: Prentice-Hall, 1988 (WEN).

The reader is assumed to have a general understanding of the terminology of musical form as it relates to tonal music. One departure from conventional terminology should be noted: no distinction is made in this chapter between "part forms" or "song forms" and the longer "compound forms." For instance, ABA will be labeled "ternary" and ABACA will be labeled "rondo" without regard to the length or complexity of the component parts.

## BINARY FORM

Binary form (AA′ or AB) is found as the structure of short pieces or movements or of sections within longer works. Examples are as varied as Hindemith's "A Swan" (1939) (BUR, p. 491), John Cage's Sonatas and Interludes (1948), Nos. 1 and 5 (TUR, p. 829), "Vocalise 2: Invocation," from George Crumb's *Apparition* (1980) (WEN, p. 91), and Ligeti's Sonata for Solo Viola (1994), fifth movement (K-G, p. 582). In its application, the binary principle is little changed in the twentieth century from earlier times, except that the traditional |I–V||V–I| and |i–III||III–i| tonal schemes are seldom used.

## TERNARY FORM

The ternary principle is a flexible one that can be applied to small or large segments of music, and the contrast can be achieved in various ways. In a simple tonal piece like Schumann's "Humming Song" (1848) (BUR, p. 311), the contrast provided by the B section might be in little more than pitch level. More often, though, the contrast involves several elements. In Kenneth Gaburo's *Exit Music II: Fat Millie's Lament* (1965), an electronic piece, the A sections use voice and percussion sounds recorded at various tape speeds, while the B section is an excerpt from a jazz piece by Morgan Powell, providing a contrast in almost every aspect of the music.[1]

Many full-length movements are in ternary form, one example being the "Pastorale" from Britten's Serenade for Tenor, Horn, and Strings (1943) (K-G, p. 565), but it is also not uncommon to cast individual themes or sections in ternary form. An instance of this is the cornet solo in the third tableau of Stravinsky's *Petroushka* (1911) (WEN, p. 213).

One of the most obvious examples of ternary form in tonal music is the *song form with trio*, which is often found as a minuet or scherzo with trio, followed by a *da capo*, in multimovement sonatas (symphonies, string quartets, piano sonatas, and so forth). While less common in the twentieth century, such forms do occur, as in the fifth movement of Schoenberg's Suite, Op. 25 (1923) (WEN, p. 175). A more complicated example is the third movement of Bartók's String Quartet No. 5 (1934). Here the trio is differentiated from the scherzo partly by its time signature ($^{4+\frac{2}{8}+3}$ in the scherzo, $^{3+2+\frac{2}{8}+3}$ in the trio) and partly by its faster tempo, as well as by more traditional thematic means. The *da capo* is written out and considerably varied, concluding with a coda (m. 58) that starts out with some very fast polymetric imitation.

Ternary form in tonal music generally exhibits something of a balance between the two A sections, whereas works with a shortened return of the A material are categorized by some writers as *rounded binary*. No such balance is expected in twentieth-century ternary forms, and no distinction need be made between ternary and rounded binary. An example of an unbalanced ternary structure from Debussy's Preludes appears in Example 7–1. Here the A section is found in mm. 1–10, the B in mm. 11–24, and the return of A in mm. 25–31. Actually, only two measures of the A material return (mm. 25–26), but this reference to the opening of the piece is enough to give the listener a feeling of return after contrast, the essence of ternary form.

**EXAMPLE 7–1    Debussy: Preludes, Book I (1910), "Dancers of Delphi" (complete)**

*doux mais en dehors*

## RONDO FORMS

The usual outlines of the rondo form in tonal music were the five-part rondo (ABACA or ABABA) and the seven-part rondo (ABACABA). The term *sonata rondo* is sometimes used for the seven-part structure, especially if the C part includes development of earlier material. The key structure of the rondo required that the A theme always occur in the tonic key and that the B and C themes provide some kind of tonal contrast, except that the return of the B theme in the seven-part rondo was in the tonic key. Unlike sonata form, however, tonal contrast in a rondo could be achieved simply through change of mode. This occurred most often in the C themes of both five- and seven-part rondos.

Both five- and seven-part rondos are found in twentieth-century music, but the traditional tonal plans are not always used. Debussy's "Reflections in the Water" ("Reflets dans l'eau") (1905) follows fairly closely the conventional tonal scheme of a five-part rondo:

| A | B | A | B | A |
|---|---|---|---|---|
| D♭ | A♭ | D♭ | B | D♭ |

The second movement of Hindemith's String Quartet No. 3 (1921) (WEN, p. 125) is somewhat less conventional in its key relationships:

| A | B | A | B | A |
|---|---|---|---|---|
| C♯ | E♭ | C♯ | A | E♭, C♯ |

In addition, the B section is bitonal at its beginning, the E♭ harmonies supporting a melody that starts out in E Lydian. Bitonality is carried much further in "Song of the Harvest" from Bartók's *Forty-Four Violin Duets* (1931) (WEN, p. 9). In this miniature five-part rondo the first four sections are bitonal, the two keys in each case being a tritone apart, and the A theme is in a different tonal setting in each appearance (the first B theme appears in Example 6–B–5, p. 135).

The third movement of Prokofiev's Piano Sonata No. 4 (1914) follows the traditional outline for a seven-part rondo:[2]

| A | B | A | C | A | B | A |
|---|---|---|----|---|---|---|
| C | G | C | E♭ | C | C | C |

Since the rondo form is somewhat more dependent than some others (notably sonata form) on contrast of themes as opposed to contrast of key centers, it would seem better suited to the atonal style. The fourth movement of Schoenberg's Wind Quintet, Op. 26 (1924), is a seven-part rondo written using the twelve-tone technique, usually associated with atonality. The B theme is at a different pitch level when it returns, as one would expect, but the A theme also varies in pitch level (and in other ways) at each recurrence, a departure from the classical norm. Interestingly, the movement emphasizes E♭ at its beginning and end, and E♭ remains an important pitch class at the beginning and often at the end of each movement of this otherwise atonal work.

## OTHER PART FORMS

Part forms other than binary, ternary, and rondo are frequently encountered, but many of them can be thought of as variants of more traditional structures. One that is very similar to the seven-part rondo is ABACADA. Examples of this form can be found in the last movement of Barber's *Capricorn Concerto* (1944) and in the "Interlude" from Debussy's Sonata for Flute, Viola, and Harp (1916). In the Debussy example the D section also contains elements of C. Another part form that resembles a seven-part rondo is ABACBA, one example of this occurring in the fourth movement of Bartók's Concerto for Orchestra (1943).

The interest that some composers have in various kinds of symmetry is reflected in their use of *arch form*, a term for any formal structure that reads the same forwards and backwards. Some conventional forms, such as ternary and seven-part rondo, are examples of arch form, but we usually reserve the term for less-conventional formal structures.

| Ternary: | A | B | A | | | | | | | | |
|---|---|---|---|---|---|---|---|---|---|---|---|
| Seven-part rondo: | A | B | A | C | A | B | A | | | | |
| Arch: | A | B | C | B | A or A | B | C | D | C | B | A etc. |

Examples of arch forms in music range from single movements to entire multimovement works. The third movement of Debussy's String Quartet (1893) can be analyzed as a ternary form or as a five-part arch form:

| Ternary: | A | Ba | Bb | Ba | A |
|---|---|---|---|---|---|
| Arch: | A | B | C | B | A |

The third movement of Bartók's *Music for String Instruments, Percussion, and Celesta* (1936) is a modified arch form, two of the parts being recapitulated simultaneously.

A  B  C  D  C + B  A

Bartók's String Quartet No. 5 (1934) is an arch form in terms of its overall plan:

   I. Allegro

  II. Adagio Molto

 III. Scherzo and Trio (Vivace)

 IV. Andante

  V. Finale (Allegro Vivace)

The first movement of this work combines sonata form with the arch idea in various ways, the most obvious being a reverse recapitulation.[3] The second movement (K-G, p. 481) exhibits a more straightforward arch design:

A  B  C  B′  A′

Some part forms show the influence of the sonata by including a development. The second movement of Ravel's String Quartet (1903) combines the statement of new material with the development of previous material. The A and B parts each contain two themes:

A A B + Dev A Coda
a,c♯ a,C unstable a,c♯ a

Another movement containing a development is the fourth movement of Debussy's String Quartet, which contains elements of both rondo and sonata forms:[4]

A  B  A  C  Dev

Still other part forms are unique in that they do not seem to be similar to any more conventional form or to conform to the arch principle. One example is Debussy's prelude, "Canope" (K-G, p. 455), which has the following structure:

A  B  C  D  E  B′  F  A′/D′/C′

## SONATA FORM

Sonata form was the most important musical form of the Classical and Romantic periods. Its essence involved a conflict between tonalities that would arise early in the exposition and continue until its resolution in the recapitulation. Thematic contrast was a frequent element in movements in sonata form, but it was by no means essential, as the many "monothematic" sonatas of the Classical period prove. Nor was it required that the recapitulation return the material in the original order (the "reverse recapitulation" was a possibility), or that it all return in the tonic key (the "subdominant recapitulation" brought back the first theme in the subdominant), or even that the first theme be recapitulated at all (see the first movements of Chopin's Piano Sonatas, Op. 35 [1839] and Op. 58 [1844]). Instead, the crucial elements seem to have been that the tonal conflict must be resolved by returning to the tonic key well before the end of the movement, and that any important thematic material that had been presented in a contrasting key in the exposition must return in the tonic key.

Movements in sonata form are frequently encountered in twentieth-century music. Some of them even make use of the traditional key relationships in the exposition of tonic-dominant as in Piston's Quintet for Flute and Strings (1942), I, or tonic-relative major as in Ravel's Sonatina (1905), I. But more often the tonal relationships in twentieth-century sonata forms are not the traditional ones, as in Shostakovich's String Quartet No. 3 (1946), I (K-G, p. 540), in which the main tonal centers in the exposition are F and E. More problematical, however, are those movements in sonata form—and there are many—in which the tonality of one or both of the main themes is unclear. Obviously, a struggle between tonalities cannot occur if the tonalities are not firmly established. Some would say that other elements replace the tonal aspect in such pieces; others might argue that a movement based upon a contrast of themes, for example, might be good music but is not a sonata.

The single movement of Berg's Piano Sonata, Op. 1 (1908), is an interesting mixture of traditional and experimental approaches to sonata form. The first theme, while tonally unstable, does cadence in B minor in the third measure of the exposition (although it does not do so in the recapitulation), and the exposition is even repeated. But Theme 2 (m. 29), which is tonally unstable, begins over an A9 chord in the exposition (implying D major) and a B9 in the recapitulation (implying E major), while the closing theme (m. 49) actually begins at the same pitch level in the exposition and the recapitulation.

Similar problems are encountered in the first movement of Bartók's String Quartet No. 6 (1939) (WEN, p. 11). In this work the first theme (m. 24) is in D, but the listener might be forgiven for not being certain about this until m. 60, where the first triad on D is heard. The second theme (m. 81) begins over a C pedal, which is apparently the dominant of the tonality of F, reached in m. 94. A third theme, tonally unstable and largely chromatic, begins at m. 99, climaxing at m. 110 on an E♭, but the exposition ends clearly on F at m. 157. In the recapitulation, the first theme returns in D, more or less, but the second theme returns over a C♯ pedal (m. 312), presumably the dominant of F♯, but certainly not in the tonality of D. The third theme climaxes on a B♭ chord at m. 343, but a D major triad is reached at m. 352, and the remainder of the movement is in D.

Tonal uncertainty is obviously a problem, in regard to sonata form, in the Berg and Bartók works discussed above, and the traditional objectives of sonata form are clearly achieved in neither instance. This is not a criticism, of course; both compositions are highly organized in their own ways, and each is a successful and well-known work. What is interesting here from a formal point of view is the effort to make a tonal form function in an increasingly nontonal environment.

The whole notion of a tonal dissonance to be resolved in the recapitulation is essentially moot in any composition that is decidedly atonal, yet a good number of atonal pieces are cast in what appears to be sonata form. A good example is the first movement of Schoenberg's Wind Quintet, Op. 26 (1924), an early twelve-tone atonal composition. In this movement the first theme (m. 1) is recapitulated at the same pitch level (m. 128), whereas the second and closing themes (m. 42 and m. 55) are brought back a perfect 5th lower or a perfect 4th higher, a remarkable duplication of the traditional relationships found in a major-mode sonata form.

## SECTIONAL VARIATIONS

The term *sectional variations* is used here to distinguish the theme with variations from the ground bass or continuous variations (passacaglia and chaconne). Many sets of sectional variations have been composed in the twentieth century, works as diverse as Ravel's hyperemotional and tonal *Bolero* (1927) and Babbitt's cerebral and atonal *Semi-Simple Variations* (1957) (TUR, p. 526; BUR, p. 516). While the compositions just cited use original themes, others such as Zoltán Kodály's *Variations on a Hungarian Folksong* (1939) and Frederic Rzewski's *The People United Will Never Be Defeated!* (1973) use borrowed material for the theme.

The theme of a traditional set of variations was relatively simple in order to allow for subsequent embellishment, and it was clearly set off from the music that followed so that the listener could easily identify and remember the theme. This is essentially the case with Copland's Piano Variations (1930), using a ten-measure theme that is set off from the first variation by a fermata. Carter's Variations for Orchestra (1955), on the other hand, begins with an introduction that is dovetailed into the beginning of the theme through sustained violin tones. The theme begins at the second of two tempo modulations that slow the tempo from allegro to andante, which does somewhat help the listener to identify the beginning of the theme. The theme itself is complex texturally and rhythmically; after 47 measures it runs into Variation I without pause but with another change of tempo. The nine variations are quite free, presenting a real challenge to the listener attempting to hear the relationship between them and the theme.

Some twentieth-century works that are called variations are not variations in the customary sense. This tends to be especially true of serial, or twelve-tone, "variations" such as Webern's Piano Variations, Op. 27 (1936), and Luigi Dallapiccola's Variations for Orchestra (1954). In both of these works the theme of the variations is not a short composition, as in traditional variations, but instead is the twelve-tone series itself; and though the series in both cases surely helps to unify the composition as a whole, the series is not presented initially as a tune or theme for the listener to remember. On the other hand, in some twelve-tone "variations" there is a true theme on which the subsequent variations are clearly based, an example being Schoenberg's Variations for Orchestra, Op. 31 (1928) (TUR, p. 443; WEN, p. 179).

## CONTINUOUS VARIATIONS

The traditional forms of continuous variations are the *passacaglia*, based on a repeating bass line, or ground, and the *chaconne*, based on a repeating harmonic progression.[5] Though both forms have seen use in this century, the decline of a common harmonic language has been paralleled by the relative decline of the chaconne as a compositional option.

As one would expect, passacaglia themes in the twentieth century tend to be complicated and nondiatonic. The fourth movement of Hindemith's String Quartet No. 4 (1921) consists of a passacaglia and a fugato based on the passacaglia theme, which is shown in Example 7–2. Notice that in the course of its seven measures this theme sounds every pitch class but one (E). Passacaglias using all twelve pitch classes have been used, a famous example being the passacaglia in Act I, Scene 4, of Berg's *Wozzeck* (1921). An intriguing passacaglia with a twelve-tone theme is "Little Blue Devil," from Gunther Schuller's *Seven Studies on Themes of Paul Klee* (1959) (WEN, p. 194). In this work a "jazzy" nine-bar bass line makes its way through three different (but related) twelve-tone "sets." This bass line, first heard in mm. 15–23, serves as the passacaglia theme for the movement.

EXAMPLE 7–2   Hindemith: String Quartet No. 4, Op. 32 (1921), IV, mm. 1–8   *(© by B. Schott's Soehne, Mainz, 1924. Copyright renewed. All rights reserved. Used by permission of European American Music Distributors Corporation, sole U.S. and Canadian agent for B. Schott's Soehne, Mainz.)*

Another example is Crumb's "Voices from Corona Borealis" from his *Makrokosmos*, Vol. II (1973) (K-G, p. 585), which uses a sixteen-note passacaglia theme in the upper register.

The use of isorhythms (review Chapter 6, p. 133) can be thought of as an extension of the passacaglia principle. This is especially true when there is a pitch pattern associated with the rhythmic pattern, as in the "Crystal Liturgy" from Messiaen's *Quartet for the End of Time* (1941) (TUR, p. 511). Of course, the pitch pattern (the *color*) must not be the same length as the rhythmic pattern (the *talea*), or an ordinary ostinato would result. In the Messiaen work the rhythmic pattern contains 17 attacks and the pitch pattern contains 29 notes (10 different pitch classes), so the rhythmic pattern would have to be repeated 29 times before the beginnings of the two patterns would again coincide (because 493 is the lowest common multiple of 17 and 29). Messiaen stops the process long before that point.

## CANON AND FUGUE

Canon and fugue are not "forms" in the sense that rondos and sonatas are. Instead, they are contrapuntal procedures that can be cast in any of a number of formal designs. Nevertheless, musicians customarily have referred to both "homophonic forms" and "contrapuntal forms," and it will be convenient in this chapter to follow that tradition.

The canon, a form that saw relatively little use in the century and a half after Bach, has enjoyed a new popularity among twentieth-century composers. Whole sets of canons have been written, such as Webern's Five Canons, Op. 16 (1924) (WEN, p. 271), and canons frequently appear as a major portion of a longer work, examples being the trio of the minuet from Schoenberg's Suite, Op. 25 (1923) (WEN, p. 177), and the second movement of Webern's Variations for Piano, Op. 27 (1936) (BUR, p. 485). In both of these works, the canonic imitation happens to be by contrary motion. The uninformed listener would almost certainly be unaware of the canon in the Webern work, and the same would be true of the sixth movement of Arvo Pärt's *Magnificat Antiphons* (1988) (K-G, p. 591), in which a canon by augmentation is hidden in the Soprano II and Tenor II parts. Canons also frequently appear as passages in otherwise noncanonic movements. For instance, although Schoenberg's "Summer Morning by a Lake," Op. 16, No. 3 (1909) (BUR, p. 424), is not a canon, it contains canonic passages, two of the clearest being mm. 3–9 and mm. 32–38.

Much of the challenge in writing a canon in the tonal idiom is to control the dissonance while at the same time creating harmonic interest. To a certain extent these difficulties are alleviated in twentieth-century music because of the "emancipation of the dissonance" and the lack of traditional harmonic progressions. Both can be seen and heard in the works cited in the preceding paragraph. In another example, the "Song of Harvest" from Bartók's *Forty-Four Violin Duets* (1931) (WEN, p. 9), the first canonic phrase (see Example 6–B–5 on p. 137) finds the violins a tritone apart, with no attempt at conventional preparation and resolution of the dissonances that result.

Terry Riley's *In C* (1964) (TUR, p. 540; BUR, p. 531) is an interesting canon in which the performers begin together but progress through the music at different rates. Each performer plays the same 53 musical segments for an indeterminate amount of time, usually for at least a minute, with each performer proceeding to the next segment on his or her own initiative, but not without regard for what the other players are doing. The resulting canon is a good example of phase music, or minimalism, to be discussed in more detail in Chapter 15.

The renewed interest in counterpoint in this century can also be seen in the collections of fugues composed after the model of *The Well-Tempered Clavier*. Hindemith's *Ludus Tonalis* (1942) is a famous collection of twelve fugues separated by eleven interludes, the entire work beginning with a prelude and ending with a postlude. Instead of arranging his fugues in chromatic order, as Bach did in *The Well-Tempered Clavier*, Hindemith follows Series 1 from his *Craft of Musical Composition*, an ordering that he first derives when discussing tuning. Hindemith felt that this ordering represented a "diminishing degree of relationship" with the beginning tonality of C:[6]

C   G   F   A   E   E♭   A♭   D   B♭   D♭   B   F♯

Fugue 5 from the *Ludus Tonalis* (TUR, p. 504) is a good representative of Hindemith's contrapuntal style.

Another collection of twentieth-century fugues is Shostakovich's *Twenty-Four Preludes and Fugues*, Op. 87 (1951). Here the order of keys is more traditional: C–a–G–e–D–b–A–f♯, etc. As in Bach's collection, each fugue is preceded by a prelude in the same key.

Fugues are also commonly encountered as individual movements within a longer work, as in the first movement of Bartók's *Music for String Instruments, Percussion, and Celesta* (1936) (BUR, p. 453) and the "Fantasy" from Elliott Carter's *Eight Etudes and a Fantasy Woodwind Quartet* (1950) (WEN, p. 57), or as a portion of a movement, as in Berg's *Wozzeck* (1921), Act III, Scene 1, consisting of a theme with seven variations followed by a fugue based on the theme.

The tonal conventions of the Baroque fugue need not restrict the twentieth-century composer, and frequently they do not, but it is remarkable how often the traditional tonal relationships are found in the expositions of twentieth-century fugues. Three examples:

Bartók: Sonata for Solo Violin (1944), II

Shostakovich: String Quartet No. 8 (1962), V

Rochberg: String Quartet No. 4 (1977), II

Each of the movements cited above begins with a fugue exposition in which the first and third statements of the subject are in the tonic and all the others are in the dominant. Coincidentally, each also happens to be in the key of C.

## PROPORTION: THE GOLDEN MEAN

Some twentieth-century composers and writers have been interested in the "golden mean" or "golden section," a proportion used for centuries in art and architecture to obtain aesthetically pleasing designs. To understand this ratio, consider a line ac with line segments ab and bc:

If the proportion of ab to bc is the same as the proportion of bc to the whole line, then ac is segmented according to the golden mean. This relationship can be expressed as:

$$\frac{ab}{bc} = \frac{bc}{ac}$$

The resulting fraction is about .618.

Integers (whole numbers) that approximate the golden mean can be generated by means of a **Fibonacci sequence,** an endless series of numbers in which each number is the sum of the previous two. The farther you go in the sequence, the closer you get to the true value of the golden mean:

| Integers | 1 | 2 | 3 | 5 | 8 | 13 | 21 | 34 etc. |
|----------|-----|-----|-----|------|------|------|------|---------|
| Ratios: | | .5. | .67 | .6 | .625 | .615 | .619 | .618 |

The most obvious way that this ratio can be used musically is in the proportions of a musical form. For example, the beginning of "Minor Seconds, Major Sevenths," from Bartók's *Mikrokosmos* (BUR, p. 483), could be subdivided in this way:

m.  8 = Strong cadence; first whole-note chord.

m.21 = Strong cadence; first appearance of "glissando."

m.21 = End of long accelerando and of first main section.

There is some evidence that Bartók used the golden mean not only in formal proportions but in other aspects of his music as well,[7] and this is also true, if to a lesser extent, of some other twentieth-century composers.[8]

## NONTHEMATIC DELINEATORS OF MUSICAL FORM

The primary determinants of musical form in tonal music were tonality and theme, with contrast of tonalities being a generally stronger force than contrast of themes. The decline in tonality as an organizing force has often led to a greater reliance on thematic contrast; but in many pieces, themes, in the sense of melodies, play a small or nonexistent part. The most obvious example is electronic music, where texture, register, dynamics, and especially timbre are usually more important as shaping elements than themes are. Rhythmic activity is another organizing factor, as in Bartók's "Increasing—Diminishing" from the *Mikrokosmos* (1937), where rhythmic activity creates an arch form. Another work in which nonthematic elements are important in delineating the form is the second movement of Webern's Concerto, Op. 24 (1934) (K-G, p. 502).

The ABCB form of the first movement of Arvo Pärt's *Collage on B-A-C-H* (1964) is delineated by nonthematic means. The A section (see Example 7–3a) begins with a repeated B♭4 that unfolds in m. 2 to a B♭ major triad. The triad arpeggiates slowly outward until it spans four octaves by m. 7. The B section (Example 7–3b) also consists of repeated notes, but here the sonorities are dissonant and include sixteenth-notes. The repeated notes in part C (Example 7–3c) also create dissonances, but here they are staccato and pit downbeats against upbeats. The dissonant climax of the movement in mm. 47–48 is followed by eight measures of retransition and the return of the B material. The movement ends with an unexpected *p* B minor triad in mm. 81–84. While the form is clear to the listener, nothing resembling a melody is heard.

EXAMPLE 7–3  Pärt: *Collage on B-A-C-H* (1964), I, mm. 2, 11, 30  *(© 1964, Musikverlag Hans Sikorski, Hamburg.)*

## NONORGANIC APPROACHES TO MUSICAL FORM

A traditional painting depicts something, and if the painting is a good one, every part of the canvas contributes to the effectiveness of the visual message that the artist is trying to convey. In traditional literature every passage has its purpose—fleshing out a character, setting the mood, developing the plot, and so on. The same is generally true of music in the European tradition: the composition is considered to be greater than the sum of its parts, a work of art in which each passage has a function that is vital to the overall plan of a work. Think of any tonal work that you know well, and imagine what it would be like if its parts—themes, transitions, and so forth—were randomly rearranged. It might be interesting to see how it would turn out, but the piece would almost certainly not be as effective as a whole.

There has been a reaction by some composers against this traditional "organic" (or "teleological") approach to musical composition. One such reaction led to what Karlheinz Stockhausen has called "moment form," an approach that treats every portion of a piece as an end in itself, without any intentional relationship to what precedes or follows it. The listener is not supposed to try to identify traditional shaping forces such as motivic development, dynamics, and rhythmic activity in an attempt to understand where the music is going, because it is not going *anywhere*, in the traditional sense. Even the beginning and ending of the work lose their traditional functions, because "a proper moment form will give the impression of starting in the midst of previously unheard music, and it will break off without reaching any structural cadence, as if the music goes on, inaudibly, in some other space or time after the close of the performance."[9]

Stockhausen first used the term "moment form" in discussing *Contact* (1960), a work for prerecorded tape, piano, and percussion, but other works by various composers, both before and since, show the same avoidance of linear growth. Some of these are works employing a high degree of chance, an early example being Cage's *Williams Mix* (1952), a tape piece composed by juxtaposing at random hundreds of prerecorded sounds. Tape music and the use of chance in music are both discussed in more detail in later chapters.

### SUMMARY

All of the forms of the tonal era survived into the twentieth century, in spite of problems relating to the function of tonality in those forms. Not only was there a decline in the influence of tonality upon form, but in many twentieth-century compositions the "theme" also ceased to be an important element of form. Formal proportions are often less balanced than in the Classical period, but interest in the golden mean by some composers, notably Bartók, shows a desire for a systematic aesthetic. Coexisting with the traditional forms are a large number of works that do not conform to earlier models. Some of these can be thought of as variants of traditional part forms or as related to the sonata; others are arch forms; and still others would seem to be unique in the sense that they do not have traditional analogues. Even more radical is the nonorganic approach to musical form seen in the "moment form" works of Stockhausen and others and in some works composed using chance procedures.

## NOTES

1. Barry Schrader, *Introduction to Electro-Acoustic Music*, p. 33.

2. For a detailed analysis of the form of this work, see Wallace Berry, *Form in Music*, pp. 216–24.

3. For a detailed analysis of this movement, see Mary Wennerstrom, "Form in Twentieth-Century Music," in Wittlich, ed., *Aspects of Twentieth-Century Music*, pp. 19–33.

4. For an analysis of this movement, see Gail de Stwolinski, *Form and Content in Instrumental Music*, pp. 546–48.

5. These definitions are used for convenience, but the difference between the two was not so clearly defined in the Baroque period, during which both the passacaglia and the chaconne first flourished.

6. Paul Hindemith, *The Craft of Musical Composition*, Vol. I, p. 56. The derivation of this series of tones is found on pp. 32–43.

7. Ernö Lendvai, *Béla Bartók: An Analysis of His Music*.

8. Jonathan D. Kramer, "The Fibonacci Series in Twentieth Century Music."

9. Jonathan D. Kramer, "Moment Form in Twentieth Century Music," p. 180.

## EXERCISES

### Part A: Score Analysis

Each of the pieces below can be found in one of the three anthologies listed at the beginning of this chapter. Analyze the form of whatever piece you are assigned, including a diagram down to the phrase level, if possible. Be sure to include measure numbers.

1. Bartók: *Mikrokosmos* (1931), No. 94, "Tale" (K-G, p. 477).
2. Berg: *Wozzeck* (1921), "Marie's Lullaby" (WEN, p. 28).
3. Debussy: Preludes, Book I (1910), "The Engulfed Cathedral" ("La Cathédrale engloutie") (BUR, p. 421).
4. Debussy: Preludes, Book I (1910), "The Hills of Anacapri" ("Les Collines d'Anacapri") (K-G, p. 449).
5. Hindemith: *Ludus Tonalis* (1942), Fugue in C (BUR, p. 490) and Fugue in A (WEN, p. 140). Before beginning work on these fugues, review the terms "double fugue" and "triple fugue."
6. Ives: Sonata No. 2 for Violin and Piano (1910), II (WEN, p. 147). Though this movement is not a canon, it contains some canonic passages. Locate and comment upon each one.
7. Schoenberg: *Six Short Pieces for Piano*, Op. 19 (1911), No. 6 (WEN, p. 173).
8. Schoenberg: *Pierrot Lunaire*, Op. 21 (1912), No. 8 (TUR, p. 438).
9. Schoenberg: Variations for Orchestra, Op. 31 (1928), Var. 2 (TUR, p. 443). Concentrate on the issue of imitation in this variation.

10. Shostakovich: String Quartet No.3, Op. 73 (1946), I (K-G, p. 540).
11. Webern: Five Movements for String Quartet, Op. 5 (1909), IV (BUR, p. 484).

## Part B: Aural Analysis

Listen several times to any of the works listed below. Name the form, and provide a dia-gram of the main parts. For each section, provide the approximate time at which it begins and try to sketch or describe the salient features (rhythms, contours, etc.) of each section.
1. Barber: Piano Concerto, Op. 38 (1962), III.
2. Bartók: String Quartet No. 6 (1939), II.
3. Dallapiccola: *Quaderno Musicale* (1952), No. 3.
4. Hindemith: String Quartet No. 3 (1921), V.
5. Piston: Symphony No. 5 (1956), I.
6. Prokofiev: Symphony No. 5 (1944), IV.
7. Walter Ross: Trombone Concerto (1971), II, "Canzona."
8. Shostakovich: String Quartet No. 1 (1935), II.
9. Stravinsky: Septet (1953), I.
10. Stravinsky: *Symphony of Psalms* (1930), II.
11. Stravinsky: Septet (1953), II.
12. Arnold Walter, Myron Schaeffer, and Harvey Olnick: *Summer Idyll* (1959).

## FURTHER READING

BERRY, WALLACE. *Form in Music.* This text—like de Stwolinski's, cited below—does not deal exclusively with twentieth-century music.

DE STWOLINSKI, GAIL. *Form and Content in Instrumental Music.*

HOWAT, ROY. "Bartók, Lendvai, and the Principle of Proportional Analysis."

KRAMER, JONATHAN D. "The Fibonacci Series in Twentieth Century Music."

———. "Moment Form in Twentieth Century Music."

LENDVAI, ERNÖ. *Béla Bartók: An Analysis of His Music.* See the sections titled "Golden Section," pp. 17–26, and "Chromatic System," p. 35–66.

WENNERSTROM, MARY. "Form in Twentieth-Century Music," in Gary Wittlich, ed., *Aspects of Twentieth-Century Music*, pp. 1–65.

---EIGHT---

# Imports and Allusions

## INTRODUCTION

This chapter is concerned with some of the external influences that had an effect on the music of the twentieth century. These influences came chiefly from three sources:

*The Past*

  Neoclassicism
  Quotation

*The Present*

  Folk music
  Jazz

*The Unfamiliar*

  Music from other cultures

There is little new technical information in this chapter, and few exercises follow it. In many ways it deals more with music history than with music theory. But the currents outlined here are important ones, and they had a significant role in shaping the sound of twentieth-century music.

## INFLUENCES FROM THE PAST

Composers in this century have shown a greater awareness of and concern for the music of past centuries than did any of their predecessors. In earlier chapters we have seen the revival of modal scales and isorhythm and renewed interest in older forms like the passacaglia. This

**157**

historical consciousness has also led to the developments discussed in the next two sections: neoclassicism and quotation. *Neoclassicism* was a reactionary movement in the sense that it rejected the chromatic saturation and other characteristics of both the late Romantic style and atonality. While it was not truly an attempt to revive the Classical style, as the term might suggest, it did reflect a desire for clarity, balance, and greater detachment, and the music of the Baroque and Classical periods provided a starting place for the style.

*Quotation* of already existing music was not unknown before the twentieth century. The use of plainsong melodies in Renaissance polyphonic compositions and the borrowed themes for sets of variations are but two examples. But quotation in the twentieth century is of a different sort, at times a dramatic juxtaposition of contrasting styles, at others an almost poetic allusion to another composer. Thus "quotation music" has become another catchword of twentieth-century music.

## Neoclassicism

"Let's say that I was a kind of bird, and that the eighteenth century was a kind of bird's nest in which I felt cozy laying my eggs."[1] In this picturesque way Stravinsky characterized his own involvement in neoclassicism, an approach to composition that was especially widespread from around 1920 to around 1950. Many composers wrote works in the neoclassical style—Hindemith and Poulenc, for example—but the central figure in the movement was Stravinsky. Important neoclassical works by Stravinsky include the Octet for Wind Instruments (1923), the *Symphony of Psalms* (1930), the Symphony in C (1940), and the Symphony in Three Movements (1945).

Donald Jay Grout defines neoclassicism as "adherence to the Classical principles of balance, coolness, objectivity, and absolute (as against Romantic program) music, with the corollary characteristics of economy, predominantly contrapuntal texture, and diatonic as well as chromatic harmonies.[2] William Austin, referring to Stravinsky's neoclassical works in particular, writes:

> They presumed sophistication. They alluded not simply to Bach and Beethoven, but to separate traits of the classical styles. They treated those traits with such dry irony, such jerky stiffness, and such evident distortion that even a sympathetic listener needed several hearings to penetrate beneath the wit and skill to the glowing warmth of the melodies and the subtle continuity of the forms.[3]

From these definitions it is clear that neoclassicism was not an attempt to compose new works in the style of Haydn and Mozart. For one thing, it made use of Baroque techniques as well as Classical ones. But more important, neoclassicism was a reaction against the style of late Romanticism in favor of a sparser texture and less chromaticism, using clear rhythms and definite cadences, all combined with twentieth-century developments in melody, meter, and the treatment of dissonance.

The techniques of neoclassicism are not new, and all of them have been discussed in earlier chapters of this text. The best way to get acquainted with the style is through listening and score study, but Example 8–1 is included here as a representative of several aspects of neoclassicism. First of all, notice the metric subtleties between the bass-clef instruments and the treble-clef instruments. The changing time signatures accurately reflect the rhythm of Trumpet I and the Clarinet; however, the bass-clef instruments move along with a steady pattern of eighth-notes followed by eighth rests, sometimes agreeing with the time signature and sometimes not, ironically creating through their steady pulse a destabilizing polymeter. Meanwhile, in the Flute and Trumpet II, which imitate Trumpet I, the $\frac{3}{4}$ measure four bars from the end is notated in $\frac{2}{4}$, creating a third polymetric element.

Another aspect to be noted in Example 8–1 is the prevailing pandiatonicism (see p. 108). Since Trumpet II sounds in unison with the Flute (but two octaves lower), the only pitches in the excerpt that are not diatonic to E♭ major are the D♭'s in Bassoon I and Trombone II. But there is no harmonic progression in the traditional sense, even though the bass-clef accompaniment is triadic, and no attempt is made to control the dissonances that occur among the treble-clef instruments or between them and the bass-clef accompaniment.

**EXAMPLE 8–1**    Stravinsky: Octet for Wind Instruments (1923), "Sinfonia," last 9 mm.

*(© Copyright 1924 by Hawkes & Son (London) Ltd. Copyright renewed. Reprinted by permission of Boosey & Hawkes, Inc.)*

The ballet *Pulcinella* (1920) is one of Stravinsky's earliest neoclassical works. An excerpt from the Suite Italienne (1932), derived from the ballet, appeared earlier as Example 3–10 (p. 51), and it will serve as our second example of neoclassicism. Here the rhythm is quite straightforward, as is the harmonic progression, but the nontraditional treatment of dissonance in this excerpt is a fine example of the dry irony to which Austin referred in the passage quoted earlier.

Though the neoclassical style has nearly died out, music of the past still attracts the interest of many composers. A more recent movement, dubbed *neoromanticism*, will be discussed in the final chapter of this book.

### Quotation, Arrangement, and Paraphrase

Neoclassicism rarely involved the actual quotation of already existing music, exceptions including Stravinsky's *Pulcinella* (1920) and *The Fairy's Kiss (Le baiser de la fée)* (1928), which used the music of Perolesi and Tchaikovsky, respectively. But many other twentieth-century composers not connected with the neoclassical style have quoted, arranged, and paraphrased earlier music extensively. Though this practice has become especially common since the mid-1960s, earlier examples include Debussy, who quoted Wagner in "Golliwog's Cakewalk" from *The Children's Corner* (1908) and Bach in *In Black and White (En blanc et noir)* (1915), and Berg, who quoted Wagner in the last movement of the Lyric Suite (1926) and Bach in the concluding "Adagio" movement of the Violin Concerto (1935). The style of another composer from the early part of the century, Charles Ives, depended to a great extent on the quotation of music—hymn tunes, popular songs, and the like—familiar to most Americans in the early part of the century. Patriotic songs were grist for his mill as well, as seen in Example 8–2, where "America," "Columbia, the Gem of the Ocean," and the "Marseillaise" can all be heard. Notice as well the polymeter in the first few measures, where the piano sounds as if it is in $\frac{3}{4}$.

**EXAMPLE 8–2**   Ives: "In Flanders Fields" (1917), mm. 30–35   *(© Copyright 1955 by Peer International Corporation. Used by permission.)*

Other works that quote national anthems include Debussy's "Fireworks" (Example 5–6, p. 106) and Stockhausen's *Hymns (Hymnen)* (1966), an electronic work in which the "program" is not nationalistic, as Ives's presumably was, but instead is concerned with world unity.

A composer does not always quote existing music for programmatic reasons. The second act of George Rochberg's *Music for the Magic Theater* (1965) begins with a "transcription" (actually a rather free arrangement) of the fourth movement from Mozart's Divertimento in B-flat, K. 287 (1777). In the preface to the score Rochberg discusses the reaction of the audience:

> It seems to test the perceptual courage of listeners (musicians and laymen alike) by putting in question the whole concept of what is "contemporary," how far that concept may be stretched today and what it can include. The presence of the transcription abrogates the 19th to early 20th century notion of "originality."[4]

Rochberg goes on to provide more insight into the compositional aesthetic that justifies quotation in his music:

> The world of this music is surreal more than it is abstract. In its combinations of the past and the present, seemingly accidental, unrelated aural images whose placement in time obeys no conventional logic, it attempts to create a musical soundscape which is strangely and oddly familiar.[5]

This idea of juxtaposing seemingly unrelated ideas was encountered in Chapter 7 in the discussion of "nonorganic approaches to musical form." Crumb takes up the same topic in discussing his *Ancient Voices of Children* (1970), which contains a quotation from Bach: "I was conscious of an urge to fuse various unrelated stylistic elements. I was intrigued by the idea of juxtaposing the seemingly incongruous. . . ."[6]

Juxtaposition of the incongruous is certainly a feature of Example 8–3. The work from which the example is taken is a chillingly dramatic representation of the anguished madness of King George III. Various composers are quoted, or suggested, in the course of the piece, the most recognizable being from Handel's *Messiah* (1742), which was composed when George III was a child. In Example 8–3 a "Country Dance" is interrupted by the famous "Comfort ye" quotation from the *Messiah*, which is then continued and grossly distorted by the mad king. Both lines are sung by the same performer, who must play both a female vocalist and the king in this excerpt. It is said that Roy Hart, the singer for whom the work was written, could sing chords, as you see at the end of the excerpt. This use of multi-phonics for the voice is very unusual, although they are frequently called for in instrumental writing. Multiphonics will be discussed in more detail in Chapter 11.

**EXAMPLE 8–3**   Davies: *Eight Songs for a Mad King* (1969), VII   *(© Copyright 1971 by Boosey & Hawkes Music Publishers Ltd. Reprinted by permission of Boosey & Hawkes, Inc.)*

The material borrowed by a composer is often transformed, or paraphrased. This was true to some extent of the Ives excerpt in Example 8–2. Electronic compositions might use recorded excerpts, with or without alteration, as in Kenneth Gaburo's *Exit Music II* (see p. 141) and Stockhausen's *Opus 1970* (1969). The pair of excerpts in Example 8–4, drawn from Examples 108 and 109 of Messiaen's *Technique of My Musical Language*, illustrate how Messiaen paraphrased part of a plainchant in the melody of a work for organ.

**EXAMPLE 8–4**   Messiaen: *Technique of My Musical Language*, Examples 108 and 109 (excerpts)   *(© 1944 Editions Alphonse Leduc. Used by permission of the publisher.)*

Quotation in Bernd Alois Zimmermann's music is an important stylistic element rather than the exceptional event, a good example being *Photoptosis* (1968), an orchestral work with quotations from various sources. In *Petroushkates* (1980), Joan Tower has composed a sort of paraphrase variation on Stravinsky's original. Direct quotations in *Petroushkates* are most apparent at the beginning, but chords, rhythms, and melodic figures drawn from Stravinsky can be heard throughout the work, most of which maintains the exhilarating spirit of the opening of *Petrushka*.

Bach's Partita in E Major for solo violin serves as the basis for the third movement of Lukas Foss's Baroque Variations (1967). Far removed from the traditional theme and variations, this dramatic and effective work often views the Bach work through a wildly distorted lens. Chapter 14 includes additional discussion of this movement.

Perhaps the most famous example of quotation is the third movement of Berio's Sinfonia (1968), a work for eight voices and orchestra. The entire movement is based on the third movement of Mahler's Symphony No. 2 (1894), sometimes obviously but often more subtly, with additional quotations from Bach, Berg, Brahms, Debussy, Ravel, Schoenberg, Strauss, Stravinsky, and others, these quotations being alluded to on occasion by the chorus.[7] Most of the text, however, is drawn from Samuel Beckett's novel *The Unnameable*. The connections between Mahler, Joyce, Beckett, and Berio have been convincingly shown, including the suggestion that Joyce's stream-of-consciousness style of writing has its parallel in Mahler's music, and presumably in Berio's as well.[8] The result is a musical collage but also a complex and fascinating work, much more than a haphazard pastiche.

Alfred Schnittke is a Russian composer who has been using quotations and stylistic allusions in his music since the late 1960s, one example among many being his *Moz-art*, a blend of Mozartean gestures and twentieth-century dissonances, multiphonics, and other effects. His use of earlier materials is sometimes humorous and sometimes serious.

> Sometimes I'm tweaking the listener. And sometimes I'm thinking about earlier music as a beautiful way of writing that has disappeared and will never come back; and in that sense, it has a tragic feeling for me.[9]

## INFLUENCES FROM FOLK MUSIC, JAZZ, AND ROCK

Composers of the nineteenth century were certainly not unaware of folk music, as witnessed by the influence of Polish folk music on Chopin and the arrangements of German folk songs by Brahms. The rise of nationalism in the late nineteenth century spawned an increased interest on the part of composers of all countries in the music that was indigenous to their own cultures, and this interest continued into the twentieth century, especially in the first several decades.

Probably the composer whose name first comes to mind in connection with folk music in the twentieth century is Béla Bartók. Shortly after the beginning of the century, he and his compatriot Zoltán Kodály began a serious study of folk music, at first only Hungarian, but soon including that of neighboring countries as well. Bartók's interest in this area is seen explicitly in the titles of many of his works; for example, the following titles appear in Volumes 4–6 of the *Mikrokosmos:*

An excerpt from No. 148 appeared as Example 2–21 (p. 36), and the beginning of No. 112 is given in Example 8–5. The folk-song melody appears in octaves in mm. 1–8. The first variation follows without pause, parallel 6ths in the right hand being imitated canonically in the left hand at the 12th below.

**EXAMPLE 8–5**   Bartók: *Mikrokosmos* (1926–37), No. 112, "Variations on a Folk Tune," mm. 1–17

*(© Copyright 1940 by Hawkes & Son (London) Ltd. Copyright Renewed. Reprinted by permission of Boosey & Hawkes, Inc.)*

The music of composers like Bartók, Kodály, and the Czech composer Leoš Janáček often shows the influence of folk music even when folk materials are not being explicitly quoted—hence the frequent references to their "folklike" melodies and rhythms. But it would be a serious mistake to think of the music of these composers only in terms of folk songs. Though folk music is an important element in their work, it merges with the currents of change in twentieth-century music, to which these composers made significant contributions.

Interest in folk music was of some importance in all European countries, but less in countries like Germany that had a great musical tradition of their own. Spain had a particularly strong nationalist movement in the music of Isaac Albéniz, Enrique Granados, and Manuel de Falla. Representative figures in the New World included Heitor Villa-Lobos in Brazil and Carlos Chávez and Silvestre Revueltas in Mexico.

In the United States the influence of folk song is seen in the music of Ives, Copland, and Roy Harris, among others. One of the first to make use of the folk songs of black Americans was the English composer Samuel Coleridge-Taylor, whose father was African. His *Twenty-Four Negro Melodies* (1905) may have inspired the black American composers William Grant Still and William Dawson. Another English work that uses black folk music is Michael Tippett's *A Child of Our Time* (1941), an oratorio dealing with racial persecution.

Jazz music first caught the attention of "serious" composers around the end of World War I (1918). A large number of works were composed over the next few decades that borrowed certain obvious features from jazz. Some of the better-known of these compositions include:

Igor Stravinsky: *Ragtime* (1918)

Paul Hindemith: *Chamber Music No. 1 (Kammermusik No. 1)* (1922)

Darius Milhaud: *The Creation of the World (La création du monde)* (1923)

George Gershwin: *Rhapsody in Blue* (1924)

Aaron Copland: *Music for the Theater* (1925)

Aaron Copland: Piano Concerto (1927)

Ernst Křenek: *Johnny Plays On (Jonny spielt auf)* (1927)

Kurt Weill: *The Three Penny Opera (Die Dreigroschenoper)* (1928)

Maurice Ravel: Concerto for the Left Hand (1930)

George Gershwin: *Porgy and Bess* (1935)

Igor Stravinsky: *Ebony Concerto* (1945)

One of the first such pieces was the "Ragtime" from Stravinsky's *The Soldier's Tale (L'histoire du soldat)* (1918), the beginning of which is seen in Example 8–6. The syncopations and dotted rhythms are evident here, as is an imitation of the functions of bass and percussion in an early jazz band, while later in the piece "jazzy" trombone glissandos are used. Of course, this music does not really sound like jazz, any more than neoclassical music sounds Classical; in fact, Stravinsky's comment concerning his neoclassical style (see p. 158) is equally appropriate here.

**EXAMPLE 8–6** Stravinsky: *The Soldier's Tale* (1918), "Ragtime," mm. 1–8 *(Copyright © 1924 (Renewed) by Chester Music Ltd. International copyright secured. All rights reserved. Reprinted by permission of G. Schirmer Inc. (ASCAP))*

With some important exceptions, jazz does not seem to have exerted much influence on concert music after World War II (i.e., since 1945). The main exception to this has been the so-called Third Stream movement, chiefly associated with Gunther Schuller, which attempted to blend jazz and concert music without condescending to either. In Example 8–7 Schuller evokes the sound of a blues through the "walking" bass line in the bassoon, the prevailing compound meter (Schuller instructs the performers to accent the eighth-note in any figure), the bends and glissandos in the horn, and other means as well. Another of Schuller's Third Stream pieces, "Little Blue Devil" (1959) is discussed on pp. 149–150.

**EXAMPLE 8–7**    Schuller: *Suite for Woodwind Quintet* (1957), II, mm. 16–23    *(Copyright © 1957 by Josef Marx. Used by permission of McGinnis & Marx Music Publishers.)*

Third Stream music never seemed to "catch on" to the extent that might have been expected, but jazz-influenced music is still being created by composers such as David Amram and Anthony Davis, whose operas *X (The Life and Times of Malcolm X)* (1986) and *Amistad* (1997) resemble Gershwin's *Porgy and Bess* in its combination of jazz idioms with serious subject matter. The use of jazz styles even found its way into Schnittke's first quotation piece, his First Symphony (1972). Nevertheless, Reginald Smith Brindle is no doubt correct when he points out that most jazz has three characteristics that avant-garde composers since 1945 generally have wanted to avoid: clear melodic lines, conventional harmonic progressions, and a strong beat.[10] Ironically, "progressive jazz" itself seems to have done away with those characteristics one at a time—first by means of the disjunct, complex melodies of bebop in the 1940s, then through the harmonic stasis of the "time-no changes" style associated with Miles Davis in the 1960s,[11] and finally, in the performances of musicians like Keith Jarrett, by the development of an ametric approach to rhythm. In fact, some of the experimental jazz ensembles that exist today play compositions that resemble in significant ways some postwar avant-garde music.

All jazz by definition contains some improvisation, usually a significant amount, and this is the primary difference between jazz and most of its concert-hall derivatives. But improvisation has been an important aspect of certain "serious" music in recent decades (see Chapter 14), and the improvisatory styles of Charlie Parker and his heirs may well have had an influence on the performers of this kind of music. In addition, some of the instrumental timbres introduced into concert music in the twentieth century—notably the vibraphone and the cup mute for brass instruments—probably got there by way of the jazz band.

For whatever reason, composers of concert music have not shown the interest in rock music that Third Stream composers had for jazz, even though their colleagues in musicology and music theory have been dealing seriously with rock for some years now. However, there is a recent approach to musical composition that some refer to as "totalism" and that allows—even encourages—the combining of many musical resources and styles, from world music to serial, and totalist composers do display some interest in rock music. Totalism will be discussed further in Chapter 15.

## MUSIC FROM OTHER CULTURES

Composers have shown occasional interest since the late eighteenth century in the music of "exotic" lands, which in this context means anything from the islands of the Western Pacific to the Middle East to Africa. A broader definition could easily include Hungary and Spain, since each had absorbed a certain amount of Eastern culture through long periods of occupation. Under such a definition, Debussy's "La Puerta del Vino" (1910) and Ravel's *Bolero* (1927) would be examples of musical exoticism.

Until the twentieth century, most examples of musical exoticism, such as the "Alla Turca" movement from Mozart's Sonata in A Major K. 331 (1783) and Rimsky-Korsakov's *Scheherazade* (1888), made use of only the most superficial elements of the musical style being imitated. Two obvious ways of evoking the sound of the Orient are through timbre—the use of gongs, wood blocks, and pitched percussion instruments in imitation of the gamelan orchestra—and through certain compositional techniques such as parallelism and pentatonic scales.

Debussy makes use of some of these in Example 8–8. The upper two voices move in parallel motion up and down a four-note scale: (C♯–D♯–F♯–G♯), while the entrance of the bass in m. 29 provides a B, which when added to these four produces a pentatonic scale.

EXAMPLE 8–8   Debussy: *Estampes (Stamps)* (1903), "Pagodas," mm. 27–30

The middle voice in the texture moves more quickly than the bass but more slowly than the upper pair, and it seems to emphasize the important notes of the topmost voice. The total effect—pentatonicism, slow-moving bass, heterophony between topmost and middle voices—resembles some of the characteristics of the Javanese gamelan orchestra, indicating that Debussy had perhaps absorbed more of the authentic technique of exoticism than had his predecessors.

Composers became still more sophisticated about the music of other cultures as the century progressed: Messiaen, who studied the music of India and adapted its rhythms and scales to his own purposes, and Lou Harrison, who studied in Japan, Taiwan, and Korea, are but two examples. Some representative works:

Gustav Holst: *Choral Hymns from the Rig-Veda* (1910)
Albert Roussel: *Padmâvatî* (1914)
Henry Cowell: *Persian Set* (1957)
Messiaen: *Sept haïkaï* (1953)
Alan Hovhaness: *Fantasy on Japanese Woodprints* (1965)
Karlheinz Stockhausen: *Telemusik* (1966)

This blending of Western and Eastern musical styles has been furthered by various non-Western composers, including the Japanese composers Toru Takemitsu and Toshiro Mayuzumi, the Chinese Chou Wen-chung, and Jacob Avshalomov, a Chinese-born American.

Harrison's *Concerto in Slendro* (1961) is a work for violin, celesta, two tackpianos (pianos in which a thumbtack is pressed into each hammer), and percussion, including gongs, triangles, washtubs, garbage pails, pipes, and wooden sticks. The term "Slendro" refers to certain Indonesian tunings of the pentatonic scale, and Harrison states in the score that the piece may be performed with or without these tunings. The third movement is a blend of Indonesian timbres and compositional practices with Western ones (for example, the recurring strict canons). In Example 8–9 (Harrison does not provide here the key signature of four sharps given at the beginning of the movement), one of the tack pianos provides a pedal point on F♯ while the violin and celesta play in heterophony, a texture in which simple and ornamented versions of a melody are played simultaneously.

**EXAMPLE 8–9**   Harrison: *Concerto in Slendro* (1961), III, mm. 19–23   *(© 1978 by C. F. Peters Corporation. Used by permission.)*

Oriental philosophy (or at least the Western understanding of it) has also been important for some twentieth-century composers, especially for John Cage. Questioning the whole notion that art can "communicate" anything, Cage turned to Indian aesthetic theory, where he found the idea that "the purpose of music is to sober and quiet the mind, thus making it susceptible to divine influences."[12] His study of Zen, which "leads to a mistrust of the rational mind and a searching out of ways to nullify its powers of decision,"[13] led Cage to compose music by chance, the compositional decisions being made by the use of chance procedures from the *I-Ching*, a Chinese treatise on probabilities (discussed in more detail in Chapter 14). For Cage the influence of Zen was central to his development as a composer; he has said that "without my engagement with Zen I doubt whether I would have done what I have done."[14]

Cross-cultural influences continue today, of course, in many facets of our lives and no doubt will do so increasingly as means of communication proliferate in the future. While it is unlikely that this will ever lead to some kind of unified "world music," it does open up doors to creative and aesthetic experiences that can only enrich our musical lives.

## SUMMARY

In many ways the music of the twentieth century has broken with the past as completely as has any period in history. Neoclassicism and quotation, while providing important connections to the music of earlier times, are in no sense equivalent to the veneration of the past represented by the *stile antico* of the Baroque. As if to fill the void, some composers have reached out in other directions—to folk music, to jazz, to the music of other cultures—and have adapted these new materials and techniques to their own needs. These trends are an important part of the amazing diversity of styles found in twentieth-century music.

## NOTES

1. Robert Craft, *Stravinsky: The Chronicle of a Friendship, 1948–71*, p. 103.
2. Donald Jay Grout, *A History of Western Music*, pp. 714–15.
3. William Austin, *Music in the 20th Century*, p. 330.
4. George Rochberg, *Music for the Magic Theater*, p. 6. "Notion" appears as "notation" in the original.
5. Ibid., p. 6.
6. George Crumb, *Ancient Voices of Children* (New York: C. F. Peters, 1970).
7. A thorough list is given in Chapter 4 of David Osmond-Smith's *Playing on Words*.
8. Michael Hicks, "Text, Music, and Meaning in the Third Movement of Luciano Berio's *Sinfonia*."

9. Allan Kozinn, "An Eclectic Mix, Through a Contemporary Prism."

10. Reginald Smith Brindle, *The New Music*, pp. 137–38.

11. Ian Carr, *Miles Davis*, p. 145.

12. Ev Grimes, "Ev Grimes Interviews John Cage," p. 48.

13. Brindle, *The New Music*, p. 123.

14. Michael Nyman, *Experimental Music*, p. 43.

## EXERCISES

### Part A: Analysis

1. Bartók: *Fourteen Bagatelles*, Op. 6 (1908), No. 4, mm. 1–8. This excerpt contains the beginning of a folk-song harmonization by Bartók (the remainder of the piece simply repeats mm. 5–8). Bartók uses different compositional techniques in the harmonization of each phrase. Analyze both the song and the accompaniment in detail, summarizing your findings in prose with musical examples. Do not neglect such issues as voice leading and scale formations.

2. List the chords used in the accompaniment (bassoons and trombones) in Example 8–1. How much of this conforms to traditional harmonic progressions in E♭? Point out some dissonances between the accompaniment and the upper parts that would be difficult to explain in traditional terms. Comment on imitation in this excerpt.

3. A very basic harmonic pattern for a twelve-bar blues in B♭ is:

| B♭ | ╱ | B♭7 | ╱ | E♭7 | ╱ | B♭ | ╱ | F7 | E♭7 | B♭ | ╱ ||

Discuss how Example 8–7 compares to the first eight measures of that pattern. Remember to transpose the clarinet and horn parts.

4. The B♭ "blues scale" can be derived by combining the three seventh chords listed in the previous exercise, producing a nine-tone scale: B♭–C–D♭–D–E♭–F–G–A♭–A. Part of the flavor that we associate with the blues results from the use, either melodically or harmonically, of the altered and unaltered "blues notes" (D♭/D and A♭/A) in close proximity. Point out any examples that you can find of this technique in Example 8–7.

## Part B: Listening

Listen to as many examples as you can. For each one, explain how the example is relevant to the present chapter, and try to describe how the music *sounds*—how the use of folk materials or quotation, for example, helps to give the music its own particular sound.

1. David Amram: Triple Concerto for Woodwind, Brass, and Jazz Quintets, and Orchestra (1970), I
2. Béla Bartók: *Fifteen Hungarian Peasant Songs* (1917)
3. Luciano Berio: Sinfonia (1968), III
4. Aaron Copland: *Appalachian Spring* (1944)
5. Manuel de Falla: *Nights in the Gardens of Spain* (1916)
6. Lou Harrison: Double Concerto for Violin and Cello with Javanese Gamelan (1982)
7. William Grant Still: *Afro-American Symphony* (1933)
8. Igor Stravinsky: Octet for Wind Instruments (1923)

## FURTHER READING

BRINDLE, REGINALD SMITH. *The New Music*. See Chapter 13, The Search Outwards—The Orient, Jazz, Archaisms.

CHOU, WEN-CHUNG. "Asian Concepts and Twentieth-Century Western Composers."

COPE, DAVID H. *New Directions in Music*. See the sections titled "Non-Western Influences," pp. 109–13, and "Quotation," pp. 355–57.

GANN, KYLE. *American Music in the Twentieth Century*. See Chapter 11, Interfaces with Rock and Jazz.

GRIFFITHS, PAUL. *Modern Music and After*. See the section titled "Of Elsewhen and Elsewhere," pp. 151–70.

GROUT, DONALD JAY. *A History of Western Music*. See the sections titled "Musical Styles Related to Folk Idioms," pp. 685–700, and "Neo-Classicism and Related Movements," pp. 700–22.

RINGO, JAMES. "The Lure of the Orient."

SIMMS, BRYAN R. *Music of the Twentieth Century*. See Chapter 10, Neoclassicism in France, Germany, and England, and Chapter 15, Eclecticism.

# ─────NINE─────

# Nonserial Atonality

## INTRODUCTION

In the first decade of the twentieth century, a few composers developed an approach to composition that, in retrospect, was perhaps inevitable. The chromaticism of the nineteenth century had chipped away at the tonal system so successfully that it was only a natural outcome for the system eventually to be abandoned altogether. This new music without a tonal center eventually became known as "atonal" music, although not without objection by some of the composers who originated the style.

Atonality is one of the more important aspects of twentieth-century music, and it is a major factor that distinguishes much of the music of this century from any other music in the Western tradition. Nonserial, or "free," atonality led in the 1920s to a more organized atonal method called serialism or twelve-tone music, but nonserial atonal music continued to be composed and is still being composed today. We will discuss serialism in later chapters. For now we are concerned only with nonserial atonal music, which, for the present, we will refer to simply as atonal music.

It is not surprising that the analysis of atonal music has required the development of new theoretical terms and approaches. Although analytical methods are still being developed and experimented with, most of the current literature derives from the work of Allen Forte, whose book *The Structure of Atonal Music* is a standard reference on the subject.[1] Most of the information in this chapter derives from Forte's work or from that of his followers. Although the basics of this theory may be totally unfamiliar to you, the concepts are not very difficult, and you will find them applicable to a wide range of twentieth-century styles.

## CHARACTERISTICS OF ATONAL MUSIC

There are several characteristics of atonal music that set it apart from other styles. The first of course, is that it lacks a tonal center. This aspect is a subjective one, for any two listeners might differ concerning the degree to which a tonal center is audible in a particular work; nevertheless, a great many pieces are widely accepted as being atonal. This atonality is achieved by avoiding the conventional melodic, harmonic, and rhythmic patterns that help to establish a tonality in traditional tonal music. In their place we find unresolved dissonances, a preponderance of mixed-interval chords, and pitch material derived from the chromatic scale. Textures often are contrapuntal, with themes or melodies in the traditional sense occurring less often, and the metric organization is frequently difficult for the listener to follow.

Example 9–1 is from the beginning of one of the earliest atonal works. Although it is not the most representative example that could have been chosen, it does have the advantage of being easy to play, and you will get more out of the following discussion if you play the example several times before going on. The piece opens with a slow tremolo between D and F over a sustained F, perhaps suggesting D minor. (Octave doublings such as the octave here on F were soon discarded by some atonal composers on the theory that they put too much emphasis on a single pitch class.) The melody that enters in m. 2 does little to confirm D as a tonality. Two short melodic phrases, one beginning in m. 2 and the other in m. 3, use the pitch classes C, D♭, D, E♭, A♭, and A, with many of these pitches being freely dissonant against the accompaniment. Following the rest under the fermata, a third phrase interrupts the tremolo figure in the low register and closes the excerpt. Melodically this third phrase begins with an expressive motion up to D (notice the accompanying chords here do not suggest a D tonal center), followed by the same pitch classes that ended the second phrase: C–E♭–D♭. The tremolo figure returns as the melody settles in on its last two notes. Whereas in this excerpt the D/F *dyad* (pair of notes) in the accompaniment is clearly in opposition to the D♭ in the melody, neither D nor D♭ is strongly established as a tonal center, and this, along with the prevailing chromaticism, leads us to classify this music as atonal rather than polytonal (review Chapter 5).

**EXAMPLE 9–1** Schoenberg: *Three Piano Pieces* (1909), Op. 11, No. 2, mm. 1–5

*(Used by permission of Belmont Music Publishers.)*

It is doubtful that the listener would be able to identify the time signature used in these opening measures. The opening undulating figure is notated in groups of three notes but contains only two pitches, so the listener is not sure whether the first six eighth-notes constitute two or three beats (assuming the eighth-note is heard as a division of the beat). The melody in its first phrase works out nicely in $\frac{12}{8}$, but, to express the meter as notated, the melody should start at the beginning of the measure instead of on the third eighth-note (Example 9–2a). The melody of the second phrase could easily be heard as two measures of $\frac{3}{4}$ with an anacrusis (Example 9–2b). Later portions of the piece (not shown) suggest $\frac{3}{4}$, $\frac{2}{4}$, and $\frac{6}{4}$, among others, although there are passages that are clearly in $\frac{12}{8}$.

**EXAMPLE 9–2** The Melody Renotated

a.                                            b.

## PITCH-CLASS SETS

It soon became clear to musicians that the pitch aspect of atonal music required a new vocabulary if the analysis of this music was ever to be more than descriptive. It was recognized that atonal music often achieved a certain degree of unity through recurrent use of a new kind of motive. This new kind of motive was given various names, including **cell**, **basic cell**, **set**, **pitch set**, **pitch-class set**, and **referential sonority**. It could appear melodically, harmonically, or as a combination of the two. The set also could be transposed and/or inverted (that is, in mirror inversion; for example, G–B–C inverts to G–E♭–D), and its pitches could appear in any order and in any register. Most pieces were found to employ a large number of different kinds of pitch sets, only a few of which might be important in unifying the piece. The analysis of atonal music usually includes the process of identifying and labeling these important pitch sets, a process that involves **segmentation**.

Segmentation is in some ways much more difficult than the analysis of chords in traditional tonal music. The first problem is that, when beginning the analysis, one usually does not know which sets will turn out to be significant in the piece and which ones will not, meaning that various musically convincing segmentations may have to be tried and discarded before the significant ones appear. We will demonstrate the process of segmentation throughout this chapter.

A second problem is labeling the sets for ease of comparison, and it is in this area that Allen Forte's work has proved so helpful. Because an atonal chord or melodic fragment can consist of any combination of pitches, thousands of different sets are possible. As we shall see, Forte's system of pitch-class sets reduces this number considerably.

## OCTAVE EQUIVALENCE, TRANSPOSITIONAL EQUIVALENCE, AND NORMAL ORDER

In the analysis of tonal music, we routinely reduce sonorities to basic forms. For instance, through the theories of **octave equivalence** and chord roots we analyze all of the chords in Example 9–3a as C major triads and all of those in Example 9–3b as F major triads. In addition, we consider C major triads and F major triads to be **transpositionally equivalent**, to be members of a class of sonorities referred to collectively as major triads. These concepts are so obvious to us that it seems trivial to mention them, but in fact the theory that classifies the sonorities in Example 9–3 into one chord type is only a few centuries old.

EXAMPLE 9–3   Major Triads

In order to analyze and compare the pitch-class sets in atonal music, we need a process that will reduce any set to some basic form in the same way that we reduce the chords in Example 9–3 to the three notes of the major triad in root position. This basic form in pitch-set analysis is called the **normal order**. The procedure to follow in determining the normal order will be illustrated by means of the segmentations shown in Example 9–4. All of the segmentations are circled except for Sets 3 and 4; these sets are the three-note chords that accompany the melody.

EXAMPLE 9–4   Schoenberg: *Three Piano Pieces* (1909) Op. 11, No. 2, mm. 1–5

*(Used by permission of Belmont Music Publishers.)*

The normal order of a pitch-class set is that ordering of the pitches that spans the smallest possible interval. In that sense, it is similar to putting a triad into root position. Some instructors prefer to use pitch-class integers (C = 0, C♯/D♭ = 1, etc.) when figuring out the normal order, but in this text we will use musical notation.

To find the normal order of a set, notate the pitches as an ascending "scale," within a single octave, as in Example 9–5a. You can begin the scale on any one of the notes, and the notes may be spelled enharmonically if you wish. Leave out any duplicated pitch classes, but continue the scale up to the octave (the second D♭ in Example 9–5a). Now find the largest interval between any two adjacent notes (the tritone in Example 9–5a); the *top* note of this largest interval (the A in Example 9–5a) is the *bottom* note of the normal order. The normal order of set 1 is shown in Example 9–5b. Notice that in Example 9–5 we have labeled the interval A–D♭ as a major 3rd even though it is notated as a diminished 4th. While enharmonic substitution is usually discouraged in tonal analysis, it is essential in analyzing atonal music. To write out a normal order without using musical notation, separate the note names with commas, and enclose the normal order between brackets, as in [A, Db, Eb].[2]

EXAMPLE 9–5    Normal Order of Set 1

When we put Set 2 into normal order in Example 9–6b, we discover that it is [Ab, C, D], the same as Example 9–5b, but a minor 2nd lower; in other words, Set 2 is transpositionally equivalent to Set 1.

EXAMPLE 9–6    Normal Order of Set 2

Sets 3 and 4 are the three-note chords that accompany the melody in m. 4. The normal orders of these two sets are shown in Example 9–7. Notice that Set 4 [Eb, G, A], is transpositionally equivalent to Sets 1 and 2, but Set 3 is not.

EXAMPLE 9–7    Normal Orders of Sets 3 and 4

Sets 5, 6, and 7 result from a different segmentation of m. 4. Each one contains four pitch classes. The first column of Example 9–8 shows these sets in scalar form. Notice that in Set 7 the G♯ and C♯ have been spelled enharmonically for convenience. The normal orders of these sets are shown in the second column of Example 9–8. None of these sets is transpositionally equivalent to any of the others.

**EXAMPLE 9–8    Normal Orders of Sets 5, 6, and 7**

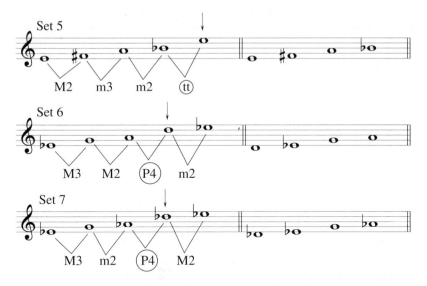

We are making good progress here in learning how to put pitch sets into normal order, which, you will recall, means that order that spans the smallest interval. A complication that occasionally arises is a set in which there is not a single largest interval, but instead two or more intervals are tied for largest. Set 8 is an example of such a set. Notice in Example 9–9a that there are two major 3rds and that all of the other intervals are smaller. This means that we have two candidates for the normal order, Example 9–9b and Example 9–9c. The tie is broken by comparing the intervals between the first and next-to-last notes in both versions (A–E♭ in Example 9–9b versus C♯–F in Example 9–9c). The normal order is the version with the *smaller* interval—Example 9–9c—because that version is the one that is packed most tightly to the left.

**EXAMPLE 9–9    Normal Order of Set 8**

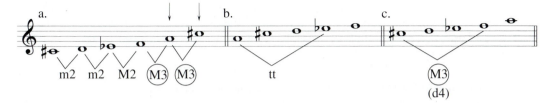

If the intervals between the first and next-to-last notes in Example 9–9b and Example 9–9c had been the same, we would have proceeded to the intervals between the first and third-to-last notes, and so on, until the tie was broken. In some sets, however, the tie cannot be broken. Consider the set in Example 9–10a (not taken from the Schoenberg excerpt). It contains two instances of its largest interval, the minor 3rd, so there are two candidates for the normal order. These are shown in Example 9–10b and Example 9–10c. The interval successions in the two versions are identical (because they are transpositionally equivalent), so it is impossible to break the tie. In this case, either of the tied forms may be selected as the normal order. A set such as this is called a **transpositionally symmetrical set**, because it reproduces its own pitch-class content under one or more intervals of transposition. In the case of the set in Example 9–10, transposition at the tritone reproduces the set.

EXAMPLE 9–10    A Transpositionally Symmetrical Set

## INVERSIONAL EQUIVALENCE AND BEST NORMAL ORDER

We have seen that tonal and atonal analyses share the concepts of octave equivalence and transpositional equivalence. Atonal analysis goes a step further, however, and considers pitch-class sets that are related by inversion to be equivalent. (To "invert" a set in atonal music means to reverse the order of the intervals.)

This would not be a useful approach in tonal music, because the major and minor triads, for example, are related by inversion, as are the dominant 7th chord and the half-diminished-7th chord, and we need to be able to distinguish between them in tonal analysis. But in atonal music a set and its inversion are considered to be different representations of the same set class.

If we are going to have a single classification for any set and its inversion, then we will have to carry the concept of the normal order a step further, to something called the **best normal order**. This concept is important because the best normal order is the generic representation of all the possible transpositions and inversions of a set. In order to find the best normal order of any set, first find its normal order and then notate its inversion. The inversion will already be in normal order *unless* there are two or more occurrences of the largest interval (discussed later). Finally, compare the two normal orders: the "better" of the two is considered to be the best normal order.

Let us see how this works with Set 1 from Example 9–4. Its normal order was given in Example 9–5. An easy way to invert the normal order of a set is to use the same top and bottom notes, and then fill in the remaining notes by reversing the order of the intervals. In Example 9–11a the intervals of the normal order are analyzed. Then, keeping the outer notes the same, these intervals are reversed in Example 9–11b to form the inversion. Finally, we choose between the two orders by comparing the intervals between the first and next-to-last notes in both versions, just as we did with Example 9–9. We select as the best normal order the version with the smaller interval—in this case, Example 9–11b.

EXAMPLE 9–11   Set I and Its Inversion

Looking back over Examples 9–5, 9–6, and 9–7, you can see that Sets 1, 2, and 4 were transpositionally equivalent to one another, and that all three were inversionally equivalent to Set 3. In other words, all four sets have the same best normal order and therefore are all representatives of the same set class.

Set 5 is analyzed in Example 9–12. The normal order of the original set is in Example 9–12a, and its inversion is in Example 9–12b. When the two normal orders, Example 9–12a and 9–12b, are compared, we see that the major 3rd (diminished 4th) in Example 9–12b is smaller than the perfect 4th in Example 9–12a, so Example 9–12b is selected as the best normal order. If the intervals between the first and next-to-last notes in Example 9–12a and Example 9–12b had been the same, we would have proceeded to the intervals between the first and third-to-last notes, and so on, until the tie was broken.

EXAMPLE 9–12   Best Normal Order of Set 5

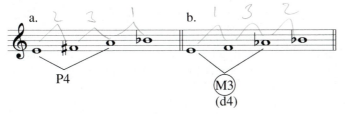

In Example 9–13 Set 6 is analyzed. The normal order of the original set, Example 9–13a, turns out to be the best normal order.

EXAMPLE 9–13   Best Normal Order of Set 6

Set 7 is analyzed in Example 9–14. The best normal order is Example 9–14b. Because the best normal orders of Sets 6 and 7 (Example 9–13a and Example 9–14b) are transpositionally equivalent, Sets 6 and 7 are representatives of the same set class.

EXAMPLE 9–14   Best Normal Order of Set 7

It is not uncommon to find a set in which the normal order of the set and the normal order of its inversion are identical or transpositionally equivalent. An example is Set 9, shown in normal order in Example 9–15a. In Example 9–15b the normal order is inverted, and we see that the normal order of the inversion is the same as the original. A set such as this is called an **inversionally symmetrical set** because it reproduces its pitch-class content at one or more levels of inversion.

EXAMPLE 9–15   Best Normal Order of Set 9

The method that we have been using so far to find the best normal order will not always work with pitch-class sets that have more than one occurrence of the largest interval (such as the one in Example 9–9). Consider the set in Example 9–16a. There are two occurrences of the largest interval, the major 3rd, so we have to consider the two candidates for the normal order in Examples 9–16b and 9–16c. The interval between the first and next-to-last notes in Example 9–16b is smaller than that in Example 9–16c, so the normal order is [E, G, A♭, C].

EXAMPLE 9–16   A Pitch-Class Set

The normal order of this set is given again in Example 9–17a along with its inversion in 9–17b. However, because we know that there are two occurrences of the largest interval (the major 3rd), we have to consider another ordering of the inversion, shown in Example

9–17c. Comparing our three candidates for best normal order, we see that two of them span a major 3rd between the first and next-to-last notes, which eliminates Example 9–17b from the competition. We now back up one interval and compare the intervals between the first and third-to-last notes in Examples 9–17a (minor 3rd) and 9–17c (minor 2nd), looking for the smaller interval. As it turns out, the last version of our set wins out over the other two and is in fact the best normal order. The lesson here is that you must try out as many orderings of the inversion as there are occurrences of the largest interval or you may not discover the best normal order.

**EXAMPLE 9–17** The Normal Order Inverted

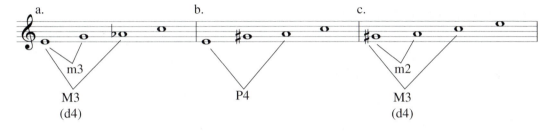

## PRIME FORMS AND SET CLASSES

Once we know the best normal order of a set, we need to be able to give it a name, which is done by applying numbers to the best normal order. The resulting series of numbers is called the **prime form**, and it represents all of the pitch-class sets in that **set class**, just as "major triad" represents all possible major triads in all possible arrangements. The first number of a prime form is always 0, and it stands for the lowest note of the best normal order. The other numbers give the distance in half steps each successive note is above that lowest note. For instance, in Example 9–11b we notated the best normal order of Set 1 as [A, B, E♭]. Because B is two half steps above A and E♭ is six half steps above A, the name of this set class is [026], and [026] represents all transpositions and/or inversions of Set 1. Sets 1, 2, 3, and 4 are all [026] trichords. Notice that the set class is enclosed in brackets and that the numbers are not separated by commas or spaces. In the event that you need a 10 or 11 in a set name, use T or E; a whole tone scale would be [02468T].

A few more illustrations: The best normal order of Set 5 (Example 9–12b) is [E, F, A♭, B♭], yielding [0146] as a prime form. The best normal order of Set 6 (Example 9–13a) is [D, E♭, G, A], so its prime form is [0157], and Set 7 (Example 9–14b) is also a [0157] tetrachord. Set 9 (Example 9–15a) is a [0145] tetrachord.

By adopting the concepts of transpositional and inversional equivalence, the thousands of possible pitch combinations have been reduced to a manageable number of prime forms or set classes. The following table shows how many set classes there are for combinations of from two to ten pitch classes.

|     |                                |
|-----|--------------------------------|
| 6   | Dyads (2 pitch classes)        |
| 12  | Trichords (3 pitch classes)    |
| 29  | Tetrachords (4 pitch classes)  |
| 38  | Pentachords (5 pitch classes)  |
| 50  | Hexachords (6 pitch classes)   |
| 38  | Septachords (7 pitch classes)  |
| 29  | Octachords (8 pitch classes)   |
| 12  | Nonachords (9 pitch classes)   |
| 6   | Decachords (10 pitch classes)  |
| 220 | TOTAL                          |

## THE INTERVAL-CLASS VECTOR

Most of pitch-set analysis is concerned with identifying sets that recur in a piece in compositionally significant ways. This includes, of course, transpositions and inversions of the original set, since we recognize transpositional and inversional equivalence. But analytical theory is much less advanced when it comes to comparing nonequivalent sets. Consider, for example, Sets 5 and 6 from the Schoenberg excerpt, reproduced here in best normal order beginning on G.

EXAMPLE 9–18   Sets 5 and 6

[0146]                    [0157]

It would appear that [0146] and [0157] are very similar, the only difference being the interval between the second and third notes; thus, [0157] is a kind of expansion of [0146]. But there are other differences, one of them being that [0157] contains two perfect intervals (G–C and G–D), while [0146] contains only one (A♭–C♯). This may mean that [0157] is potentially a more consonant sound than [0146]. One way of comparing sets that contain the same number of pitch classes, as these do, is to tabulate their interval contents. Because inversional equivalence is still in effect, we will consider the minor 2nd and the major 7th to be the same interval, also the major 2nd and the minor 7th, and so forth. We then have six **interval classes** ("interval class" is sometimes abbreviated as "IC"):

| Interval Class | Traditional Interval |
|----------------|----------------------|
| 1 | m2, M7 |
| 2 | M2, m7 |
| 3 | m3, M6 |
| 4 | M3, m6 |
| 5 | P4, P5 |
| 6 | A4, d5 |

To analyze a set according to its interval content, tabulate all the ICs between each note in the set and all the notes *above* it. This way, the interval between each pair of notes in the set will be counted only once. The tables below demonstrate this procedure for Sets 5 and 6 (refer again to Example 9–18).

| Set 5 | | |
|---|---|---|
| From | Up to | IC |
| G | A♭ | 1 |
| G | B | 4 |
| G | C♯ | 6 |
| A♭ | B | 3 |
| A♭ | C♯ | 5 |
| B | C♯ | 2 |

| Set 6 | | |
|---|---|---|
| From | Up to | IC |
| G | A♭ | 1 |
| G | C | 5 |
| G | D | 5 |
| A♭ | C | 4 |
| A♭ | D | 6 |
| C | D | 2 |

You can see from this that Set 5 contains exactly one occurrence of each IC. Set 6, on the other hand, contains two occurrences of IC5 but none of IC3. This information is usually presented in the form of an **interval-class vector** (or ICV), which lists the number of occurrences of each IC, beginning with IC1 and continuing through IC6. In this text we will enclose the list with angled brackets, as in <001110>. Set 5, as it contains one of each IC, has an interval-class vector of <111111>, whereas the interval-class vector for Set 6 is <110121>. The interval-class vectors of Sets 5 and 6 illustrate their similarity and give us a general picture of their potential consonance or dissonance.

The interval-class vector provides one tool for comparing pitch-class sets of the same size, but it is not without its problems. At the beginning of Example 3–B–8 (p. 72) Berg employs two set classes in alternation (the chords marked a, b, c, d, and e). The first two chords are shown in Example 9–19, both in their original versions (but compressed spacing) and in their best normal orders, transposed to begin on G. The first chord is set class [0137], and the second is [0146], the same as Set 5 from the Schoenberg excerpt. The surprising thing here is that both sets have an interval-class vector of <111111>. Because they are different set class, we know they are not related by transposition or inversion, yet their interval-class vectors are identical. Pairs of sets that share the same vector (they come only in pairs) are known as **Z-related sets**. This is the only pair of Z-related tetrachords, but there are three pairs of Z-related pentachords and fifteen pairs of Z-related hexachords. It is obvious from this that the interval-class vector alone cannot be used to compare set classes, although it does provide some useful information.

EXAMPLE 9–19   Two Chords from Berg's "Warm Is the Air"

One thing an ICV can do is to predict how many pitch classes will be retained under any level of transposition. For example, the ICV of a major triad (or a minor one, for that matter) is <001110>. This means that if we transpose a triad up *or* down by minor 3rd, a major 3rd, or a perfect 4th, exactly one pitch class will be held **invariant**—that is, it will be retained. Conversely, transposing a triad by any other interval will produce a fresh crop of three new pitch classes. (Prove this to yourself by starting with a C major triad.) An important point, however, has to do with IC6: transposition by a tritone will keep *twice* the number of pitch classes invariant as are found in the last digit of an ICV. For instance, Set 6 from the Schoenberg example was an [0157] set with an ICV of <110121>. If it is transposed by a tritone, two—not one—pitch classes will be retained:

## FORTE LABELS

Music theorists often use the labels for prime forms that are found in Allen Forte's *Structure of Atonal Music*. Once you know the prime form of a set, you can look up its Forte label as well as its ICV in the appendix in the back of this book. A Forte label has three parts: a number that indicates how many pitch classes the set contains, a hyphen, and a number that is sometimes preceded by the letter Z. For example, the chromatic trichord, [012], has 3–1 as its Forte label, while the augmented triad, [048], is 3–12. The letter Z is used for pairs of sets that have identical interval–class vectors. You may recall that [0137] and [0146], discussed earlier, both have an ICV of <111111>, so their Forte labels include a letter Z, as in 4-Z29 and 4-Z15, respectively. Forte labels are frequently used in the theoretical literature, so it is useful to know where you can look them up and find their associated prime forms.

## SUBSETS

Sometimes pitch-class sets that do not belong to the same set class may be related to each other as **subsets** of a larger set. For example, suppose that the following four trichords (each given in normal order but not necessarily best normal order) appear in a passage:

[Ab, B, C]   [014]
[F, B, C]    [016]
[F, Ab, C]   [037]
[F, Ab, B]   [036]

These trichords belong to four different set classes, but they are related in that they are all subsets of this set:

[F, Ab, B, C]  [0147]

Going a step further, if we accept transpositional and inversional equivalence, we could say that *any* [014] is a subset of *any* [0147], as are [016], [037], and [036], even if the subsets are not **literal subsets** but are instead transposed and/or inverted.

A special kind of subset is the **scalar subset**, which is a subset that is derived from a particular scale type, usually diatonic (as in the white keys of the piano), octatonic, or whole-tone. For example, even if a passage is not based upon a single whole-tone scale, it would be of interest to discover that most or all of its sets are whole-tone subsets. In Example 9–20a, the violin states a figure that, while not octatonic, is constructed from octatonic subsets. The piano a few measures later answers with some octatonic subsets of its own with another non-octatonic figure (Example 9–20b).

**EXAMPLE 9–20**   Zwilich: Sonata in Three Movements (1974), III

*(Copyright 1978 by Elkan-Vogel, Inc.)*

## AGGREGATES

Nonserial atonality does not offer a systematic method of achieving atonality, as serialism does, but atonal composers have at times shown a concern that all twelve pitch classes be heard within a fairly short period, which is one of the fundamental notions of twelve-tone serialism. The term **aggregate** is used to refer to any such statement of all twelve pitch classes, *without regard to order or duplication.* In atonal analysis, it is sometimes helpful to look for aggregates, especially at the beginning of a piece or major section, or even within certain parts of the texture.

Concerning his Bagatelles Op. 9, a nonserial atonal work, Anton Webern wrote, "While working on them I had the feeling that once the twelve tones had run out, the piece was finished."[3] This does not mean that each Bagatelle is only twelve notes long, although they are quite short, but it might mean that Webern has used aggregates in significant ways in these pieces. The first half of the fifth Bagatelle (Example 9–21) contains an extreme example of what Webern was talking about.

In the first measure of this piece, Webern introduces a nearly chromatic set, C–C#–D#–E, which is filled in by the D in m. 2, giving us:

| C | C# | D | D# | E |
|---|----|---|----|---|
| ├── | mm. 1–2 | ──┤ | | |

Measure 3 begins with a chord that extends the chromatic set by two more pitches:

| B | C | C# | D | D# | E | F |
|---|---|----|---|----|---|---|
| 3 | ├── | mm. 1–2 | ──┤ | | | 3 |

The chord in m. 4 expands the chromatic set to nine pitches:

| B♭ | B | C | C# | D | D# | E | F | G♭ |
|----|---|---|----|---|----|---|---|----|
| 4 | 3 | ├── | mm. 1–2 | ──┤ | | | 3 | 4 |

Measure 6 continues the set upwards by two notes:

| B♭ | B | C | C# | D | D# | E | F | G♭ | G | A♭ |
|----|---|---|----|---|----|---|---|----|---|----|
| 4 | 3 | ├── | mm. 1–2 | ──┤ | | | 3 | 4 | 6 | 6 |

And the chromatic set is completed by the A in m. 7:

| A | B♭ | B | C | C# | D | D# | E | F | G♭ | G | A♭ |
|---|----|---|---|----|---|----|---|---|----|---|----|
| 7 | 4 | 3 | ├── | mm. 1–2 | ──┤ | | | 3 | 4 | 6 | 6 |

What we have in mm. 1–7 is an aggregate, but it is a highly unusual one in that the pitch classes are introduced according to a preconceived pattern and within a single octave (A3 to A♭4). Even the pitch classes that are repeated, like the E and E♭ in m. 3, recur in the same octave, with the single exception of the C5 in m. 5.

**EXAMPLE 9–21**   Webern: Six Bagatelles for String Quartet, Op. 9 (1913), V, mm. 1–7

Aggregate completion is also important in the first movement of Ligeti's *Ten Pieces for Wind Quintet* (1968). In this twenty-five-measure work, the composer employs eleven pitch classes, omitting only C♯, until the middle of m. 16, where C♯s are introduced to produce the climax of the movement.

## MORE ABOUT SEGMENTATION

Earlier in this chapter we said that atonal analysis is largely a matter of segmentation, or identifying and labeling significant pitch-class sets. The Schoenberg excerpt provided some experience with this process. Segmentation is largely a hit-or-miss analytical procedure, because a set that occurs only once and is not significantly related to any more important set is not really of much interest. In the Webern excerpt (Example 9–21), for instance, you might isolate these three sets in m. 1:

> C–C♯–E            [014]
> C–D♯–E            [014]
> C–C♯–D♯–E       [0134]

The fact that the first two sets are representatives of the same pitch-class set is encouraging to the analyst, but they may or may not recur later in the piece. Another segmentation that could be tried would be to join the "melodies" in the violins:

> C♯–D♯–D–F–E♭     [0124]

Other musically defensible segmentations could be made on the basis of timbre (for instance, *am steg* versus *pizzicato*) or register. The most important thing is that the segmentations should reflect the way the music sounds and should not divide musical units such as chords or melodic figures in unmusical ways. Good atonal analysis requires a high degree of musical sensitivity and a very keen ear.

### SUMMARY

The most essential characteristic of nonserial atonal music is its atonality, which is achieved by avoiding the melodic, harmonic, and rhythmic patterns used to establish tonality in tonal music. Some of the other characteristics of nonserial atonal music include unresolved dissonances, a preponderance of mixed-interval chords, contrapuntal textures, ambiguous metric organization, and use of the chromatic scale.

An important aspect of atonal analysis is the segmentation of the texture into smaller sets, or cells, which are then identified according to set class. This process involves arranging each set in normal order and then in best normal order for the identification of its set class, represented by its prime form. This classification process depends on both transpositional and inversional equivalence in order to reduce to 220 the number of possible sets that contain between two and ten pitch classes. Forte labels provide reasonably short names for each of these set classes. Some set classes are transpositionally or inversionally symmetrical, or both.

Nonequivalent sets may be compared by means of their interval-class vectors, by subset relationships (including scalar subsets), and by other means not introduced here. Aggregate completion is another element to look for in the analysis of atonal music, especially at the beginning of a piece.

Probably the best way to analyze atonal music, as well as tonal music, is at the piano keyboard. Finding the best normal order and prime form becomes considerably faster at the piano. More important, as you work at the analysis, you hear the sound of the set and gradually learn to associate the sounds with the set classes.

### NOTES

1. Allen Forte, *The Structure of Atonal Music.*
2. The conventions for notating normal orders and other constructs introduced in this chapter are still in flux. Your instructor may wish to employ other conventions that are equally useful.
3. Webern, *The Path to the New Music*, p. 51.

## EXERCISES

### Part A: Fundamentals

1. Analyze the pitches in each exercise below as a single pitch-class set. Notate the set in its normal order and in its best normal order (which may or may not be different), and write the prime form (e.g., [0157]) underneath the best normal order.

2. Provide the interval-class vector for each set in Exercise A.1.
3. Classify each set from Exercise A.1 as (1) transpositionally symmetrical, (2) inversionally symmetrical, (3) both transpositionally and inversionally symmetrical, or (4) neither transpositionally nor inversionally symmetrical.
4. Notate the four trichordal subsets that can be derived from Exercise A.1.f. Notate them in normal order, not in best normal order. Which two belong to the same set class?

### Part B: Analysis

1. See Example 3–15 (p. 54). What trichord type (prime form) is featured in the piano?
2. See Example 3–21 (p. 59). What trichord type (prime form) is featured in this passage from a tonal composition by Debussy?
3. See Example 3–27 (p. 62). What is the prime form of this hexachord? Is this set class transpositionally symmetrical, inversionally symmetrical, or both?
4. See Example 3–29 (p. 64). The same two tetrachord types appear in each measure on beats 1 and 2. What are the prime forms of these tetrachords? Are either or both of them transpositionally and/or inversionally symmetrical?
5. See Example 3–B–8 (p. 72). We saw in connection with Example 9–19 that the music alternates between [0137] and [0146] in the first two measures. What trichord type is found in the right hand in those measures? What set class ends the piece?
6. See Example 4–4 (p. 79). What tetrachord begins the flute part? The voice part? Where is the first aggregate completed? Is this a structurally significant location, such as a climactic pitch or the end of a phrase?
7. See Example 4–6 (p. 81). What trichord type appears under each of the three phrase marks?

8. See Example 4–7 (p. 82). Using reasonable segmentations of the bassoon part, find two recurrent tetrachords.

9. See Example 4–B–1 (p. 93). One way to segment this would be into three tetrachords and a final trichord. Analyze each one.

10. See Example 4–B–2 (p. 94). Analyze this melody in terms of set classes and large-scale (mostly chromatic) motion.

11. See Example 5–4 (p. 104). What trichord type is most prominent in this excerpt?

12. See Example 9–1. Where in this excerpt is the first aggregate completed? Is this a structurally significant location?

13. Takemitsu: *And then I knew 'twas Wind* (1992), mm. 1–10 (harp). Takemitsu presents some of the important pitch material in this piece in m. 1, where six pitch classes are heard. Determine the set class of this hexachord, and then analyze the set classes of the circled trichords in the following measures. All of the pitch material in mm. 3–10 comes from m. 1 except for the mysterious B♮ in m. 8.

(Takemitsu: *And then I knew 'twas Wind* (1992), mm. 1–10 (harp))

14. Crumb: Madrigals, Book I (1965), No. 1, "To see you naked is to remember the earth," mm. 1–6 (see p. 195). This excerpt is based primarily on one set class. Decide what that set class is and mark its occurrences in the music. Try to make your segmentations musically justifiable.

Crumb: Madrigals, Book I [1965], No. 1, "To see you naked is to remember the earth," mm. 1–6  (© 1971 by C. F. Peters Corporation. Used by permission.)

## *Part C: Composition*

1. Compose an instrumental melody based on the [0157] tetrachord in various transpositions and in inversion. Every fourth note should be the end of one statement of the tetrachord and the beginning of another:

Because the [0157] tetrachord has an interval-class vector of <110121>, your melody can have a good deal of intervallic variety. Include an analysis of your melody.

2. Continue the example below or compose one of your own, basing the passage on a single trichord type, used both melodically and harmonically. Circle all occurrences of the set. The trichord used in the example is [016].

3. Compose a fanfare for three trumpets, based upon one melodic trichord type and a different harmonic trichord type. Label all of the trichords.

4. Compose a harmonic "progression" in four parts using a single tetrachord type. The pitch content of each chord should be a transposition of the preceding one, and you are to use all six ICs as intervals of transposition. Label the transpositions. Keep any invariant pitch classes in the same voices, and move the remaining voices as smoothly as possible. What is the interval-class vector of your tetrachord? How does that interval-class vector relate to the invariants?

## FURTHER READING

COPE, DAVID. *Techniques of the Twentieth Century Composer.* See Chapter 7, Pitch-Class Sets.

FORTE, ALLEN. *The Structure of Atonal Music.* See Part I, Pitch-Class Sets and Relations.

KOSTKA, STEFAN, AND DOROTHY PAYNE. *Tonal Harmony with an Introduction to Twentieth-Century Music.* See pp. 511–520.

LANSKY, PAUL, AND GEORGE PERLE. "Atonality," in Stanley Sadie, ed., *The New Grove Dictionary of Music and Musicians.*

LESTER, JOEL. *Analytic Approaches to Twentieth-Century Music*. See Unit 2, Pitch Structures.

PERLE, GEORGE. *Serial Composition and Atonality*. See Chapter 2, "Free" Atonality.

RAHN, JOHN. *Basic Atonal Theory*.

SCHMALFELDT, JANET. *Berg's Wozzeck*. See pp. 14–24.

SIMMS, BRYAN. *Music of the Twentieth Century*. See Chapter 2, Harmonic and Motivic Associations and the "Emancipation of Dissonance."

STRAUS, JOSEPH N. *Introduction to Post-Tonal Theory*. See Chapter 2, Pitch-Class Sets.

WILLIAMS, J. KENT. *Theories and Analyses of Twentieth-Century Music*. See Chapters 2 through 6.

WINOLD, ALLEN. *Harmony: Patterns and Principles*. See Chapter 28, Integer Notation and Analysis.

WITTLICH, GARY. "Sets and Ordering Procedures in Twentieth-Century Music," in Gary Wittlich, ed., *Aspects of Twentieth-Century Music*. See pp. 455–470.

# *TEN*

# Classical Serialism

## INTRODUCTION

When Schoenberg composed the first twelve-tone piece in the summer of 1921,[1] the "Prelude" to what would eventually become his Suite, Op. 25 (1923), he carried to a conclusion the developments in chromaticism that had begun many decades earlier. The assault of chromaticism on the tonal system had led to the nonsystem of free atonality, and now Schoenberg had developed a "method [he insisted it was not a "system"] of composing with twelve tones that are related only with one another."

Free atonality achieved some of its effect through the use of aggregates, as we have seen, and many atonal composers seemed to have been convinced that atonality could best be achieved through some sort of regular recycling of the twelve pitch classes. But it was Schoenberg who came up with the idea of arranging the twelve pitch classes into a particular series, or row, that would remain essentially constant throughout a composition.

Various twelve-tone melodies that predate 1921 are often cited as precursors of Schoenberg's tone row, a famous example being the fugue theme from Richard Strauss's *Thus Spake Zarathustra* (1895). A less famous example, but one closer than Strauss's theme to Schoenberg's method, is seen in Example 10–1. Notice that Ives holds off the last pitch class, C, for 3½ measures until its dramatic entrance in m. 68.

In the music of Strauss and Ives the twelve-note theme is a curiosity, but in the music of Schoenberg and his followers the twelve-note row is a basic shape that can be presented in four well-defined ways, thereby assuring a certain unity in the pitch domain of a composition.

This chapter presents the basics of "classical" serialism, the serial technique developed by Schoenberg and adopted by Webern and Berg (somewhat more freely by the latter), as well as many other composers. Chapter 13 will deal with more advanced serial topics, concentrating on integral serialism.

EXAMPLE 10–1    Ives: *Three-Page Sonata* (1905), mm. 62–68    *(© 1949 Mercury Music Corporation. Used by permission of the publisher.)*

## BASIC TERMINOLOGY

The core of the twelve-tone system is the *tone row (basic set, series)*, an ordered arrangement of the twelve pitch classes (not twelve pitches), with each one occurring once and only once. The row itself has four basic forms:

1.  **Prime**: the original set (not to be confused with the prime form of an unordered set, discussed in Chapter 9)
2.  **Retrograde**: the original set in reverse order
3.  **Inversion**: the mirror inversion of the original set
4.  **Retrograde Inversion**: the inversion in reverse order

The row that Schoenberg used for his first serial work is shown in its four basic forms in Example 10–2. The notes could have been written here in any octave and with enharmonic spellings—it would still be the same row. We follow the convention in this and in similar examples of omitting natural signs; any note without an accidental is natural. The numbers under the notes are called *order numbers* and simply indicate each note's position in the row form.

EXAMPLE 10–2    Schoenberg: Suite, Op. 25 (1923), row forms    *(Used by permission of Belmont Music Publishers.)*

In addition, each of the four basic forms has twelve transpositions—that is, each one may be transposed to begin with any of the twelve pitch classes—so a single row has 4 × 12, or 48, versions that are available to the composer. In simple terms, a twelve-tone work consists of the presentation of various row forms at various transpositions, though the details of how this is done vary from composer to composer and from piece to piece.

When analyzing a serial composition we label the row forms using abbreviations:

*P* = Prime

*R* = Retrograde

*R* = Inversion

*RI* = Retrograde Inversion

After the abbreviation comes a number, from 0 to 11, which specifies the transposition level of the row. A prime form or an inversion that begins on C would have a transposition level of 0 (P-0 or I-0), one beginning on C♯/D♭ would have a transposition level of 1 (P-1 or I-1), and so on to the pich class B which is represented by an 11. However, the transpositional level of an R or RI form is indicated by the pitch class that *ends* the row: R-0 and RI-0 would both *end* with a C because they are the retrogrades of P-0 and I-0.[2] Therefore, the row forms in Example 10–2 are P-4, R-4, I-4, and RI-4.

## THE TWELVE-TONE MATRIX

It is sometimes helpful when composing or analyzing serial music to be able to see all forty-eight versions of the row. The **matrix**, or "magic square," allows you to see all forty-eight versions after writing out only twelve of them. Example 10–3 is the matrix for the row for Schoenberg's Suite. The prime forms can be read from left to right along the rows of the matrix, while the retrogrades are read from right to left. The inversions are read along the columns from top to bottom, and the retrograde inversions from bottom to top. The transposition number is next to the first note of each row form. Looking down the left-hand side of the matrix, you can see that P-4 begins on E, P-3 on D♯, P-1 on C♯, and so on. To fill in the matrix, follow these steps:

1. Write the prime form of the row along the top row of the matrix. It does not matter what transposition level you choose.

2. Fill in the main diagonal (the one that runs from upper left to lower right) with the first note in the top row of the matrix.

3. In the next row of the matrix, identify the interval between the note in the main diagonal and the note immediately above it.

4. Transpose the other eleven notes of that row by the same interval. Use simple spellings (not B♯ or F♭, for example), and make sure that there are exactly five notes with accidentals when you finish the row. (In Example 10–3, we have used all sharps, but you could use all flats or a combination of the two.)

5. Repeat Steps 3 and 4 until all twelve rows are filled.

6. Fill in the trasposition levels along the top and left borders (only), with C = 0, C♯/D♭ = 1, and so on.

7. Copy the numbers from the left border onto the right border, and from the top border to the bottom one.

EXAMPLE 10–3   Matrix for Schoenberg's Suite, Op. 25

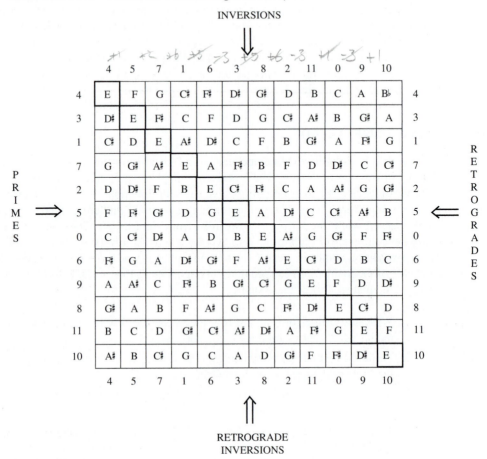

# A FIRST EXAMPLE

Before going on to some more technical information, it would probably be of interest at this point to see how Schoenberg used the row we have been discussing. The beginning of the work is given in Example 10–4. Since this is the first serial piece that Schoenberg composed, you might expect it to be fairly simple in terms of row usage, but this is really not the case. While reading the discussion that follows the example, be sure to find in the matrix (Example 10–3) every row that is mentioned.

   The Prelude is the first movement of the Suite, and the first row form to be used is P-4. Here the first row form occurs in the treble clef, beginning on E and ending on B♭. P-4 is accompanied at the beginning by P-10, and the careful listener will hear the imitation between the two voices at this point:

P-4:          E        F        G        D♭
        P-10:                    B♭    C♭      D♭        G

P-10 continues toward the end of m. 2 in the tenor voice: C–A–D–G♯, in imitation of G♭–E♭–A♭–D in the soprano, while beneath the tenor the bass sounds the last four notes: F–F♯–E♭–E. Notice that notes 9–12 here do not follow notes 5–8, but occur simultaneously with them.

The B♭ that ends P-4 becomes the bass for a time, and it also serves as the first note of I-10, the next row form. Trace the first four notes of this row form, B♭–A–G–D♭, as they move from the bottom staff to the top staff and finally, in m. 5, to the melody. Some listeners would be able to recognize that the sixteenth-note line, B♭–A–G, is the inversion of the opening motive, E–F–G, and that G–D♭ occurs here in the same octave as in m. 1. The highest voice from the end of m. 3 through m. 4 is made up from notes 5–8, A♭–C♭–G♭–C, while the alto sounds notes 9–12, E♭–D–F–E.

To recapitulate: We have seen that P-4 and P-10 were used in counterpoint at the beginning, whereas in the next measures a single row form, I-10, accompanied itself. We have also seen that the row does not always have to proceed strictly from the first note to the last, but instead that segments of the row may appear simultaneously.

EXAMPLE 10–4    Schoenberg: Suite, Op. 25 (1923), Prelude, mm. 1–5    *(Used by permission of Belmont Music Publishers.)*

## ANALYZING A ROW

Since the tone row serves as the source of the pitch material of a composition, we really should analyze the row itself before beginning the analysis of the piece. The first step should be to play (or sing) it several times. Listen for sequences or familiar patterns. In general, composers avoid using in a row any combination of pitches that would recall tonal music, such as triads, scale segments, and traditional bass or melodic formulas. If the composer chooses to include such patterns, as occasionally happens, you should make note of this and its effect on the music. For example, play through the series Berg used for his *Lyric Suite* (1926):

| F | E | C | A | G | D | G# | C# | D# | F# | A# | B |
|---|---|---|---|---|---|----|----|----|----|----|---|
| 1 | 2 | 3 | 4 | 5 | 6 | 7  | 8  | 9  | 10 | 11 | 12 |

This row contains triads on A minor and D# minor, and the row ends with a figure that suggests a B tonality, F#–A#–B. (The end of the retrograde, C–E–F, would suggest an F tonality.) The first hexachord (the first six notes) is diatonic to C major or F major, and the second hexachord is diatonic to F# major or B major. Schoenberg's row (Example 10–2) contains fewer tonal references, but it ends with the retrograde of the famous B–A–C–H motive (in German B♭ is written as B, and B♮ as H), and we might expect Schoenberg to do something with this in the piece.

The next step in the analysis might be to label the ICs (interval classes; review Chapter 9) found between adjacent notes of the row. For instance, for Schoenberg's Op. 25 we find:

| IC: | 1 | | 2 | | 6 | | 5 | | 3 | | 5 | | 6 | | 3 | | 1 | | 3 | | 1 | |
|-----|---|---|---|---|---|---|---|---|---|---|---|---|---|---|---|---|---|---|---|---|---|
| Note: | E | | F | | G | | C# | | F# | | D# | | G# | | D | | B | | C | | A | | B♭ |

| Totals: | IC1 | IC2 | IC3 | IC4 | IC5 | IC6 |
|---------|-----|-----|-----|-----|-----|-----|
|         | 3   | 1   | 3   | 0   | 2   | 2   |

We see from the totals (do not confuse this interval tabulation with the interval vector, discussed in Chapter 9) that there are no appearances of IC4 (major 3rd or minor 6th) and that IC1 (minor 2nd, major 7th) and IC3 (minor 3rd, major 6th) predominate. Some rows are composed so as to emphasize particular intervals, as is the case here, while others are not. The **all-interval row**, when spelled in an *ascending* fashion, contains exactly one appearance of each interval, from the minor 2nd through the major 7th. For example, the row from Berg's *Lyric Suite:*

| M7 | m6 | M6 | m7 | P5 | TT | P4 | M2 | m3 | M3 | m2 |
|----|----|----|----|----|----|----|----|----|----|----|
| F | E | C | A | G | D | G# | C# | D# | F# | A# | B |

If the row that you are analyzing has two of each IC except for IC6, which appears once, check to see if it is an all-interval row.[3]

Some rows use the first three, four, or six notes as a pattern from which the rest of the row is derived: such a row is called a *derived set.* In such a set the pattern is transposed, inverted, retrograded, or inverted and retrograded to "generate" the remainder of the set. For example, the first hexachord of Berg's row from the *Lyric Suite* in the previous paragraph in retrograde and transposed by a tritone would produce the second hexachord, so the row is a derived set. The row of Webern's Concerto, Op. 24 (1934), is generated by applying the RI, R, and I operations to the first trichord:

| B | B♭ | D | | E♭ | G | F♯ | | G♯ | E | F | | C | C♯ | A |
|---|---|---|---|---|---|---|---|---|---|---|---|---|---|---|
| 1 | 2 | 3 | | 4 | 5 | 6 | | 7 | 8 | 9 | | 10 | 11 | 12 |

|  pattern  |  RI of 1–3  |  R of 1–3  |  I of 1–3  |

Even if the row is not a derived set, it may well contain patterns that are transposed, inverted, or retrograded. Patterns of ICs that are repeated or reversed may help us to find these pitch-class patterns. In Schoenberg's Suite the repeated 3–1 at the end of the row is caused by two overlapping statements of a trichordal pattern:

| IC: | 1 | | 2 | | 6 | | 5 | | 3 | | 5 | | 6 | | 3 | | 1 | | 3 | | 1 | |
|---|---|---|---|---|---|---|---|---|---|---|---|---|---|---|---|---|---|---|---|---|---|---|
| Note: | E | F | G | C♯ | F♯ | D♯ | G♯ | D | B | C | A | B♭ |
| | | | | | | | | [ D | B | C ] | |
| | | | | | | | | | [C | A | B♭] |

The pattern 6–5 within the row is reversed later as 5–6, and it is also part of a larger palindromic pattern: 6–5–3–5–6. Such patterns may indicate that a segment of the row is its own retrograde or retrograde inversion. Here the patterns 6–5–3–5–6, 3–1–3 and 1–3–1 reproduce themselves under retrograde inversion. As it turns out, two of these segments are duplicated in RI-5, whereas the third is duplicated in RI-7, as shown in Example 10–5.

**EXAMPLE 10–5** Recurring row segments

These patterns that we have found may have implications in the piece motivically, and in this case they certainly have implications in the area of **invariance**. An invariant pitch class is one that is shared by any two collections of pitches (two chords, for example). Similarly, an **invariant subset** is one that appears intact in two forms of the row. The order of the notes was not important when dealing with unordered sets in Chapter 9, but it is important when talking about rows. Looking again at Example 10–5, you can see that RI-5 is a reorganized version of P-4, beginning with notes 9–12 from P-4, then notes 3–8, and ending with notes 1–2. Each prime row transposition in the matrix has a similar RI "cousin," and there also are twelve similar I/R pairs. The matrix of a derived set may exhibit even more invariance. The row from Berg's *Lyric Suite*, for instance, has only twenty-four different row forms instead of the usual forty-eight, because each R form is the same as some P form, and each RI form is the same as some I form.

The next step in a thorough analysis is to analyze the subsets in terms of the pitch-class set types we learned in Chapter 9. This is not the same thing as the row segment analysis we were doing above, because there we were looking for exact transpositions (or inversions, etc.) of row segments. Here we are looking for set types, and we know that the notes of a pitch-class set may appear in any order and may be inverted to find the best normal order and the prime form. For example, there are ten trichords in any row, the first one made up of notes 1–3, the second of notes 2–4, and so on, with the last one made up of notes 10–12. There are also nine tetrachords, eight pentachords, and seven hexachords. The set types contained in Schoenberg's row are the following:

| First Note | Trichords | Tetrachords | Pentachords | Hexachords |
|---|---|---|---|---|
| E | [0,1,3] | [0,2,3,6] | [0,1,2,3,6] | [0,1,2,3,4,6] |
| F | [0,2,6] | [0,1,2,6] | [0,1,2,4,6] | [0,1,2,3,5,7] |
| G | [0,1,6] | [0,1,4,6] | [0,1,2,5,7] | [0,1,2,5,6,7] |
| C♯ | [0,2,5] | [0,2,5,7] | [0,1,2,5,7] | [0,1,2,4,7,9] |
| F♯ | [0,2,5] | [0,1,4,6] | [0,1,4,6,9] | [0,1,3,4,7,9] |
| D♯ | [0,1,6] | [0,1,4,7] | [0,1,3,4,7] | [0,1,3,4,6,7] |
| g♯ | [0,3,6] | [0,2,3,6] | [0,1,3,4,6] | [0,1,2,3,4,6] |
| D | [0,1,3] | [0,2,3,5] | [0,1,2,3,5] | |
| B | [0,1,3] | [0,1,2,3] | | |
| C | [0,1,3] | | | |
| A | | | | |
| B♭ | | | | |

In practice, it is usually enough to analyze only the trichords and tetrachords; the first and last hexachords will always be either of the same type or Z-related,[4] and most of the pentachords and hexachords overlap too much to be of interest. The trichord analysis shows us that [0,1,3] and [0,1,6] are unifying elements in the set; the composer might possibly make use of them as melodic motives or as chords to help unify the piece. The set [0,2,5], although it occurs twice, is less useful because its two appearances overlap. The tetrachords [0,2,3,6] and [0,1,4,6] also might fulfill a unifying function, although the two appearances of [0,1,4,6] overlap by two notes.

## COMPOSITIONAL USES OF THE ROW

There are a number of ways in which rows are actually used in compositions. Generally, a twelve-tone work consists of the presentation of various row forms at a number of transpositions, the forms being used sometimes in succession and sometimes simultaneously. The notes may appear in any octave, and the order of the notes of each row form is usually preserved, but there are exceptions. Notes can be sounded simultaneously, as in a chord, and there is no "rule" as to how the notes in this case must be arranged. Repeated notes are not considered to alter the order of the row, and neither are tremolo figures—using two of the notes repeatedly in alternation. You may also occasionally encounter overlapped segments of a row (as in Example 10–4) and arbitrary reordering of the row for compositional purposes.

Because most music involves more than a single line, the composer must either present two or more row forms simultaneously or distribute a single row form among the various voices. Both of these approaches are widely used, which complicates the task of determining the original row at the beginning of an analysis. Turn back to Example 10–4 for a minute, and imagine that you had no prior knowledge of the row. You might notice that the melody in the right hand comes to a stop after eight notes (on the D) and that the left hand in the same passage contains four notes, making twelve in all, so you would check out the possibility that the row has been distributed between the two lines. This could have been done in various ways, such as:

```
1    2    3         6    8    9              11    12
          4    5         7         10
```

or

```
1    2    3         4    5    6         7    8
          9    10        11        12
```

The first of these diagrams is the more commonly used method of distributing a row, but we could not rule out the second possibility. Even if we want to go ahead on the assumption that the first diagram is basically correct, we still would not be sure of the entire order, because some of the notes are played simultaneously (3–4 and 7–8), and notes in a simultaneity do not have to be arranged in any particular vertical order with respect to the row. In any case, we would have to analyze more of the piece to find out the answers to these questions.

As it turns out, we can see that Schoenberg has not distributed the row between the two hands, because the eight notes in the treble and the four in the bass include only ten of the pitch classes: C and A are missing, and D♭ and G occur twice. Instead, P-4 continues through the B♭ in m. 3, while P-10 is used in the bottom staff. In mm. 3–6 Schoenberg uses the other basic approach, which is to distribute a single row form among the voices. In this and in some of his other works. Schoenberg breaks his row into three tetrachords, which he then uses somewhat independently. That is, he might begin with the third tetrachord in some voice and introduce the first and second tetrachords later. Sometimes the order of pitches within each tetrachord is maintained, and at other times it is not. A more frequently used method is the one shown in the first diagram above, where the notes of the row are presented in order.

Turn back to Example 4–7 (p. 82) for an especially interesting example of row technique. (Remember that in this example the horn is written at concert pitch.) The excerpt, from Schoenberg's Wind Quintet, Op. 26, consists of three statements of P-3 (plus a final E♭) of the following row:

| E♭ | G | A | B | D♭ | C | B♭ | D | E | F♯ | G♯ | F |
|----|---|---|---|----|---|----|---|---|----|----|---|
| 1 | 2 | 3 | 4 | 5 | 6 | 7 | 8 | 9 | 10 | 11 | 12 |

Schoenberg distributes the notes so that the horn melody (the H symbol designates the primary line) uses each member of the row only once (disregarding immediate repetitions):

```
Horn:        1            6 7              12      2          5          8           11
Bassoon:         2 3 4 5          8 9 10 11        1       3 4      6 7      9 10           12

(Horn, cont.)                3 4              9 10
(Bassoon, cont.)   1 2        5 6 7 8         11 12 1
```

The resulting succession of twelve pitch classes in the horn forms a new twelve-tone row, drawn from but distinct from the original row.

Ernst Křenek demonstrates another approach in Example 10–6. The row upon which this work is based is:

| C | E♭ | D♭ | G♭ | D | B♭ | A | A♭ | B | G | F | E |
|---|----|----|----|---|----|---|----|---|---|---|---|
| 1 | 2 | 3 | 4 | 5 | 6 | 7 | 8 | 9 | 10 | 11 | 12 |

Here Křenek keeps the initial pitch of P-0 as a pedal point, doubled at the octave, while the other instruments unfold the remainder of the row in a harmonic progression until the cadence on F. The next two measures (not shown) are similar, ending with a strong B♭–F cadence. Although this is a serial work, it is clear that the C's here are acting as a dominant of the F, and both pitch classes are prominent at the end of the opera as well.

**EXAMPLE 10–6**   Křenek: *Karl V* (1933), I, mm. 1–4   *(© 1933 Universal Edition. All rights reserved.*
*Used by permission of European American Music Distributors Corporation, sole U.S. and Canadian*
*agent for Universal Edition.)*

## SET SUCCESSION

Although a composer has forty-eight row forms available, few twelve-tone compositions make use of all of them—in fact, some works use only the prime form and at a single transposition. One of these is another of Schoenberg's early serial works, the fourth movement from his Serenade, Op. 24 (1923), for voice and seven instruments. The text features eleven-syllable lines, which Schoenberg sets to permutations of his row:

> Line 1: notes 1–11
>
> Line 2: notes 12–10
>
> Line 3: notes 11–9
>
> etc.

Not many twelve-tone works are so restricted, however. Most employ all four basic forms and several transpositions. One of the more difficult tasks of the analyst is attempting to determine why a particular row form and transposition have been chosen. It is not enough to put the label "R-3" on the score without considering why a retrograde form was chosen and why R-3 instead of some other transposition, even though we may not be able to find an explanation in every case.

Invariance is frequently a factor in the choice of transpositions. In the Schoenberg excerpt, Example 10–4, B♭ is the invariant pitch class in m. 3 between P-4, where it is the last note, and I-10, where it is the first. It is not uncommon for one or more pitch classes to serve as common tones between two row forms in this manner. Schoenberg's reasons for choosing P-10 as the first row in the left hand are not hard to guess. Presumably he chose imitation at the tritone as an effect analogous to the imitation at the dominant so much a part of Baroque style, and it offered the advantage of keeping intact the pitch classes that form the two tritones in the top voice:

> G/D♭ answered by D♭/G
>
> A♭/D answered by D/G♯

Also, Schoenberg's choice of I-10 and P-10 conforms to his overall plan for the work, which is to use only P-4, P-10, I-4, I-10, and their retrogrades. Each of these row forms begins on E and ends on B♭ (or the reverse), and each contains the tritone G/D♭ (or D♭/G).

Luigi Dallapiccola's overall plan for "Fregi," the sixth movement of his *Musical Notebook for Annalibera (Quaderno Musicale di Annalibera)* (1952), goes as follows:

1. Compose a melody for mm. 1–6 to be played by the right hand.

2. In mm. 7–12, invert that melody and give it to the left hand.

3. In order to carry the idea of inversion a step further, accompany mm. 1–6 with an I form, and mm. 7–12 with a P form.

The prime form of the row is:

| A♯ | B | D♯ | F♯ | G♯ | D | D♭ | F | G | C | A | E |
|----|---|----|----|----|---|----|---|---|----|----|----|
| 1 | 2 | 3 | 4 | 5 | 6 | 7 | 8 | 9 | 10 | 11 | 12 |

Notice that this row has tonal implications (for example, the triads on B and A) that we might expect Dallapiccola to make use of. The melody in mm. 1–6 actually consists of two row forms, P-10 (mm. 1–4) and R-5 (mm. 4–7). Here the link between the rows is the E, which is the *second* note of R-5:

| B | Ⓔ | G | D | C | G♯ | A | E♭ | D♭ | B♭ | G♭ | F |
|---|---|---|---|---|----|---|----|----|----|----|---|
| 1 | 2 | 3 | 4 | 5 | 6 | 7 | 8 | 9 | 10 | 11 | 12 |

This allows a diatonic "progression" from the A minor triad at the end of P-10 to the E minor triad at the beginning of R-5. It also allows for a quintal chord (A–E–B) that is beautiful in context. All of this happens in the fourth measure of Example 10–7. The accompaniment in mm. 3–6 is provided by I-8:

| A♭ | G | E♭ | C | B♭ | Ⓔ | F | D♭ | B | F♯ | A | D |
|----|---|----|---|----|---|---|----|---|----|---|---|
| 1 | 2 | 3 | 4 | 5 | 6 | 7 | 8 | 9 | 10 | 11 | 12 |

**EXAMPLE 10–7**  Dallapiccola: *Musical Notebook for Annalibera* (1952), "Fregi," mm. 1–8

Just as P-10 is ending and R-5 is beginning in m. 4, I-8 in the accompaniment needs an E, the shared pitch class between P-10 and R-5. Dallapiccola puts the E for I-8 in the *top* staff, stem up, and all three rows come together at this point. The use of I-8 also allows the first half of the piece to end in m. 6 on an inversionally symmetrical sonority, A–D–G♭–F, or [0347], which means that when the first half of the piece is inverted to form the second half, the final sonority will be a (transposed) duplication of this one.

The only remaining row choice to be discussed is the transposition level for the inversion of the melody, which begins with the C♭ in the bottom staff at the end of m. 6. The obvious answer is that I-11 is the only inversion that keeps the opening two dyads invariant:

P-10    (A♯ B)    (D♯ F♯)

I-11    (B A♯)    (F♯ D♯)

Another consideration might have been the nice G♭ major-7th sonority in m. 7 formed by the end of R-5 and the beginning of I-11.

## COMBINATORIALITY

Sometimes the choice of row forms or transpositions is governed by a desire to form aggregates (without duplication of pitch class) between portions of row forms. For example, in the following diagram, the row that Schoenberg used for his *Piano Piece*, Op. 33a (1929), is followed by its RI-3 form. Notice that when the second hexachord of P-10 is combined with the first hexachord of RI-3, they form an aggregate. In effect, we have created a new row, called a **secondary set**, by combining two hexachords from two different row forms.

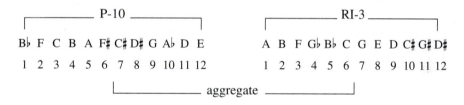

This combining of row forms to form aggregates is called **combinatoriality**, and it is an important aspect of some serial compositions. Most often, however, the combining is done *vertically*:

| P–10: | B♭ | F | C | B | A | F♯ | C♯ | D♯ | G | A♭ | D | E |
|---|---|---|---|---|---|---|---|---|---|---|---|---|
| I–3: | D♯ | G♯ | C♯ | D | E | G | C | B♭ | G♭ | F | B | A |
| | 1 | 2 | 3 | 4 | 5 | 6 | 7 | 8 | 9 | 10 | 11 | 12 |

aggregate            aggregate

This diagram is seen in notation in Example 10–8. The first aggregate occupies m. 14 through the first two notes of m. 16, and the second aggregate occupies the rest of the excerpt. Notice that Schoenberg freely retrogrades or repeats row segments, as in C–B–A–B–C in mm. 14–15.

EXAMPLE 10–8   Schoenberg: *Piano Piece*, Op. 33a (1929), mm. 14–18   *(Used by permission of Belmont Music Publishers.)*

Schoenberg's row is so constructed that any pair of row forms that can be combined hexachordally to form twelve-tone aggregates can also be combined tetrachordally to form three sets of eight pitch classes each:

| RI-3: | A | B | F | F♯ | A♯ | C | G | E | D | C♯ | G♯ | D♯ |
|-------|---|---|---|----|----|---|---|---|---|----|----|----|
| R-10: | E | D | A♭ | G | D♯ | C♯ | F♯ | A | B | C | F | B♭ |
|  | 1 | 2 | 3 | 4 | 5 | 6 | 7 | 8 | 9 | 10 | 11 | 12 |

└───octachord───┘   └───octachord───┘   └───octachord───┘

Though this does not produce twelve-tone aggregates in the way that the combined hexachords do, the technique is similar. In Example 10–9 each pair of tetrachords occupies approximately one measure.

EXAMPLE 10–9   Schoenberg: *Piano Piece*, Op. 33a (1929), mm. 3–5   *(Used by permission of Belmont Music Publishers.)*

    Other rows are constructed to produce tetrachord aggregates by combining three rows vertically, or trichord aggregates by combining four rows vertically; however, hexachordal combinatoriality is the approach most commonly used.

    Combinatoriality guarantees a more controlled recycling of the twelve pitch classes, and to some it seems a necessary extension of the twelve-tone aesthetic. Schoenberg invented this technique, although he obviously was not using it in his Suite (see the juxtaposed G/D♭ and D♭/G in Example 10–4). Nor was Dallapiccola interested in combinatoriality in his *Notebook* (notice the duplicated G's in m. 3 of Example 10–7). In fact, most rows cannot by their nature be used combinatorially (except with their retrogrades) and must instead be specially constructed for that use. But combinatoriality has been of considerable interest to some composers, and a large number of pieces are combinatorial throughout.

## THE ANALYSIS OF SERIAL MUSIC

    In analyzing the use of rows in a serial piece, it is often enough to label the row forms (P-0, etc.) without writing the order numbers on the music. If the texture is complex or if some unusual row technique is being employed, it may be necessary to write the order numbers near the noteheads and even to join them with lines. Always work from a matrix. If you get lost, try to find several notes that you suspect occur in the same order in some row form, and scan the matrix for those notes, remembering to read it in all four directions.

    It is important to understand that the labeling of row forms and the consideration of the details of their use is only a part of the analysis of a serial composition, somewhat analogous to identifying the various tonalities of a tonal work. Questions regarding form, thematic relationships, texture, rhythm, and other matters are just as relevant here as in the analysis of more traditional music. The music of classical serialism is not especially "mathematical," and it is not composed mechanically and without regard to the resulting sound or the effect on the listener. Probably the best way to appreciate the processes and choices involved in serial composition is to try to compose a good serial piece. The exercises at the end of this chapter will provide some practice at attempting this.

*SUMMARY*

The pitch materials of a serial work are derived from the twelve-note row, so an analysis should begin with the row itself. Two special types of row are derived sets and all-interval sets. A composition may make use of the prime row, its retrograde, its inversion, and its retrograde inversion, each of which can appear at any of twelve transpositions. This pitch material may be conveniently displayed in the form of a matrix.

Row forms may be used compositionally in a number of ways. For example, a single row form may be distributed among the voices, or more than one row form may be used at the same time. The choice of row forms is often related to invariance or combinatoriality, among other reasons.

Analysis of serial music includes identification of the row forms and consideration of the reasons for choosing a particular row form and transposition, but a thorough analysis cannot be confined only to serial matters.

*NOTES*

1. Jan Maegaard, "A Study in the Chronology of Op. 23–26 by Arnold Schoenberg." See the chart on p. 108.
2. Another approach (and one that was used in previous editions of this book) labels the first appearance of the row as P-0, no matter what pitch class it begins with, and numbers the transpositions chromatically from that pitch class. Also, some authors have employed the letters S or O instead of P for the prime form of the row.
3. Another type of all-interval row contains all of the intervals only if some of them are ascending and others are descending. The Dallapiccola row discussed in this chapter is one example.
4. The so-called "hexachord theorem." See John Rahn, *Basic Atonal Theory*, p. 105.

*EXERCISES*

*Part A: Fundamentals*

1. Suppose P-7 begins on G and ends on B♭:

   | Form | Begins on | Ends on |
   |------|-----------|---------|
   | (a) P-6 | _____ | _____ |
   | (b) P-11 | _____ | _____ |
   | (c) R-0 | _____ | _____ |
   | (d) R-5 | _____ | _____ |
   | (e) I-1 | _____ | _____ |
   | (f) I-9 | _____ | _____ |
   | (g) RI-2 | _____ | _____ |
   | (h) RI-7 | _____ | _____ |

2. Analyze the row from Dallapiccola's *Musical Notebook for Annalibera* (p. 209).
3. Analyze the row from Schoenberg's Wind Quintet, Op. 26 (p. 208), and construct a matrix.
4. The following set is P-0 from the first of Milton Babbitt's *Three Compositions for Piano* (1947). Analyze it and construct a matrix.

Bb    Eb    F    D    C    Db    G    B    F#    A    G#    E

5. Do the same for the following set, from Webern's Symphony, Op. 21.

A    F#    G    G#    E    F    B    Bb    D    Db    C    Eb

6. The following row consists of two [014589] hexachords (also referred to in Chapter 2 as the "hexatonic" or "augmented" scale). This row can be used combinatorially with three traspositions each of the P, I, R, and RI forms of the row. Find the three transpositions of the P form and the three transpositions of the I form that will work combinatorially with P-3. You may find it helpful to construct a matrix before beginning.

Eb    Ab    G    B    C    E    Bb    A    C#    F#    F    D

## Part B: Analysis

1. Turn back to Example 6–3 (p. 119). Note that each accidental effects only the note it procedes.

   (a) Analyze the row forms used in the excerpt using the matrix you constructed for Exercise A.4.

   (b) Is the row usage in m.10 combinatorial? How about m.11? Explain both of your answers.

   (c) Is there a secondary set formed by the last hexachord of m.9 and the first hexachord in the left hand in m.10? If so, write out the secondary set. Does something similar happen the right hand from the end of m. 11 through the beginning of m. 12? Explain.

2. Turn back to Example 2–B–3 (p. 40).

   (a) Analyze the row forms using the matrix you constructed for Exercise A.5. (*Hint:* Four row forms are used simultaneously.)

   (b) Is this excerpt combinatorial? How can you tell?

   (c) Is the excerpt canonic? Explain.

3. Schoenberg: Wind Quintet, Op. 26 (1924), III, mm. 8–15. This excerpt is a continuation of Example 4–7 (p. 82). We discussed the use of the row in Example 4–7 in the section titled "Compositional Uses of the Row," and you constructed a matrix for this row in Exercise A.3. This excerpt features a duet between the clarinet and horn, with a secondary duet in the flute and oboe.

   (a) Analyze the row forms in the clarinet and horn. The Eb in the bassoon is part of the first row, but the F# in the horn is not and may be ignored.

(b) Compare the row usage here with that in Example 4–7. Be sure to review the discussion concerning that example.

(c) Do you find any other similarities between Example 4–7 and this duet between the clarinet and horn?

(d) Analyze the row forms in the flute and oboe.

(e) In what ways is this duet similar to the one in the clarinet and horn? In what ways is it different?

(Schoenberg: Wind Quintet, Op. 26 [1924], III, mm. 8–15)

4. In discussing Example 10–4 we identified P-4, P-10, and I-10. What row form ends the excerpt? Remember (a) that this is one of Schoenberg's tetrachord pieces, in which the three tetrachords of a row form may be introduced in any order, and (b) the possibility of common tones linking the row forms. Use the matrix in Example 10–3 for help.

5. Webern: "Das dunkle Herz" (1934), Op. 23, No. 1, mm. 1–11

   (a) In this song the row begins with the D that is the first note in the piano. Because of the chords that occur in that piano in the first two measures, you will need to do a certain amount of detective work to determine the correct order of the pitch classes. Once you have discovered P-2, construct a matrix.

   (b) Label all the row forms used in the excerpt. Remember that notes may occasionally serve functions in two row forms, either in the same part (voice or piano) or between parts.

(c) This piece is more concerned with the unifying effect of invariants than it is with combinatorial aggregates. For example, the vocalist enters on an F that has just been heard in the piano and then sings three of the notes contained in the chord at the end of m. 2 (G–E–E♭). Find similar pitch-class connections that help bring the voice and piano parts together. (Obviously, this technique has much to do with explaining why the various row forms were chosen.)

(d) Use the pitch-class set terminology you learned in Chapter 9 to study Webern's use of motives. For example, the four-note chord is an important accompanimental motive. In terms of pitch-class set types, how do these chords compare? Consider the other motives in a similar fashion. Do not neglect the voice. Are there any motivic connections between the two?

6. Play through and sing the row from Dallapiccola's *Musical Notebook for Annalibera* (p. 209) until you are able to sing it without accompaniment, then listen carefully to several or all of the movements from that work. In which ones is the unifying effect of the row apparent? How is this accomplished? Is there any particular part of the row that is more memorable, or perhaps more emphasized by the composer, than others?

## *Part C: Composition*

1. Compose a twelve-tone row that avoids tonal references and is not predictable in its use of patterns. Be sure to do this at a piano or other instrument, and play (or sing) the row as you compose it.
2. Analyze your row, and construct a matrix. Then compose an unaccompanied melody for some instrument in your class, using three different row forms from your matrix. Label the row forms and transpositions. Try to emphasize in some way any recurrent subsets or other significant features that the row contains, and explain what you are attempting. Include tempo, dynamics, and phrasing.
3. Compose an instrumental duet using a single form of your row distributed between the two instruments in a manner similar to that used by Schoenberg in Example 4–7 (p. 82), discussed under "Compositional Uses of the Row." Try to give the duet a musical shape, with some amount of motivic unity and a climax in the second half of the duet. Analyze your work.
4. Use your row for a simple piano piece in a homophonic (melody-and-accompaniment) texture. Use different row forms in the melody and accompaniment. Label all row forms.
5. Compose a twelve-tone row in which the first hexachord contains the notes: C♯, D, E♭, F, A, and B♭. Put the notes in any order you choose, except that D should be the first note. The second hexachord should contain the remaining notes, in any order. Then compose a duet beginning with P-2 in one part and I-7 in the other. These two forms are combinatorial, so be sure to line up the hexachords to form aggregates. Then continue the duet with two different combinatorial pairs (such as P-4 and I-9). Label the row forms.

## *FURTHER READING*

ANTOKOLETZ, ELLIOTT. *Twentieth-Century Music.* See Chapter 3, Vienna Schoenberg Circle: The Twelve-Tone System.

BRINDLE, REGINALD SMITH. *Musical Composition.* See Chapter 12, "Serialism."

————. *Serial Composition.* See Chapters 1–7.

COPE DAVID. *Techniques of the Contemporary Composer.* See Chapter 6, Serialism.

DALLIN, LEON. *Techniques of Twentieth Century Composition.* See Chapter 14, The Twelve-Tone Method.

FENNELLY, BRIAN. "Twelve-Tone Techniques," in John Vinton, ed., *Dictionary of Contemporary Music.*

GRIFFITHS, PAUL. "Serialism," in Stanley Sadie, ed., *The New Grove Dictionary of Music and Musicians.*

KOSTKA, STEFAN, AND DOROTHY PAYNE. *Tonal Harmony with an Introduction to Twentieth-Century Music.* See pp. 520–532.

KŘENEK, ERNST. *Studies in Counterpoint.*

LESTER, JOEL. *Analytic Approaches to Twentieth-Century Music.* See Chapters 10 through 13.

MORGAN, ROBERT P. *Twentieth-Century Music.* See Chapter 9, The Twelve-Tone System.

PERLE, GEORGE, AND PAUL LANSKY. "Twelve-Note Composition," in Stanley Sadie, ed., *The New Grove Dictionary of Music and Musicians.*

SIMMS, BRYAN R. *Music of the Twentieth Century.* See Chapter 4, Serialism, pp. 68–74 and 78–83.

STRAUS, JOSEPH N. *Introduction to Post-Tonal Theory.* See Chapter 5, Basic Twelve-Tone Operations.

WILLIAMS, J. KENT. *Theories and Analyses of Twentieth-Century Music.* See Chapter 15, Serialism.

WITTLICH, GARY. "Sets and Ordering Procedures in Twentieth-Century Music," in Gary Wittlich, ed., *Aspects of Twentieth-Century Music.* See pp. 388–430.

WUORINEN, CHARLES. *Simple Composition.* See Chapter 7, The 12-Tone Pitch System: Elements and Operations.

# ELEVEN

# Timbre and Texture: Acoustic

## INTRODUCTION

It may be that the way twentieth-century music *sounds* sets it apart from earlier styles as much as anything. This seems obvious, since music is about sound, after all, but what "sound" means in this context is a little narrower. Here we are referring especially to timbre and texture, two aspects of music that have received much attention from twentieth-century composers. **Timbre** means tone color, and it can refer to the tone color of an individual instrument or of an ensemble. As we will see, the timbral ranges of both have expanded greatly in the twentieth century. **Texture** is a little harder to define, although most of us have a pretty good idea of its meaning. We could say that texture refers to the relationships between the parts (or voices) at any moment in a composition; it especially concerns the relationships between rhythms and contours, but it is also concerned with aspects such as spacing and dynamics. Not infrequently the line between timbre and texture is unclear, especially when a large ensemble is involved.

Some of the exploration of new timbres and textures, especially the former, was partly the result of outside influences—jazz and folk music, oriental and Latin American music. In fact, few really new instruments have been invented and successfully introduced in this century, most of the exceptions being percussion instruments (the vibraphone, for instance). A very important exception is electronic music, an area significant enough to require its own chapter (see Chapter 12).

## NEW TIMBRAL EFFECTS FROM TRADITIONAL INSTRUMENTS

Composers in the twentieth century have required performers to learn many new techniques of producing sound with traditional instruments, so many that we can only hope to provide a good sampling in this discussion.[1] One problem that has not been entirely solved at this point is how to notate many of these new techniques, although progress is being made here as successful approaches become recognized and imitated.

Some techniques have been required of all performers, regardless of instrument, including tapping on the instrument or on some other surface, whistling, and a wide variety of vocal sounds. In these cases the performer is not performing as a clarinetist, for example, but as a percussionist, whistler, or vocalist. In Example 6–10 (p. 126) thirteen wind players whistle approximately the same pattern (the exact pitches are unspecified), but beginning at different times and proceeding independently. Notice also in the same example the use of glass crystals, or tuned water glasses. Electronic amplification and distortion are other timbral devices that can be used with any performing medium.

## WIND INSTRUMENTS

Some techniques for winds used in contemporary scores are not entirely new but represent an intensification or development of earlier usages. This would include, for example, the use of mutes and glissandi. The brasses use a wider variety of mutes than previously, many of them of jazz origin, and even the woodwinds have been muted in a number of ways. The "bend," which might be considered a special type of glissando, also derives from jazz. Both the bend and the glissando were seen in Example 8–7 (p. 168), where the horn imitates a jazz trombone solo. Other techniques sometimes associated with jazz include the flutter-tongue (see mm 9–12 of Example 4–4, p. 79) and the enharmonic trill, in which the performer rapidly alternates between two fingerings for the same pitch.

Removal of the mouthpiece permits performing on the mouthpiece alone, without the rest of the instrument, or performing only on the rest of the instrument without the mouthpiece. Wind players are also required to produce breath sounds through their instruments instead of pitches, and in some cases to sing and play simultaneously. Harmonics, though not practicable on brasses, have been used on woodwinds, especially the flute and the clarinet. Several of these techniques are illustrated in a lighthearted way in Example 11–1.

EXAMPLE 11–1    David Amram: Quintet for Winds (1968), III, mm. 106–11    *(© 1971 by*
*C. F. Peters Corporation. Used by permission.)*

An important development, again available only on woodwinds, is the use of **multi-phonics,** the production on a single instrument of two or more pitches (as many as six are possible) simultaneously. Multiphonics rarely sound like the instrument played in a conventional manner. In Example 11–2 three flutes using multiphonics combine to produce chords of up to six notes. Notice that multiphonics are not simply two harmonics played at once. None of the multiphonics in Example 11–2 are produced as harmonics, and most of them create dissonant intervals, not the consonances associated with the harmonic series. Multiphonics are often difficult to produce, and in a footnote in the score Heiss suggests that the performers "secure the upper note" of each pair and "let the lower one sound more quietly if necessary." Notice also the fingering instructions in the score. Performance instructions such as these are a feature of many works composed since World War II. In his *Moz-art* (1980), Alfred Schnittke even goes so far as to direct the oboist to certain pages of Heinz Holliger's *Pro musica nova* for instruction on performing the multiphonics.

EXAMPLE 11–2    John Heiss: *Four Movements for Three Flutes* (1969), III, mm. 40–45

(© *Copyright 1977 by Boosey & Hawkes, Inc. Reprinted by permission.*)

## STRINGED INSTRUMENTS

A large number of special effects are found in the contemporary string repertoire. As with the winds, these devices are in many cases not the invention of twentieth-century composers, but they are employed much more frequently in contemporary scores. These would include the use of mutes, open strings, harmonics (both natural and artificial), nonstandard tunings (scordatura), multiple stops, and glissandi. In Example 9–B–14 (p. 195) the lowest string of the contrabass, the E string, is tuned to E♭ instead. The same excerpt also illustrates glissandi and natural harmonics. Remember that the contrabass sounds an octave lower than written.

The traditional pizzicato is still used, but other methods have been developed, including left-hand pizzicato, snap pizzicato, nail pizzicato, buzz pizzicato (the string vibrates against the fingernail), plectrum pizzicato (use of a guitar pick), and strumming. A device that might be considered a kind of pizzicato is silent fingering, in which the player only fingers the notes with the left hand, producing a subtle, semipitched sound. An early use of snap pizzicato is seen in Example 11–3, where the device is indicated by the small circle with a vertical line at the top. All of the instruments are being played pizzicato here, the viola and cello triple-stops being strummed. The arrows in the cello part indicate that the strumming is to be in descending fashion; the "O" specifies that the A3 is to be played on an open string.

**EXAMPLE 11–3**    Bartók String Quartet No. 4 (1928), IV, mm. 45–51    *(© Copyright 1929 in the USA by Boosey & Hawkes, Inc. Copyright renewed. Reprinted by permission.)*

Bowing techniques in common use in twentieth-century music include tremolo, bowing with the wood, various kinds of rebounding bow strokes, and nonpitched bowing, in which the idea is to obtain a scratchy sound rather than a pitch. In addition to bowing on the usual part of the string, the player may bow at the bridge, as in Example 9–21 (p. 191), or over the fingerboard, or the two may be combined in circular bowing. Other works call for the performer to bow between the bridge and the tailpiece, or under the strings, or on the body of the instrument. Penderecki's *Threnody: To the Victims of Hiroshima* (1961) is famous for its string techniques, among other things. In Example 11–4 each player performs a series of seven special effects as fast as possible. The wavy lines in some of the parts call for a slow quarter-tone vibrato, performed here on the highest possible note for each instrument.

Seven special effects are specified in Example 11–4, and they appear in a different order in each of eight lines in the example. These effects, as seen in the top line of the ten cellos, are (1) strike the upper sounding board, (2) play the highest note on the instrument pizzicato, (3) play a fast tremolo between the bridge and the tailpiece, (4) play an arpeggio on the four strings behind the bridge *legno battuto* (beating with the wood of the bow), (5) strike the upper sounding board twice, (6) play the highest note on the instrument arco and tremolo, and (7) play between the bridge and the tailpiece.

EXAMPLE 11–4  Penderecki: *Threnody: To the Victims of Hiroshima* (1961), mm. 6–7

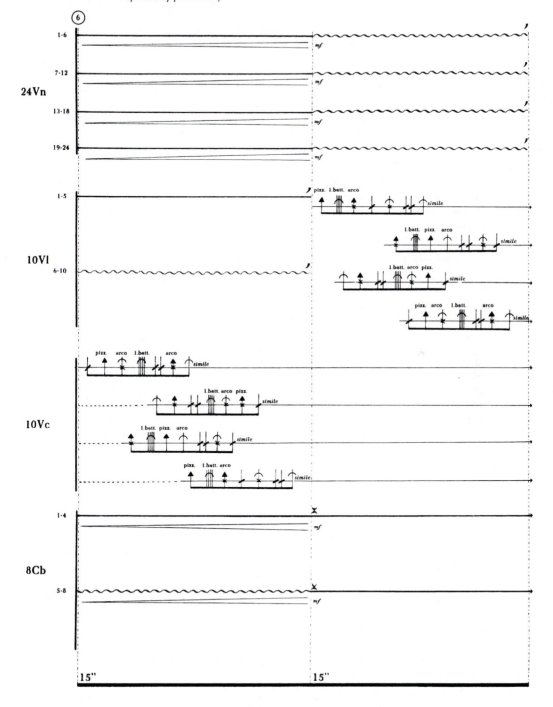

New techniques have also been developed for those stringed instruments traditionally played by plucking: the banjo, the guitar, the mandolin, and above all the harp. In fact, according to Gardner Read, "No modern instrument... has undergone such a metamorphosis in the twentieth century as the harp,"[2] with many of the new effects being devised by one composer, Carlos Salzedo. These include a wide variety of glissandi and of ways of activating the strings, as well as a number of percussive effects.

## PERCUSSION INSTRUMENTS

One of the most important developments in twentieth-century music is the greatly expanded role of percussion. The percussion section of the orchestra, to be discussed in more detail below, has been expanded from the classical norm of one timpanist to a varying number of performers playing an ever-expanding array of instruments. Some of these instruments are newly invented, but most are instruments that already existed in Western music (in bands or folk music, for example) or in the music of other cultures. An incomplete but representative list of instruments that are now commonly employed would include the following:[3]

| *Pitched Instruments* | *Unpitched Instruments* | |
|---|---|---|
| Almglocken | Anvil | Snare drum |
| Antique cymbals | Bass drum | Tam-tam |
| Brake drums | Bell tree | Tambourine |
| Chimes | Bongos | Temple blocks |
| Crotales | Castanets | Tenor drum |
| Flexatone | Claves | Timbales |
| Glockenspiel | Congas | Tom-toms |
| Marimba | Cymbals | Triangle |
| Musical saw | Field drum | Vibraslap |
| Roto-toms | Gong | Wind chimes |
| Timpani | Maracas | Wood block |
| Vibraphone | | |
| Xylophone | | |

As if this were not enough, composers freely introduce sounds produced by every-day materials. Examples include a resonant piece of furniture to be struck with a club, silk and sheets of paper to be torn apart, a metal tray filled with dishes to smash, a wooden bowl filled with marbles to rattle, and a tree stump to be hit with an ax.[4]

The more traditional percussion instruments are now played in new ways. Most of these basically consist of unconventional methods of striking the instrument (rim shots, dead-stick strokes), unconventional beaters (wire brushes, knuckles), and striking the instrument in unconventional places (the casing, tuning screws). Dead-stick strokes were illustrated in Example 9–B–14) (p. 195). Another interesting technique is the use of a string-bass bow to produce sounds from cymbals and gongs.

The percussion ensemble is one of the more important new ensemble types created in the twentieth century. Example 11–5 is an excerpt from a famous early work for percussion ensemble, in this case an ensemble of thirteen players, each player being responsible for at least three instruments:

| Player | Instruments |
| --- | --- |
| 1 | Crash cymbal, bass drum, cowbell, high tam-tam |
| 2 | Gong, high tam-tam, low tam-tam, cowbell |
| 3 | Bongos, tenor drum, two bass drums |
| 4 | Snare drum, tenor drum |
| 5 | High siren, string drum |
| 6 | Low siren, slapstick, güiro |
| 7 | Three wood blocks (high, medium, and low registers) |
| 8 | Snare drum, high and low maracas |
| 9 | Thin snare drum, snare drum, suspended cymbals |
| 10 | Cymbals, sleigh bells, tubular chimes |
| 11 | Güiro, castanets, glockenspiel |
| 12 | Tambourine, two anvils, very deep tam-tam |
| 13 | Slapstick, triangle, sleigh bells, piano |

The passage quoted in Example 11–5 features the pitched instruments, including the piano, which we do not always think of as a percussion instrument. Notice the clusters on the bottom staff. The use of sirens (performers 5 and 6) was innovative at the time, but perhaps is more amusing than novel to today's audiences.

EXAMPLE 11–5   Edgard Varèse: *Ionisation* (1931), mm. 75–81   *(© 1934 and 1967 by Colfranc Music Publishing Corporation–New York. Reproduced by courteous permission of E. C. Kerby Ltd., Toronto, General Agent.)*

## THE PIANO

The piano has been a particularly fertile field for those interested in experimenting with new sounds. Clusters, introduced in Chapter 3, were at first only a keyboard device; early examples included Henry Cowell's *The Tides of Manaunaun* (1912) and Charles Ives's Piano Sonata No. 2 *(Concord)* (1915), which calls for the use of a board to produce the cluster. Piano clusters are typically either diatonic (white keys), pentatonic (black keys), or chromatic. The clusters in Example 11–5 are chromatic clusters, played with the forearm.

A much more extreme alteration of the piano's timbre is accomplished by means of a **prepared piano,** in which objects are placed on and between the strings before the performance. Although predecessors date back at least to Ravel, Cage's *Bacchanale* (1938) is usually considered the first work for prepared piano. Cage's most famous composition for prepared piano is probably his *Sonatas and Interludes* (1948), a set of sixteen "sonatas," each in two-reprise form, with four interludes. A detailed set of instructions explains how bolts, screws, and pieces of hard rubber and plastic are to be used to prepare 45 of the 88 available notes. The resulting sounds are difficult to describe, some of them percussive, others tinny, still others sounding like the gongs of a gamelan orchestra (an early example of the oriental influence in Cage's music). The score itself gives little impression of the actual sound of these pieces, so there is no point in reproducing a musical example here, but the student is urged to listen to this intriguing work at the earliest opportunity.

Clusters and prepared notes are both played by the pianist at the keyboard, but a large array of other techniques call for the performer to reach inside the piano. These include plucking, striking, and scraping the strings using the fingers, fingernails, drumsticks, and so forth. Cowell was an innovator in this area as well, in pieces like *Aeolian Harp* (1923) and *The Banshee* (1925). Piano harmonics are also possible, as is hand muting, and it is possible to create interesting sounds by pulling threads through the strings. Yet another way to produce sounds from the piano is to have another instrument played into the piano while the damper pedal is depressed, causing the sympathetic vibration of some of the strings.

## THE VOICE

The best-known vocal technique that originated in this century is **Sprechstimme,** a method that lies somewhere between speech and singing. Schoenberg first used it in *Pierrot Lunaire* (1912), an excerpt from which appears in Example 5–2 (p. 102). The small "x" on each stem of the vocal part is the symbol commonly employed to specify *Sprechstimme*. Notice that the voice part is labeled "Recitation."

Singers are also required to make any number of vocal "noises"—grunts, shouts, and so forth—and even to perform multiphonics, as in Example 8–3 (p. 163). The computer part for Charles Dodge's *The Waves* (1985), a work for voice and computer, was derived in part from recorded vocal multiphonics and "reinforced harmonics," which Dodge explains as "intoning in such a way that arpeggiating among adjacent harmonics can be clearly heard above the fundamental frequency."[5] All of these are part of a general tendency to treat the voice as another instrument and not only as a means of presenting a text. Another illustration can be seen in Example 9–B–16 (p. 195), where the "text" is not language at all, but sounds specified by means of the International Phonetic System.

## INSTRUMENTATION AND ORCHESTRATION

Music of the nineteenth century tended to be composed for several standard ensembles: orchestra, string quartet, piano trio, and so forth. Though all of these combinations still exist, their dominance of the compositional scene has diminished. For one thing, it is commonplace today to add or omit instruments as demanded by the composer's conception of the way a piece should sound. The instruments added to an orchestra, for instance, might consist of anything from saxophones to wind machines to a toy piano. A number of new "standard" ensembles have attracted the attention of composers. One of these, the percussion ensemble, has already been discussed; others would include chamber orchestra, the concert band, and the woodwind ensemble. But in addition there are numerous works that call for an ad hoc ensemble—one that is unique, or almost unique, to the particular composition. Examples would include Debussy's Sonata for Flute, Viola, and Harp (1916) and Crumb's Madrigals, Book I, for soprano, vibraphone and contrabass (1965), among many, many others. There are even a number of works that leave the instrumentation unspecified, such as Stockhausen's *Sternklang* (Star-Sound) (1971), for five groups of performers, each one consisting of four instrumentalists and/or singers and a percussionist. Nevertheless, a fair proportion of twentieth-century works are for the symphony orchestra, and the next few paragraphs will outline some of the new approaches to orchestration.

An important development has been the expansion of the percussion section both in numbers of performers and, especially, in variety of instruments employed (see the section on percussion above). The more traditional orchestral instruments are expected to play in a much wider range than previously; the typical orchestral range has been expanded from about 5½ octaves to 7½ octaves and more.[6] The conventional spacing of a sonority, with wide intervals at the bottom and fairly even distribution in the middle and high registers, is now treated as only one of countless possibilities. The opening chord of Stravinsky's *Symphony of Psalms* is a famous example of unconventional spacing (see Example 11–6).

**EXAMPLE 11–6**   Stravinsky: *Symphony of Psalms* (1930), I, mm. 1–4   *(piano reduction)*
*(Excerpted from the International Music Co. edition, New York, NY 10018.)*

The use of multiple divisi in the strings (see for instance Example 11–4) illustrates the greater reliance on orchestral performers as potential soloists, while the nineteenth-century preference for heterogeneous doublings—that is, doublings involving two or more of the three main instrumental choirs—has been discarded in many works in favor of pure colors. Doubling frequently involves unconventional pairings or spacing, as in mm. 2–3 of Example 11–6, where the melody is played by bassoon and flute two octaves apart.

Octave doublings were, of course, a necessary part of conventional orchestration. One could hardly score a triad effectively for full orchestra without a number of octave doublings, and bass and melody lines were frequently doubled at the octave. But octave doublings were generally avoided in atonal and serial music, especially by Schoenberg and his followers, no matter what the medium, giving their orchestral music a distinctive sound. Perhaps a more far-reaching contribution by Schoenberg was his notion of **Klangfarbenmelodie,** or "tone-color melody," in which progressions of timbres would be equivalent in function to successions of pitches in a melody. Schoenberg used tone-color melody most systematically in the work from which Example 11–7 is excerpted. In this example a single chord is sustained throughout the four measures in two alternating timbres. An even more concentrated example of *Klangfarbenmelodie* is Etude No. 7 of Carter's *Eight Etudes and a Fantasy for Woodwind Quartet* (1950), which consists of a single pitch (G4) heard in varying instrumental combinations, dynamics, and articulations.

**EXAMPLE 11–7**    Schoenberg: *Five Pieces for Orchestra,* Op. 16 (1909, 1949) III, "Summer Morning by a Lake (Colors)," mm. 1–4 (reduced score)    *(© 1952 by Henmar Press Inc. Used by permission of C. F. Peters Corporation.)*

To some people, *Klangfarbenmelodie* has come to stand for simply "the principle of maximum variety of color,"[7] and as such is applied to music like that in Example 2–B–3 (p. 40). In the first six measures of that excerpt, the following solo timbres are heard:

Clarinet (low and middle registers)
Horn (low to moderately high registers)
Harp
Violin
Viola (pizzicato)
Cello (pizzicato and arco)

Perhaps a satisfactory definition of tone-color melody would be "the constant re-orchestration of a line or sonority as it proceeds through time." In Example 11–8 the violas (not the solo viola), muted and (in mm. 4–7) bowing over the fingerboard, are doubled at various points by clarinet, bassoon, and bass clarinet, creating a subtle sort of timbral modulation that might well be characterized as *Klangfarbenmelodie*.

**EXAMPLE 11–8**   William Walton: Concerto for Viola and Orchestra (1929, 1962), I, mm. 1–7
*(© 1930 Oxford University Press. Reproduced with permission.)*

Spatial effects, such as separating the performers into two distinct groups, are not unique to the twentieth century, but they are an important feature of many twentieth-century works. This might involve multiple ensembles, as in Carter's *Symphony of Three Orchestras* (1977); offstage performers, such as the strings in Ives's *The Unanswered Question* (1906); or even performers located among the audience, as in Xenakis's *Polytope* (1967). Ideally, *Polytope* is performed as in Example 11–9, where the letters "A" through "D" represent the audience, the numerals "I" through "IV" represent the four small orchestras that perform the piece, and "X" represents the conductor. Space is equally important for small ensembles, and it is not uncommon for the score of a small ensemble to include a seating plan.

EXAMPLE 11–9   Xenakis: *Polytope* (1967), seating arrangement

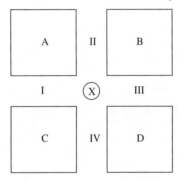

## TRADITIONAL TEXTURES AND COMPOUND TEXTURES

Discussions of traditional musical textures generally sort them into three main categories:

1. Monophonic—a single line, perhaps doubled at the octave
2. Homophonic, meaning either
   a. Melody with accompaniment, or
   b. Chordal texture
3. Contrapuntal—relatively independent lines, either
   a. Imitative, or
   b. Free

The traditional musical textures still exist, of course, and the vast majority of twentieth-century music probably can be analyzed texturally using those categories. Sometimes textures are complicated by harmonizing the individual lines, and we will refer to these as **compound textures.** Debussy's music is especially rich in compound textures, although they certainly can be found elsewhere. One instance was seen in Example 3–B–2 (p. 68), where a three-part texture is thickened into eleven voices:

Part One: Three voices on the immobile D–G–D in the highest register
Part Two: Five voices in similar motion in the middle register
Part Three: Three voices descending in parallel motion in the lowest register

A more involved example is seen in Example 11–10, the final seventeen measures of one of Debussy's preludes. A three-part texture is found in mm. 48–53:

(1), a B♭ ostinato/pedal point;
(2), a glissando/ostinato in the middle register;
(3), a melody in mm. 50–53 in the highest register.

The texture changes in mm. 54–57:

(1) and (2), continuing;
(4), a figure, G♯–E–G♯–G♯, harmonized with secundal chords;
(5), a figure, C–E–F♯, harmonized with whole-tone chords.

In mm. 58–61,

(1) and (5), continuing;
(4), shortened to two chords;
(6), a melody harmonized in parallel major 3rds.

In mm. 62–64 only two elements remain: the glissando (2) and the remnants of the last melody (6).

**EXAMPLE 11–10**   Debussy: Preludes, Book I, "Sails" ("Voiles"), mm. 48–64

Très apaisé et très atténué jusqu'à la fin

## POINTILLISM, STRATIFICATION, AND SOUND-MASS

Pointillism, stratification, and sound-mass are approaches to texture that have been developed in the twentieth century (although not without historical precedent). **Pointillism** gets its name from a technique used by some French painters in the nineteenth century that represented scenes by means of dots of color rather than lines. A pointillistic texture in music is one that features rests and wide leaps, a technique that isolates the sounds into "points."

A good example can be seen in the piano accompaniment in Example 10–B–5 (p. 218). Pointillistic textures for an ensemble frequently also involve *Klangfarbenmelodie*, because the changes in timbre cause the points of sound to seem even further isolated from each other. The texture of Example 2–B–3 (p. 40), discussed earlier in connection with tone-color melody, is an example of a pointillistic texture combined with tone-color melody.

**Stratification** (also called "block juxtaposition") is a somewhat inexact term that is sometimes used for the juxtaposition of contrasting musical textures, or, more generally, of contrasting *sounds*. Though "strata" usually means layers on top of each other, the strata in this case are *next to* each other. Any abrupt change of texture or basic sound is an example of stratification, but this term is generally used in connection with pieces in which contrasts of texture or timbre are the primary elements in shaping the form of the piece (to be discussed later).

The term **sound-mass** is sometimes used for a chord in which the pitch content is irrelevant compared to the psychological and physical impact of the sound. The most characteristic examples of sound-mass (this term seems never to be used in its plural form) are large clusters, such as the ones in Example 3–24 (p. 60) or in the piano part in Example 11–5. But sound-mass can be created by other means as well—the brutal chords at the beginning of the "Dance of the Adolescents" in Stravinsky's *Rite of Spring* (1913) are actually polychords (E♭7 over F♭), but the effect created by the *fortissimo* successive down-bowed chords is that of sound-mass. Yet another kind of sound-mass can be created by extreme activity in a large ensemble, as in the hair-raising climax to Takemitsu's *Asterism* (1968), where the effect is of every instrumentalist playing both loudly and randomly.

## TEXTURE AS A FORM DETERMINANT

We have seen in earlier chapters that tonality has lost its power to control musical form and that in many works there are really no "themes" in the traditional sense. In the absence of tonal and thematic forces, other elements have to be employed to shape a composition—to give it form. In a number of twentieth-century compositions, the primary form-determining element is texture, usually with a good deal of assistance from dynamics, timbre, and register. Many such works are electronic, but others are written for conventional media.

One example is Penderecki's *Threnody*. To this listener, the piece is in four sections, with a number of subsections:

| Section | Begins at | Material |
| --- | --- | --- |
| Part 1 | 0′0″ | High entrances, *ff, dim*, with texture thinning; "busy" sounds, random effects. |
| Part 2 | 1′50″ | Clusters *pp*, expanding, contracting, sliding, ending with stationary cluster; *ff* climax, followed by simultaneous ascent and descent. |
| Part 3 | 4′30″ | Individual entrances build up to *ff* cluster; clusters center on one pitch, slow vibrato, *dim.*; silence. |
| Part 4 | 5′45″ | Busy, random sounds (different from Part 1); high cluster superimposed, then crescendo to climax; *sub. pp;* silence; huge *ff* cluster ends the piece at 8′30″. |

Certainly there are different ways to hear this piece—more or fewer sections, and so forth—but probably every listener would agree that its shape is determined largely by texture and other elements that traditionally have had a secondary role in musical form. Incidentally, the final cluster covers the two octaves from C3 to C5 in quarter-tone intervals distributed among the fifty-two performers, obviously a prime example of sound-mass. The "busy" music from Part 1 appears above as Example 11–4.

A less extreme example of a piece in which texture is the primary form determinant is the first movement of Pärt's *Collage on B-A-C-H*, discussed in connection with Example 7–3 (p. 153).

## SUMMARY

Musical timbre has been greatly altered by twentieth-century composers. The means of producing sounds with conventional instruments have been expanded to the extent that entire books are devoted to the new techniques for a single instrument. Ensemble timbre has been changed by these new techniques, as well as by the expanded role of the percussion section. Several new techniques of orchestral writing have been developed, among them *Klangfarbenmelodie*, or tone-color melody. Other important developments include the tendency to compose for ad hoc combinations instead of the standard ensembles, and the creative use of space. Traditional textures—mono-phonic, homophonic, and contrapuntal—continue to be important in twentieth-century music. Other aspects of texture include compound textures, pointillism, stratification, and sound-mass. In many compositions texture has an important role in determining the form.

## NOTES

1. An excellent survey, with references to a large number of scores, is provided by Gardner Read's *Contemporary Instrumental Techniques*.
2. Read, *Contemporary Instrumental Techniques*, p. 185.
3. A more comprehensive list is provided in Reginald Smith Brindle's *Contemporary Percussion*.
4. Read, *Contemporary Instrumental Techniques*, pp. 183–84.
5. Charles Dodge, liner notes to *Perspectives of New Music* compact disc PNM 27.
6. Henry Brant, "Orchestration," in John Vinton, ed., *Dictionary of Contemporary Music*, p. 543.
7. Reginald Smith Brindle, *Serial Composition*, p. 127.

## *EXERCISES*

### *Part A: Fundamentals*

1. There is a pattern in the string techniques used in Example 11–4. Discover that pattern and the departure from that pattern that is apparently an error.
2. What scale (missing its Db) seems to be the basis of Example 11–6?
3. Provide the prime form of the five-note chord in Example 11–7.
4. What scale is being used in Example 11–10?

### *Part B: Analysis*

1. Debussy: Preludes, Book II, "Dead Leaves" ("Feuilles mortes"), mm. 19–35. In your analysis, consider the excerpt to be in three phrases: (1) mm. 21–24, (2) mm. 25–30, and (3) mm. 31–35.

   (a) Analyze each phrase separately in terms of texture and compositional techniques. That is, separate and identify each element of the texture and discuss the compositional techniques involved with that element. Be sure to include voice leading in your discussion where appropriate.

   (b) What scale predominates in phrase 1, even if it doesn't account for every note? And in phrase 2?

   (c) What is the tonal center of each phrase? How is it established? What elements are in conflict with it?

   (d) An F♯ major triad is the basis of phrase 3. What is the relationship between that triad and the other two triads in that phrase?

**Un peu plus allant** et plus gravement expressif

Plus lent

2. Carry out a textural analysis of Example 7–1 (p. 142). Use an approach similar to that in Exercise B.1.

3. Listen several times to a recording of Ligeti's *Ramifications* (1969), for string orchestra. Then write out an analysis similar in format to the one of Penderecki's *Threnody* (p. 239).

4. The theme that is heard in mm. 1–2 of the "Fantasy" from Carter's *Eight Etudes and a Fantasy for Woodwind Quartet* (1950) returns in mm. 121–140, augmented and in a *Klangfarbenmelodie* setting. Devise a method to show through color-coding how the timbres vary in those final measures of the piece. The clarinet is in B♭.

## Part C: Performance

Be prepared to demonstrate for the class a number of the new playing techniques that have been developed in this century for your instrument. You may find the following readings helpful in completing this assignment.

### FURTHER READING

BARTOLOZZI, BRUNO. *New Sounds for Woodwinds.*

BRANT, HENRY. "Orchestration," in John Vinton, ed., *Dictionary of Contemporary Music.*

BRINDLE, REGINALD SMITH. *Contemporary Percussion.*

———. *The New Music.* See Chapter 15, Colour—New Instrumental Usages, and Chapter 16, Vocal Music—The New Choralism.

———. *Serial Composition.* See Chapter 12, Orchestration, Texture, and Tone Color.

BROOKS, WILLIAM. "Instrumental and Vocal Resources," in John Vinton, ed., *Dictionary of Contemporary Music.*

BUNGER, RICHARD. *The Well-Prepared Piano.*

COPE, DAVID H. *New Directions in Music.* See the section titled "Sound Mass Evolution" in Chapter 3, and Chapter 4, Instrument Exploration.

———. *Techniques of the Contemporary Composer.* See Chapter 11, Percussion and the Prepared Piano, and Chapter 12, New Techniques and Instruments.

DELONE, RICHARD P. "Timbre and Texture in Twentieth-Century Music," in Gary Wittlich, ed., *Aspects of Twentieth-Century Music*, pp. 66–207.

DEMPSTER, STUART. *The Modern Trombone.*

ERICKSON, ROBERT. *Sound Structure in Music.*

HEISS, JOHN C. "Some Multiple-Sonorities for Flute, Oboe, Clarinet, and Bassoon."

HOWELL, THOMAS. *The Avant-Garde Flute.*

Kennan, Kent, and Donald Grantham. *The Technique of Orchestration*. See Chapter 17, Special Devices.

LANSKY, PAUL, AND MALCOLM GOLDSTEIN. "Texture," in John Vinton, ed., *Dictionary of Contemporary Music*.

MORGAN, ROBERT P. *Twentieth-Century Music*. See Chapter 18, Innovations in Form and Texture.

READ, GARDNER. *Contemporary Instrumental Techniques*.

SALZEDO, CARLOS. *Modern Study of the Harp*.

SIMMS, BRYAN R. *Music of the Twentieth Century*. See Chapter 6, Orchestration, Tone Color, and Texture.

TURETZKY, BERTRAM. *The Contemporary Contrabass*.

# TWELVE

# Timbre and Texture: Electronic

## INTRODUCTION

The rise of electronic music is responsible for the most important development in musical timbre in the twentieth century. In the course of less than two decades, music progressed from an almost total dependence on traditional musical instruments, some of which had not changed appreciably for centuries, to one that allowed the use of any sound that could be imagined or defined in acoustical terms. The effect of all of this development has been considerable in the area of concert and popular music.

The beginnings of electronic music go back at least to 1906, when Thaddeus Cahill installed his two-hundred-ton Telharmonium in Telharmonic Hall in New York City, an experiment that was not a complete success. More significant in the history of electronic music was the development of the Theremin (1920) and the Ondes Martenot (1928), both of which were true electronic instruments. These instruments did make an impact, especially the Ondes Martenot, which was used in Messiaen's *Turangalîla-symphonie* (1948), as well as in works by Honegger, Milhaud, Boulez, and others.

But it was not until the first studies by Pierre Schaeffer and Pierre Henry in France (1948–1949) and the development of the tape recorder that the modern history of electronic music really got started. The technological innovations that followed during the next half-century had enormous impact. For composers these developments opened a new and exhilarating soundscape never before available. As technology has become more powerful and more affordable, activities that were once the domain of government and academic institutions have become available to people working with personal computers. Radical notions of sound and music have become part of the sonic fabric of every day life, stretching from mainstream popular music, to film, to alternative forms of rock and dance music, to continued explorations by contemporary concert composers.

## CONCRETE MUSIC

Most electronic music is assembled in some way by the composer and stored on some medium for later playback. Originally, recording tape was used for both editing and storage. Over time, computers gradually replaced tape as an editing and storage medium. Eventually, the computer become responsible for generating and processing sound as well. There are two primary sound sources available for electronic music. One of these is electronically or computer synthesized sound, to be discussed in the next section. The other is simply all of the sounds available in the "natural" world, including musical instruments, voices, steam engines, dripping water, burning charcoal, or whatever the composer might wish to use. Electronic music using natural sounds as a sound source is referred to as **concrete music** (or *musique concrète*).

Although the computer has taken over the means for manipulating sound (and has greatly expanded these means), early concrete music relied entirely on manipulation of the tape on which the sound had been recorded. Initial discussions of concrete music will focus on tape manipulation and the works that grew out of this early period. The process of tape manipulation typically involved several stages of recording, rerecording, and mixing. The alterations were basically carried out in five different ways, each of which can be combined with the others:

1. Change of tape speed
2. Change of tape direction
3. Tape loops
4. Cutting and splicing
5. Tape delay

**Change of tape speed.** Playing a tape at a speed other than the speed at which it was recorded changes the pitch of the material recorded on the tape. Playing it at a speed greater than the original raises the pitch, while playing it at a slower speed lowers it. Tape speed on professional reel-to-reel decks is measured in **inches-per-second (ips)**. Playing a 15-ips tape at 7½-ips, exactly one-half the recorded speed, multiplies each frequency by one-half, lowering all the pitches by exactly one octave. Playing a 33-rpm phonograph record at 45 rpm multiplies each frequency by 45/33, approximately $\frac{4}{3}$, raising the pitch by a P4. When speed change is employed on a tape recorder that allows a wider range of speeds, a larger number of ratios can be produced, allowing more subtle graduations of pitch as well as glissandos. Change of speed also alters the timbre of a sound, because harmonics that were above the audible range in the original may become audible, or the reverse. Also, harmonics of sounds are related by multiples of the fundamental frequency. When the tape playback speed is changed, all frequencies change by the same amount, changing the relationship between fundamental and harmonics. An entertaining work that uses prerecorded sounds played at various speeds is Kenneth Gaburo's *Exit Music II: Fat Millie's Lament* (1965), briefly described in Chapter 7 (p. 141).[1] Other examples include Otto Luening's *Low Speed* (1952) and Iannis Xenakis's *Concret P.H.* (1958).

**Change of tape direction.** Playing a recorded sound backward reverses its **amplitude**, or loudness envelope, so that a sound that normally "decays," like a note played on the piano, will instead increase in amplitude. An early tape piece employing change of direction as well as speed is *Incantation* (1952), which was composed in tandem by Otto Luening and Vladimir Ussachevsky.

**Tape loops.** A piece of tape on which a sound has been recorded can be cut out and the ends spliced together to make a loop. Obviously, the longer the sound, the longer the loop. When the loop is played on a tape player, the sound is repeated over and over, creating an ostinato. The tape loop in Steve Reich's *Come Out* (1966) is simply a recording of the words "come out to show them." Two copies of the loop were played on machines that ran at slightly different speeds, the loops beginning together and moving slowly out of phase with each other; the result was recorded and made into two loops that were played again on the same machines, and so on, the process being repeated until an extremely dense texture developed.

**Cutting and splicing.** By cutting and splicing, the composer can juxtapose sounds that are normally unrelated, or the envelopes of recorded sounds can be altered by cutting out and discarding the unwanted portions, a process that can disguise the source of the original sound more than one might expect. Juxtaposition of unrelated sounds can also lead to new rhythmic patterns. An example of a piece that uses cutting and splicing extensively is Cage's *Williams Mix* (1952), discussed briefly in Chapter 7 (p. 154). While most electronic compositions from this period emerged from the composer's studio as tape recordings ready for performance, *Williams Mix* is a detailed set of instructions for splicing together six different categories of prerecorded sounds, and every "realization," or performance, of the piece will be unique.

**Tape delay.** Echo effects can be achieved by playing a prerecorded sound on a tape recorder and simultaneously rerecording the sound on the same tape. Using either one or two tape recorders, the sound is channeled from the playback head back to a record head, usually with a reduction in amplitude, creating the echo effect. For this process to work, the erase head of the tape recorder has to be disabled so that the recording process does not erase whatever sounds already exist on the tape. A work that features tape delay is *I of IV* (1966) by Pauline Oliveros. Tape delay also can be done "live" in a concert performance, as in Jacob Druckman's *Animus II* (1969) for clarinet and tape and James Tenney's *Saxony* (1978) for solo saxophone.

## THE CLASSICAL ELECTRONIC MUSIC STUDIO

The first studio for electronically synthesized music was established in Cologne, West Germany, in 1951, only a few years after the first experiments with concrete music. While many people have designated concrete music a French tradition and electronically synthesized music a German tradition, the distinctions were hardly ever absolute. One of the early synthesizers, the Ondes Martenot, was a French development. Stockhausen, one of the leading composers associated with the development of the electronic studio in

Germany, studied in Paris. Composers today feel free to employ any sounds, concrete or electronic, in their music. Stockhausen's *Song of the Youths* (*Gesang der Jünglinge*) (1956) and *Hymns* (*Hymnen*) (1967) stand as notable examples of works that employ both electronic and concrete sounds.

The "classical studios" of the 1950s and later all had their own configurations that reflected such things as the interests of the people who designed the studio, the state of the art at the time that the equipment was purchased, and constraints related to budget and space. The configurations of some studios were so distinctive that a connoisseur could sometimes identify where a composition had been realized just by the kinds of sounds that were used. The works composed at the Columbia-Princeton Studios in the 1960s and 1970s, particularly by Mario Davidovsky, epitomized such a recognizable sound that it led to widespread imitation. Davidovsky's *Synchronisms*, composed for different combinations of acoustic instruments and electronic tape, collectively and individually represent milestones of achievement from this period, particularly his *Synchronism #6* (1970) for piano and tape.

In general, most of the equipment found in a classical studio falls into one of four categories: sound-producing equipment, sound-processing equipment, controllers, and sound storage equipment. Oscillators, including noise generators, are the primary components for sound production. Sound processing was typically handled by envelope generators, filters, equalizers, reverberation units, and ring modulators. Sequencers and keyboards were typically used as controllers, so named because they allowed a composer to control a variety of sound parameters with one touch, or sequence of keys pressed. Keyboards were often modeled after acoustic piano keyboards, but in some cases the typical piano key layout was avoided so that a piano performance paradigm would not dominate compositional practice. Reel-to-reel tape recorders were an essential part of any classical electronic studio, providing a means for storing and editing electronically produced sound.

An **oscillator** is an electronic device that produces a fluctuating electrical signal, a **waveform**, at a controllable frequency. Different types of waveforms, named after the shape of the wave over time, produce different sounding timbres. Oscillators in a classical electronic studio could generally produce **sine waves** (a fundamental pitch with no additional partials); **sawtooth waves** (a fundamental pitch with all harmonics in the series); **square waves** (a fundamental pitch with odd-numbered harmonics); **triangle waves** (same as a square wave but with less energy in the upper harmonics); and **pulse waves** (a positive-amplitude only type of square wave that had a variable number and energy level of harmonics based on the relative width of the positive pulse to the overall length of the wave). **Noise generators** are special types of oscillators that produce randomly varying waveforms, theoretically with all frequencies present. Different types of noise (white, pink, yellow) have different relative amplitude levels for the frequencies present. For example, the frequencies in white noise are all at relatively equal amplitudes to one another, whercas pink noise has equal energy per octave band of frequencies. Since frequency doubles with every octave, there are many more frequencies within higher octaves than lower octaves, giving white noise a higher sound.

**Mixers** combine multiple audio signals at varying amplitudes. Used not only to combine multiple musical passages, mixers are an essential component of **additive synthesis**, where harmonically simple sounds are combined to produce more complex sounds.

Filters and equalizers reduce or increase the amplitude of some portion of the spectrum of a sound (for instance, the portion between 440 cps and 660 cps—A and E—or above 1,000 cps). Filters are an essential component of **subtractive synthesis**. Conceptually the opposite of additive synthesis, subtractive synthesis starts with a harmonically rich waveform (usually noise, sawtooth wave or pulse wave) and eliminates, or filters away parts of the spectrum to produce the final sound.

Events such as a change in frequency or amplitude can be controlled manually by various means, including knobs (or **potentiometers**) and the **keyboard**, which could be used as a tunable electronic-organ keyboard or an arbitrary collection of switches. Events can be controlled automatically by **voltage control**, an important aspect of electronic music since the development of the voltage-controlled synthesizer in the 1960s. A voltage-controlled oscillator will usually double its frequency (a change of one musical octave) when one volt is added to its control voltage input. One method of voltage control uses the fluctuating current of one oscillator to change or "modulate" the amplitude or frequency of another. For example, a very low-frequency sine wave, say at 5 cps, could be used as the *modulating signal* to control changes in frequency of another oscillator, perhaps one generating a sawtooth wave at 440 cps. The frequency of the sawtooth oscillator would change, positively and negatively, 5 times per second. How much the frequency would change depends on the amplitude of the modulating signal. The greater the modulating signal amplitude, the greater the change in frequency would be. If the frequency of the modulating signal is high enough, the change in amplitudes or frequencies occurs so fast that it produces new audible sound of its own, called **sidebands**, which may also be used compositionally. Another way to control the amplitude of a sound automatically is by the use of an **envelope generator**, a device that produces a signal that can be used to change a sound parameter over time. The kind of **sequencer** found in the classical electronic studio is a voltage-control device that produces one or more series of voltages that can be used to control frequencies, amplitudes, filter settings, or the speed of the sequencer itself. Often the series produced by the sequencer are used repetitively, resulting in a sound like that of a tape loop.

The **tape recorder** is an essential part of any classical electronic studio, for it is here that sounds are stored, either temporarily while a composition is under way, or permanently when the work is completed. Although cassette tape machines were sometimes used for producing copies in a convenient format, the professional-quality reel-to-reel tape recorder was the workhouse of the classical studio. These machines came in various configurations, with anywhere from two to twenty-four "tracks" (paths on the tape on which sound is recorded independently of other paths) using tapes ranging from ¼″ to 2″ wide at speed of 7.5, 15, or 30 inches per second. Good-quality machines allow for "overdubbing" (recording one track without erasing the others), and some allowed speed variations in small increments between the usual tape speeds. Today, digital recording has largely replaced analog recording. Digital recorders come in a variety of formats: tape recorders (two-track and multitrack), dedicated hard disk systems, and computer-based systems.

In the late 1960s modular voltage-controlled synthesizers began to replace the one-of-a-kind electronic studio as the standard. These synthesizers were designed to function as musical instruments as well as compositional devices. Their designs varied widely but usually included combinations of a variety of oscillators, filters, envelope generators, and other modules, all designed to work together as part of a single larger unit. Composers created sounds by using "patch cords" to connect the outputs and inputs of the modules to create sounds or even full gestures. Smaller units incorporated internal wiring matrices that allowed for connections to be made with buttons and switches. While the core modules were similar, different composers were able to create a remarkably wide variety of sounds, even on the same instrument. Two widely used voltage-controlled synthesizers were the Moog, used in Wendy Carlos's *Switched-on Bach* (1968), and the Buchla, used in Morton Subotnick's *Silver Apples of the Moon* (1967).

A drawback that these modular synthesizers shared with earlier electronic equipment was that it was often difficult and time-consuming to create and later try to recreate patches. This led to synthesizers that combined and routed the modules together internally with simpler buttons and knobs for limited patching and controls. The MiniMoog is a good example of this type of pre-routed synthesizer, and many software programs available today emulate its operation. As microprocessors became more common (and affordable) they were added to synthesizers, making it possible to store and recall these patch configurations and settings. This allowed composers and performers to recall even complex patches with "a push of the button."

Microprocessors rapidly became more inexpensive and incredibly more powerful. In a relatively short time commercial synthesizers became entirely digital—with the synthesizer becoming a "dedicated" music-making computer—a computer built only to make music. As personal computers have become even more powerful they have increasingly taken over synthesis and music-making functions from their "dedicated" predecessors.

## DIGITAL SYNTHESIS

Electronic music synthesis has from the beginning made use of *analog* equipment like that described in the preceding section, but since the late 1970s there has been increasing interest in *digital* synthesizers and digital synthesis software running on computers. A basic difference between the two (analog and digital synthesis) is that an analog device allows an infinite number of measurements within its range, whereas digital devices count in a limited number of steps. For example, the old-fashioned analog watch can theoretically display the time more accurately than a digital watch, because it is not limited to a fixed number of increments. With a digital system, measurements that fall between increments must be assigned the value of a nearby step. The reader can easily see the result of this *quantization*, or "rounding" of values by changing the color resolution of a computer monitor while looking at a photograph. Most computer systems display pictures with millions of colors (almost seventeen million). Lowering the resolution to "thousands of colors" (around 65,000) makes a somewhat noticeable impact on the picture quality. Setting the resolution to 256 colors changes the picture quality dramatically. For audio, quantizing creates audible noise. For CD-quality and higher, quantization noise is rarely a factor. The advantages of a digital system include its smaller size, the greater ease of "patching" the various components together, and the ability to instantly and accurately recall parameter settings.

A more important advantage is its compatibility with digital computers, which has led to the development of computer-driven digital synthesizers, and more recently the widespread development and use of high-quality, complex digital synthesis software on mainstream personal computers.

## Computer Music and Digital Sampling

Computers offer an alternative method of sound synthesis. Note that computer sound synthesis is not the same thing as computer composition, in which the computer makes compositional decisions (to be discussed in Chapter 14), although the two can work in tandem.

Computer sound synthesis systems usually fall into one of two categories: premade ("ready-to-use") or open-ended. Premade systems are found in computer-driven synthesizers, as well as most commercial applications for sound synthesis, such as Reason™, which emulates (or copies) the look and functionality of a modular analog rack of hardware synthesis equipment. Open-ended systems, such as Csound and Max/MSP, allow for the users to program their own synthesis routines and in theory are only limited by the skill of the programmer/composer to specify the details of the operation. Premade systems have the advantage of providing the composer with a relatively easy path to sound generation by means of default programs and a limited set of possible connections. Open-ended systems generally come with a more significant learning curve, but they offer greater flexibility and power to the composer. As personal computers and microprocessors have become more powerful, many attempts have been made to find middle grounds between the power and complexity of open–ended systems and their simpler premade counterparts.

Early developments in computer music synthesis were done entirely with open–ended systems, and this led to the development of specialized programming languages for sound synthesis. Most of these languages are descended from a series of MUSIC *N* programs (Music I, Music V, etc.) developed at the Bell Telephone Laboratories. The most popular descendant used today is Csound, developed by Barry Vercoe at MIT. Using these programming languages requires the composer to specify for the computer the details of the desired sound—its frequency, harmonic structure, amplitude envelope, and so on—all of which can be made to change over time. Typically, the composer defines a number of "instruments" in terms that are similar to the techniques used on analog synthesizers. The instruments play a "score" that is also defined by the composer. All of these instructions are specified in text format—not through the use of a standard musical score. The computer then calculates *samples* of the waveform at a specified rate (44,100 times per second for CD-quality audio), and stores these samples as numbers. At some point, the stored numbers are sent at the same specified rate to a **digital-to-analog converter**, which converts the numbers into voltages that can drive a loudspeaker.

In addition to the complexity of specifying synthesis instructions, the "turnaround time" from the specification of a sound to its actual production was a significant drawback to composers working with these open-ended systems. In the early days of computer music, it could take a computer working all night to produce a minute of sound. Modern computers can now usually do all but the most complex forms of synthesis in *real time*, meaning that the computer can compute and output the required samples at the same rate or faster than they are required for playback. The development of graphic audio mixing programs (such as Pro Tools, Digital Performer, Cakewalk, etc.) has also made the process of using open-ended systems easier. Before the advent of mixing programs, a computer composition had to be realized in one operation from start to finish. Naturally, a long and complex composition required the input of a large amount of data, although that data in stages could be retained, edited, and reused at will. Graphic mixing programs allow for the gathering and precise placement of a number of files, with their amplitude controlled over time by the mixing program.

One example among many of a work using a Music *N* language prior to the advent of graphic mixing programs is Charles Dodge's *Changes* (1970), which makes extensive use of digital filtering.

As with many areas of study, early research in computer music has trickled down to the consumer in a variety of ways. For example, pioneering computer music work in Frequency Modulation (FM) Synthesis by John Chowning at Stanford University, which was used in works such as *Turenas* (1972), was later adapted by Yamaha Corporation to produce a line of synthesizers, including the popular DX-7 keyboard. More recently, Granular Synthesis, Phase Vocoding, and Convolution have made their way from the research center to commercial applications.

Granular synthesis, originally developed for the computer by Curtis Roads working at the University of California, San Diego, and later at the Massachusetts Institute of Technology, builds sound by combining many short moments of audio, called *grains*. A sound grain usually has a duration between 1 ms and 100 ms. The technique can be applied to synthesized waveforms or sampled sounds. When applied to sampled sounds, granular synthesis can be used to change the pitch of a sound without changing its length, and vice versa—something not possible to do with an analog tape recorder. Granular synthesis is used by a large number of composers, often in conjunction with other synthesis techniques. Barry Truax has used the technique extensively in his music, developing his own system for generating and modifying grains. His composition *Riverrun* (1986) makes use of sampled river and water sounds, broken into sonic grains and reassembled to make more abstract sonic images of rushing water.

Phase vocoding and convolution are sound synthesis techniques that rely on computer analysis of existing recorded sounds. The analysis technique most often used is the **Fourier transform**, named after the nineteenth-century French engineer and aristocrat Jean Baptiste Joseph, Baron de Fourier (1768–1830). Fourier developed a theory that any sound, no matter how complex, could be recreated through the combination of many simple sine waves. Sound recordings consist of changing loudness values over time. Fourier analysis takes slices of time and determines what frequencies are present in a sound. That information can then be manipulated, and then through a reverse analysis process be used to "resynthesize" the sound. **Phase vocoding** changes how fast the slices of time are resynthesized, allowing the sound to be dramatically lengthened or shortened in time without changing its pitch, similar to granular synthesis. Phase vocoding can be compared to playing back a film at a different speed than it was recorded. Film usually consists of twenty-four frames, or pictures, per second. Play the film back at twelve frames per second and you get slow motion—in this case, half the original speed of movement captured on the film—without altering the individual pictures. A Fourier transform takes "pictures" of the sound at a regular rate. Phase vocoding changes the playback rate of these "frames" of sound. Roger Reynold's *Transfigured Wind IV* (1985) for flute, and digital audio, uses phase vocoding to alter recordings of flute gestures, which are then played back as accompaniment to a live flutist.

**Convolution** is a type of **cross synthesis**, which takes the frequency characteristics of one sound and applies them to the frequency characteristic of another sound. The mathematical process involves multiplication of frequencies, which means that frequencies present in both sounds will be enhanced, while frequencies present in only one sound will be eliminated. In one respect, it can be thought of as using one sound to *filter* another sound.

Other analysis/resynthesis techniques exist and have been used to good musical results. Jonathan Harvey's *Mortuos Plango, Vivos Voco* (1981) uses an analysis of a large church bell applied to the recording of a boy's voice. The effect is one of a merged boy and bell that produces unique and haunting textures. Paul Lansky's *Idle Chatter* (1985) takes analyzed vocal sounds and separates the more static portions from the fast-changing transients (the vowels from the consonants, plosives, and sibilance) to create a rhythmic chorus of nonsense vocal sounds.

The affordability, power, and versatility of this technology have led. to a resurgence of interest and compositional activity in the area of concrete music. Composers are able to alter concrete sound sources digitally to create rich textures more easily and quickly than with tape, and there is no loss of signal quality (or added noise) like that associated with analog techniques.

## THE DEVELOPMENT OF MIDI

While early programming languages required massive mainframe computers to synthesize sound (making access to them very limited) many composers today work with a variety of open-ended systems and premade systems on personal computers that provide far greater processing power than those earlier mainframes.

Most premade applications trace their history to the development of the *MIDI* (Musical Instrument Digital Interface) specification in the early 1980s. MIDI is a digital communication standard (or language) designed originally to allow the synthesizers of one manufacturer to transmit performance instructions (such as, "now play a C4, now stop playing that C4") to synthesizers made by another manufacturer. MIDI made it easily possible for computers to store and communicate performance instructions, and led to the development of *sequencing* programs that allowed composers to organize and edit computer music scores in more musically intuitive ways than afforded by early programming languages.

Despite MIDI's weaknesses (slow communication speed between devices, limited resolution of control values, and control parameters defined by keyboard performance only) the specification has remained largely unchanged since its inception. Even today, almost all new computer music synthesis programs (premade or open-ended) use MIDI as the basis for controlling parameters and communicating between applications. MIDI breaks down most of the common keyboard-based performance actions into a stream of bits (the smallest unit of binary data, 1 or 0—on or off) arranged in groups of eight to form a byte. Usually two to three bytes are arranged to form a single MIDI message, with seven bits of each byte being used to represent a value from 0 to 127. When a key is pressed on a MIDI keyboard, a message is sent that tells what key was pressed and usually how fast (or hard) the key was pressed. Since MIDI is a performance language that only transmits information when something changes, a separate message is sent when the key is released. There are a variety of MIDI messages allowing one to transmit a variety of performance information. The most common messages include the following:

> *Note on/off messages*—Transmit information about what key is pressed or released, and how it was pressed or released.
>
> *Continuous controllers*—Transmit information about loudness, vibrato, position in stereo field (left/right), sustain pedals, and a variety of similar information through the use of knobs, sliders, pedals, and aftertouch (pressing harder on a key that is already being held down).
>
> *Pitch bend*—Allows inflection of pitch.
> *Program (Patch) changes*—Selects a program to be used to produce a sound or effect, allowing one to change the sound of an instrument playing.

Whereas MIDI was designed to allow communication between synthesizers in a live performance situation, many composers use MIDI to organize communication with synthesizers and software as part of the composition process. The most common application used for this purpose is a MIDI sequencer. Although MIDI does not transmit digital audio, most sequencer applications are modeled after a multitrack tape recorder, with performance information separated into tracks based on the synthesizer or software chosen to receive the information. What is more significant than the ability to organize information into tracks is the capability to edit stored MIDI data much like a word processor does. A sequencer allows a composer to cut, copy, paste and rearrange MIDI data, change or transpose notes, change the durations of notes, change loudness, change instruments, record new information, as well as a variety of other such transformations. MIDI sequencing programs are now almost always combined with graphic audio mixing programs, and this combination forms the centerpiece of much computer music composition. Although the programs are oriented in both layout and editing commands towards more traditional (and tonal) forms of music, experienced composers have adapted them for use in more modern and abstract ways.

## SAMPLERS, PERSONAL COMPUTERS, AND RECENT TRENDS IN DIGITAL SYNTHESIS

The same principles that allow a computer to generate and record sound found their way first into dedicated devices called **samplers** and later to personal computers through the use of software. Samplers (either hardware or software) are devices that record sound digitally into memory which can then be played back, either as recorded or after being manipulated in some fashion. Early samplers were usually limited in their manipulations to transposition, looping portions of sound, applying different loudness envelopes, and playing limited portions of a recording. Samplers can also be used to substitute for actual acoustic instruments, or to expand the sound of a small number of instruments. In this capacity digital samplers have become an important tool for commercial and film music composers, both as a tool for "sketching" ideas during the compositional process as well as playing a part in the final recorded product. Hans Zimmer (*The Lion King*) and Jeff Rona (*A Perfect Storm*) make extensive use of samplers during composition and recording of their scores.

As personal computers became more powerful and adopted *Graphic User Interfaces* (*GUI*, pronounced like "gooey"), the computer with specialized software has taken over much of the task of recording, editing, and playing back sound. The use of the computer for sampling, editing, mixing, and playing back digital sound has numerous advantages over the use of hardware systems. Most of the advantages come from the more advanced GUIs available on personal computers, which allow the user to "see" the recorded sound, quickly finding edit points in one or many sounds. Example 12–1 shows how a recording of the words "how now, brown cow" would look displayed on a computer monitor, with graphic "markers" indicating the start of each word.

**EXAMPLE 12–1  Sampled Speech**

As samplers and computers have become more complex it has become possible to subject the recorded sound to extensive digital synthesis and processing techniques, like the previously discussed granular synthesis, phase vocoding, and convolution. With recent software developments focusing on virtual instruments, or recreating different types of analog synthesizers in the digital domain, a vast array of synthesis, sampling, and digital signal processing is available to the contemporary computer music composer.

## TAPE AND INSTRUMENT, LIVE PERFORMANCE, AND INTERACTIVE COMPUTER MUSIC

The performance of an electronic composition in the concert hall is a somewhat eerie experience for the uninitiated. Because there is no parade of performers onto the stage, the audience is usually alerted to the fact that the piece is about to begin by dimming the lights. Then someone (seen or unseen) starts the playback device, and the audience listens, facing an empty stage. The applause at the end of the piece is not the for the performer, who is, after all, only a tape recorder or CD player, but instead for the composer, who may or may not even be there to hear it. Though the experience may seem a bit strange to those who are new to it, there is at least an advantage in hearing the music over a sound system that is probably superior to most home systems.

Whether or not large audiences will ever warm to a concert format of this kind remains to be seen. Certainly the proliferation of CD recordings has made electronic music more widely available to the public, but the typical electronic music concert still exists outside of the mainstream of concert life. Composers have developed several responses to the situation. One response has been to design more elaborate playback systems comprised of many loudspeakers (8, 16, 32 or more), and to focus the concert on the act of distributing, or *diffusing*, the prerecorded sound throughout the available speakers. Some composers work in multichannel formats, going beyond the two channels of stereo to compose works that take advantage of special speaker installations. Initially limited to concert halls, multichannel works are finding their way into the home through the increasing popularity of DVD-Video players and their accompanying 5.1 audio channels.[2]

Combined tape music and live instrument works can be seen as another response to the empty concert stage, but they also were developed for their own aesthetic reasons. Early examples include Edgard Varèse's *Deserts* (1954), for woodwinds, brass, percussion, and tape, and Stockhausen's *Contact* (*Kontakte*) (1960), for piano, percussion, and tape (an example of "moment form," discussed in Chapter 7). The tape portions of these works used all of the tools available to the electronic composer—a wide variety of electronically synthesized sounds as well as sampled sounds. Often, these sampled sounds were derived from the acoustic instruments used in the piece, such as in Jacob Druckman's *Animus II* (1968). Davidovsky's *Synchronisms* is a series of compositions that explored ideas of ensemble between acoustic performers and tightly integrated electronic parts.

The term *live electronics* can refer to various techniques, from simple amplification of conventional instruments—George Crumb's *Black Angels* (1970) for amplified string quartet—to live performance using electronic instruments, such as keyboard synthesizers. Philip Glass created his own keyboard synthesizer ensemble to perform his early minimalist compositions, such as *Floe* found on the *Glassworks* CD (1984) More recently, the term has come to mean the use of live, computer-generated synthesis and/or interactive computer processing of acoustic instruments.

Because MIDI is primarily a set of performance instructions, it was (and is) an important tool for composers interested in creating works of highly interactive electroacoustic music. *Eight Sketches: Duet for One Pianist* (1989) by Jean-Claude Risset has the pianist playing on a special acoustic piano that sends and responds to MIDI data (such as a Yamaha Disklavier). The performance information is sent to a computer, processed, and sent back to the piano to be played while the performer plays new material. Other musicians use pitch-to-MIDI converters, devices that listen to an acoustic instrument and determine the pitch being played, so that MIDI systems can interact with live acoustic performers. The *Voyager* series of pieces by George Lewis uses software of the composer's own design to listen for musical gestures and phrases being played by a live performer. The software responds to the musical input, sometimes with recognizable variations of the acoustic material, and sometimes with new material of its own design.

One of the more important software applications that have fueled the recent boom in interactive computer music is *Max/MSP*, originally developed by Miller Puckette, with additional development by David Zicarelli. *Max/MSP* was originally designed to handle MIDI information only (as that was all early personal computers could handle), but grew to handle live audio processing as computers grew more powerful. Named after computer music pioneer Max Matthews, *Max/MSP* is a graphic programming language with a collection of MIDI and sound processing objects and user interface elements (such as sliders and knobs). The composer links together simple objects to create complex processing routines. Originally developed in Paris at IRCAM (in English, the Institute for Music/Acoustic Research and Coordination), the audio processing portion of the program originally required large mainframe computers in the 1980s. Pierre Boulez's *Repons* (1981) for clarinet, chamber ensemble, and live computer processing made use of such a large system. Later, a special add-in processing card could perform the live audio processing. Now, the software works without the need for any additional computing hardware on standard Windows and Macintosh computer systems. *Music for Clarinet and ISPW* (1992) by Cort Lippe is another example of this type of live computer processing of acoustic instrumental performance.

The greatest musical impact of electronics, from electrically amplified guitars to computer-based performance systems, has been in the various areas of commercial music. The development of electronic instruments for real-time ("live") performance over the past few decades has been phenomenal, to the point that sales of electronic instruments today exceed those of acoustic instruments. Although most live electronics are used by popular-style commercial groups, there are a number of artists who combine serious experimental techniques with a popular musical setting. Artists such as Laurie Anderson, Peter Gabriel, Björk, and Radiohead (who even quote the music of Paul Lansky) have made significant forays into experimental electronic music performance.

## NOTATION OF ELECTRONIC MUSIC

There is no standard notation for electronic music,[3] and in fact most electronic pieces do not exist in notated form at all. A primary purpose of musical notation, after all, is to allow a composition to be performed, and this purpose is not relevant to most digital audio pieces that do not involve live performers. There are exceptions, of course, such as Cage's *Williams Mix*, in which the score gives instructions for realizing the piece, and Stockhausen's *Electronic Study II* (1954), which shows detailed frequency, envelope, and durations in a graph form. Although strikingly different from standard musical notation, the Stockhausen score is really quite traditional in that it provides all of the instructions necessary to "realize," or recreate the work.

When prerecorded electronic music is to be combined with live performers, some method of coordination has to be provided. One method is for one channel of the tape to provide cues to the performer through headphones, while another is to provide the performers with a score in which some kind of representation of the tape music is given. The composition from which Example 12–2 is excerpted is for cello and two-channel tape. At this point in the piece the taped music is heard for the first time, following a long introductory cello solo. The score instructs the person operating the tape player when to start and stop the tape, and it provides cues to help the cellist coordinate with the taped sounds, but it does not contain a complete transcription of the recorded music.

**EXAMPLE 12–2**    Mario Davidovsky: Synchronisms No. 3 (1964)    *(Copyright © 1966 by Josef Marx. Used by permission of McGinnis & March Music Publishers.)*

The lack of scores and written documentation has proven to be a significant hurdle for the analysis and theoretical discussion of electronic music. Trevor Wishart has written that musical notation actually creates musical priorities as much as it reflects them.[4] Some researchers have used technology to aid in the creation of alternate forms of documentation for a piece. In his book *New Images of Musical Sound*, Robert Cogan uses spectrum photos of recorded music to study selected electroacoustic works (as well as other genres of music). Such work has continued to evolve under the umbrella term of "spectro-morphology," which focuses on the change of spectral information over time as an important organizing feature of electronic music.

*SUMMARY*

The technology that allowed electronic music to really develop was not available until the late 1940s. In just over half a century the medium has developed from concrete music to electronic synthesis, to computer music, and from a studio art to one that allows a variety of live-performance and interactive formats. The development of personal computers powerful enough to handle complex audio processing has led to a vast expansion of activity in the field, often crossing stylistic boundaries. The integration of electronic music into the mainstream concert hall has been slow, but attitudes toward new media are slowly changing in even the most traditional of organizations.

## NOTES

1. A number of the examples in this section were suggested by Barry Schrader's *Introduction to Electro-Acoustic Music*, an excellent and highly recommended text.
2. "5.1 surround sound" delivers six channels of audio—five channels of full-range audio and one channel of low frequency effects (the ".1"). In addition to the standard pair of stereo channels for left and right, there is a front center channel, and two rear "surround" channels.
3. This is not to say that no attempts have been made to develop such a notation. See, for example, Louise Gariépy and Jean Décarie, "A System of Notation for Electro-Acoustic Music: A Proposition."
4. Wishart, *On Sonic Art*, p. 11.

## EXERCISES

### Part A: Concrete Music Techniques

Simple concrete music techniques can be performed with a variety of low- and no-cost audio editors. One such free program is *Audacity*, developed by researchers at Carnegie Mellon University and available for free download through Sourceforge (<http://www.sourceforge.net>) for Windows, Linux, and Macintosh computer systems. Depending on your computer system and installed software, many people have limited edition versions of stereo audio editors such as *Peak* (Mac) and *Soundforge* (Windows). They will have the letters "LE," "DV," or "XP" after their name. They still include many basic editing and processing functions. If you have access to one of these programs, you should try the following techniques both separately and in combination. Not all of the commands may be available on your particular software. They are most successful when done as class projects. The first step is to collect a variety of sounds—musical, text, and natural—to be used as source material. For educational purposes you can use excerpted material from audio CDs.

1. *Speed (pitch) change.* Change the playback rate of the recorded sounds, which will change both the pitch and the spectra of the sounds. Most programs offer a "pitch change" command, sometimes with the option of maintaining the original duration of the sound. Don't select this particular option. With this operation and all that follow, make sure that you save your edited sound with a new file name so as not to destroy your original sound file.
2. *Pitch change.* Similar to the previous exercise, but this time select the option of maintaining the duration of the original sound, if available.
3. *Duration change.* Change the duration of the recorded sounds without changing the pitch. Programs usually offer either one or two ways to do this operation—either through granular synthesis or phase vocoding. Try both ways, if available in your program.
4. *Reverse direction.* Change the playback direction of the sound by using the "reverse" command.
5. *Looping.* Select a portion of the sound and choose the "loop" command. By zooming in on the beginning and end points of the loop you can make subtle adjustments to remove audible "clicks," if necessary.
6. *Cutting and splicing (copying and pasting).* Select different portions of the audio and choose "cut" or "copy." You can "paste" these portions of audio into a new file, changing the order of sounds, splicing sounds together from different segments, etc.
7. *Amplitude change.* Select a portion of the sound (usually after cutting it out of the original audio) and change its amplitude (or gain) envelope. This operation allows you to change the overall amplitude of a sound. You can create *forte-piano-crescendo* and other dynamic effects with otherwise steady-state sounds.
8. *Filtering.* Use a filter or equalizer (EQ) to change the spectral makeup of the sound. You can remove high frequencies, low frequencies, emphasize some frequency range, either alone or in combination.
9. *Effects.* If available, try processing your recorded sound with an audio effect, such as reverberation (reverb), echo, distortion, flanging, or something else available to you.

## Part B: Studio Visit/Concert Performance

Computer music studios take many different forms. At many universities, there is a general-purpose music technology lab that also functions as a computer music lab. Other universities will have a dedicated room, often with more elaborate recording, mixing, and synthesizer systems. Many musicians outside of universities have home studios. If possible, try to arrange for a studio demonstration. It would be particularly helpful to hear a demonstration of some of the more advanced sample processing and synthesis techniques, such as convolution, phase vocoding, and physical modeling synthesis.

Attending a concert that involves electronic music performance is especially worthwhile. Many electronic concerts make use of multiple loudspeakers, often eight or more, to provide an immersive listening experience. You may find multimedia combinations, particularly involving video and computer music. It is also possible that you could encounter interactive computer music performance.

## *Part C: Listening*

Many of the works listed were discussed in this chapter. Works not discussed in the chapter are marked with an asterisk. Select several of them to which you have access, and try to create listening guides to them. Using the CD player's counter or a watch, note the timings of what you hear as important events, and jot down brief descriptions of them. There is no right or wrong description, but try to be as musically descriptive as possible without adding external programmatic descriptions. Adding a musical program to a work changes the way it was intended to be heard, and can interfere with understanding the work. If there is definite rhythm or pitch, you may want to include this information. You could also indicate if the work uses natural or synthesized sounds as its main source material, or some combination.

Using your listening guide, draw the individual events onto a time graph (graph paper works well) at the correct time in order to create a "score." When possible, place high sounds vertically above the lower-pitched sounds, although it may not be possible to do this. If sounds appear at several transpositions, try to represent this by placing the different occurrences at different vertical locations. The graphic score of Ligeti's *Artikulation* done by Rainer Wehinger might provide some inspiration, although it is very detailed. There is also a score to Xenakis's *Mycanae Alpha*, produced by the composer. Xenakis was also a skilled architect, and he created a computer system to translate line drawings into musical compositions.

Once you have finished your score, consider the following questions.

1. Can you recognize any techniques discussed in this chapter? If so, what are the techniques? At what timings do they occur?
2. Does the piece have a form that you are familiar with?
3. Do you perceive a climax? If so, where?
4. Does the composer build tension? If so, how?
5. Does the work juxtapose many different elements, or is a limited amount of material gradually transformed?
6. Is there an overall progression in the timbre of the piece? From noise-based sounds to clear pitches, or from clear pitches to noise-based sounds? From sounds that emphasize low frequencies to sounds that emphasize high frequencies?
7. If the piece is concrete music, can you recognize the sound sources? Does this add some extramusical element to the piece?
8. Could this piece be transcribed and realized by acoustic instruments (perhaps using extended techniques)?

William Albright: *Sphaera
Luciano Berio: *Thema, (Omaggio a Joyce)
Pierre Boulez: Repons; *Dialogue de L'Ombre Double
John Cage: Williams Mix
Wendy Carlos: Switched on Bach
John Chowning: Turenas
George Crumb: Black Angels
Mario Davidovsky: Synchronisms No. 3; *Synchronisms No. 6
Charles Dodge: Changes
Paul Dresher: *Dark Blue Circumstance
Jacob Druckman: Animus 11
Kenneth Gaburo: Exit Music II: Fat Millie's Lament
Philip Glass: *Floe
Jonathan Harvey: Mortuos Plango, Vivos Voco
Pierre Henry: *Variations pour une Porte et un Soupir
Paul Koonce: *Walkabout
Paul Lansky: Idle Chatter
George Lewis: Voyager
Cort Lippe: Music For Clarinet and ISPW
Otto Luening: Low Speed
Otto Luening and Vladimir Ussachevsky: Incantation
Thea Musgrave: *Narcissus
Jon Christopher Nelson: *Waves of Refraction
Pauline Oliveros: I of IV
Steve Reich: Come Out
Roger Reynolds: Transfigured Wind IV
Jean-Claude Risset: Duet for One Pianist; *Mutations I
Karlheinz Stockhausen: Song of the Youths; Hymns; Contact; Electronic Study II
Morton Subotnick: Silver Apples of the Moon
James Tenney: Saxony
Barry Truax: Riverrun
Vladimir Ussachevsky: *Sonic Contours
Edgard Varèse: Deserts; *Poème Electronique*

## FURTHER READING

ANDERTON, CRAIG. *MIDI for Musicians.*

ANTOKOLETZ, ELLIOTT. *Twentieth-Century Music.* See Chapter 18, Musique Concrète and Electronic Music.

BATEMAN, WAYNE. *Introduction to Computer Music.*

BRINDLE, REGINALD SMITH. *The New Music*. See Chapter 10, Concrete Music, and Chapter 11, Electronic Music.

CHADABE, JOEL. *Electric Sound: The Past and Promise of Electronic Music*.

COGAN, ROBERT. *New Images of Musical Sound*.

COGAN, ROBERT, AND POZZI ESCOT. *Sonic Design*. See Chapter 4, The Color of Sound.

COPE, DAVID H. *New Directions in Music*. See Chapter 8, Analog Electronic Music, and Chapter 9, Digital Electronic Music.

————. *Techniques of the Contemporary Composer*. See Chapter 15, Musique Concrète, and Chapter 16, Electronic Music.

DAVIES, HUGH. "Electronic Music: History and Development," in John Vinton, ed., *Dictionary of Contemporary Music*, pp. 212–216.

DODGE, CHARLES, AND THOMAS A. JERSE. *Computer Music*.

EMMERSON, SIMON (ed.). *The Language of Electroacoustic Music*.

FENNELLY, BRIAN. "Electronic Music: Notation," in John Vinton, ed., *Dictionary of Contemporary Music*, pp. 216–220.

HOWE, HUBERT S. *Electronic Music Synthesis*.

LUENING, OTTO. "Origins," in John H. Appleton and Ronald C. Perera, eds., *The Development and Practice of Electronic Music*, pp. 1–21.

MANNING, PETER. *Electronic and Computer Music*.

PELLMAN, SAMUEL. *An Introduction to the Creation of Electroacoustic Music*.

PRESSING, JEFE. *Synthesizer Performance and Real-Time Techniques*.

ROADS, CURTIS. *The Computer Music Tutorial*.

SCHRADER, BARRY. *Introduction to Electro-Acoustic Music*.

SCHWARTZ, ELLIOTT. *Electronic Music: A Listeners Guide*.

SIMMS, BRYAN R. *Music of the Twentieth Century*. See Chapter 14, "Electronic Music."

SLAWSON, WAYNE. *Sound Color*.

WISHART, TREVOR. *On Sonic Art*.

# ———THIRTEEN———

# Serialism After 1945

## INTRODUCTION

The end of World War II in 1945 was followed by two major developments in music. One of these was the beginnings of electronic music, the subject of Chapter 12. The other development, the subject of this chapter, was the dissemination of the serial technique and the extension of its principles into all facets of musical composition.

Although Schoenberg composed his first twelve-tone work in 1921, serialism did not appeal at once to a large number of composers outside of his immediate circle. But when World War II ended, interest in serialism spread rapidly, and the technique was taken up with enthusiasm by the younger generation of composers as well as by established composers as diverse as Copland and Stravinsky. It may be that serialism represented to some composers a rationality that was welcome after the irrational horrors of the war, and the fact that Hitler's regime had tried to suppress serialism certainly did nothing to harm its postwar reputation. In the United States, considerably less affected by the war, interest in twelve-tone music was due in part to Schoenberg's tenure from 1936 on as a professor at the University of California at Los Angeles.

But many of the new adherents to serialism felt that Schoenberg had not taken the technique far enough. Instead of restricting serialism to the domain of pitch class, these composers felt that other aspects of composition should also be controlled by some kind of precompositional plan. This approach has been given various labels, among them "total serialization," "total control," "generalized serialism," and the one we will use, **integral serialism.**

## INTEGRAL SERIALISM

In classical serial technique, the composer constructs the pitch series before beginning the actual composition. The compositional process is thereby restricted to the extent that, once having begun the presentation of some form of the row, the notes of the row must be used in order; however, everything else is left up to the creativity and skill of the composer. As anyone who has ever composed a twelve-tone piece knows, composition using the techniques of classical serialism is far from a mechanical or automatic procedure.

Some of the areas in which the composer has complete freedom are:

Rhythm

Dynamics

Register

Articulation

Row Form

It is these areas that the proponents of integral serialism looked at most closely (though others, such as timbre, were not ignored). Many examples of integral serialism apply serial techniques to only a few of these aspects, whereas others are so thoroughly preplanned that they truly are automatic, in the sense that all of the composer's decisions were made before the actual notation of the piece was begun. In the next several paragraphs we will examine approaches to integral serialism in three very different works by composers from the United States, France, and Italy.

### MILTON BABBITT: THREE COMPOSITIONS FOR PIANO (1947) No. 1

In this composition, evidently the very first to employ integral serialism, Babbitt "serialized" the dynamics by associating a particular dynamic level with each row form:

$$P = mp \ (pp \text{ in mm. } 49–56)$$
$$R = mf \ (p)$$
$$\quad = f \ (mp)$$
$$RI = p \ (ppp)$$

There is obviously no true dynamic series here, no parallel to the series of twelve pitch classes; nevertheless, the dynamic levels are controlled precompositionally, which is the only requirement for integral serialism. Turn back to Example 6–3 (p. 119) to see an excerpt from this work. You can tell from the dynamic levels in the excerpt that the row forms used are:

|  | *m. 9* | *m. 10* | *m. 11* | *m. 12* |
|---|---|---|---|---|
| Top staff: |  | R | I | I |
| Bottom staff: | P | RI | RI |  |

The rhythm in this composition is organized around the number series 5–1–4–2, which sums to 12. This series of numbers is always associated in some way with the P form of the pitch set. To invert the number series, Babbitt subtracts each number from 6:

$$
\begin{array}{cccc}
6 & 6 & 6 & 6 \\
\underline{-5} & \underline{-1} & \underline{-4} & \underline{-2} \\
1 & 5 & 2 & 4
\end{array}
$$

Six is chosen here because it is the only value that can be used if the resulting differences are going to sum to 12 (as they must, in order to be associated with the inversion of the twelve-tone pitch series).

The resulting durational set is:

$$
\begin{array}{ll}
P = 5\ \ 1\ \ 4\ \ 2 & R = 2\ \ 4\ \ 1\ \ 5 \\
I = 1\ \ 5\ \ 2\ \ 4 & RI = 4\ \ 2\ \ 5\ \ 1
\end{array}
$$

Each member of the durational set is always associated with its corresponding row form. The durational set is expressed in a variety of ways (rests, phrase marks, and so on). In Example 13–1 groups of notes are formed by making the last note of a group longer than the others and/or following the last note by a rest. The series being stated in the excerpt are:

|  | *mm. 49–50* | *mm. 51–52* |
|---|---|---|
| Top staff: | P  (5–1–4–2) | RI  (4–2–5–1) |
| Bottom staff: | RI  (4–2–5–1) | I  (1–5–2–4) |

Notice that the rhythms of the two RI forms in the excerpt are similar but not identical.

EXAMPLE 13–1   Babbitt: *Three Compositions for Piano* (1947), No. I, mm. 49–52

*(© Copyright 1957 by Boelke-Bomart, Inc., Hillsdale, NJ.)*

The rhythm series is expressed in Example 6–3 (p. 119) in different ways. In the left hand in mm. 9–10, the P and RI rhythm series is stated by means of phrase marks and accents. The I form in the right hand, m. 12, is presented the same way. The other measures in the excerpt are organized rhythmically by using the sixteenth-note as the unit of measure. For example, in m. 10 the right hand states 2–4–1–5 by durations of two sixteenths (one eighth), four sixteenths (two eighths tied), one sixteenth, and five sixteenths (a sixteenth tied to a quarter).

Register appears to be left open, except in the voicing of trichords. When Babbitt segments the pitch series into vertical trichords, as in mm. 10–11 of Example 6–3 (p. 119), he voices the trichords in relation to the row in this way:

|   |   | *1–3* | *4–6* | *7–9* | *10–12* |
|---|---|---|---|---|---|
| P | = | Up | Down | Up | Down |
| I | = | Down | Up | Down | Up |
| R | = | Up | Up | Down | Down |
| RI | = | Down | Down | Up | Up |

That is, the members of a prime form of the row would be voiced in trichords as:

| 3 | 4 | 9 | 10 |
|---|---|---|---|
| 2 | 5 | 8 | 11 |
| 1 | 6 | 7 | 12 |

The three row forms in Example 6–3 that are used trichordally are:

m. 10, r.h.: R–10    (E  G♯  A)  (F♯  B  G)  (D♭  C  D)  (F  E♭  B♭)

m. 11, r.h.: I–11    (B  F♯  E)  (G  A  G♯)  (D  B♭  E♭)  (C  D♭  F)

m. 11, l.h.: RI–11    (F  D♭  C)  (E♭  B♭  D)  (G♯  A  G)  (E  F♯  B)

## *PIERRE BOULEZ:* STRUCTURES Ia (1952)

European composers, unaware of Babbitt's work in the United States, developed a different approach to integral serialism. In some works each note has its own duration, dynamic level, and articulation, all precompositionally assigned. The multiplicity of dynamic levels was especially troublesome for performers, but the rhythms were also difficult because they were generally ametric.

*Structures Ia* uses as its primary material the following pitch series (borrowed by Boulez from *Mode de valeurs et d'intensités* (1949), composed by his teacher, Messiaen):

| E♭ | D | A | A♭ | G | F♯ | E | C♯ | C | B♭ | F | B |
|---|---|---|---|---|---|---|---|---|---|---|---|
| 1 | 2 | 3 | 4 | 5 | 6 | 7 | 8 | 9 | 10 | 11 | 12 |

As we shall see, the pitch series is made to govern duration, dynamic level, articulation, and row choice.

The first step is to make a matrix of prime forms of the series. The second row of the matrix begins with the second note of the original series, the third row begins with the third note, and so on:

| | | | | | | | | | | | |
|---|---|---|---|---|---|---|---|---|---|---|---|
| E♭ | D | A | A♭ | G | F♯ | E | C♯ | C | B♭ | F | B |
| D | C♯ | G♯ | G | F♯ | F | E♭ | C | B | A | E | B♭ |
| A | A♭ | E♭ | D | C♯ | C | B♭ | G | F♯ | E | B | F |
| A♭ | G | D | etc. | | | | | | | | |

Notice that this is not the kind of twelve-note matrix discussed in Chapter 10.

Next, each note name is replaced with the order number that the note had in the original series. That is, every E♭ is replaced with 1, every D with 2, every A with 3, and so on:

| | | | | | | | | | | | |
|---|---|---|---|---|---|---|---|---|---|---|---|
| 1 | 2 | 3 | 4 | 5 | 6 | 7 | 8 | 9 | 10 | 11 | 12 |
| 2 | 8 | 4 | 5 | 6 | 11 | 1 | 9 | 12 | 3 | 7 | 10 |
| 3 | 4 | 1 | 2 | 8 | 9 | 10 | 5 | 6 | 7 | 12 | 11 |
| 4 | 5 | 2 | 8 | 9 | 12 | 3 | 6 | 11 | 1 | 10 | 7 |
| 5 | 6 | 8 | 9 | 12 | 10 | 4 | 11 | 7 | 2 | 3 | 1 |
| 6 | 11 | 9 | 12 | 10 | 3 | 5 | 7 | 1 | 8 | 4 | 2 |
| 7 | 1 | 10 | 3 | 4 | 5 | 11 | 2 | 8 | 12 | 6 | 9 |
| 8 | 9 | 5 | 6 | 11 | 7 | 2 | 12 | 10 | 4 | 1 | 3 |
| 9 | 12 | 6 | 11 | 7 | 1 | 8 | 10 | 3 | 5 | 2 | 4 |
| 10 | 3 | 7 | 1 | 2 | 8 | 12 | 4 | 5 | 11 | 9 | 6 |
| 11 | 7 | 12 | 10 | 3 | 4 | 6 | 1 | 2 | 9 | 5 | 8 |
| 12 | 10 | 11 | 7 | 1 | 2 | 9 | 3 | 4 | 6 | 8 | 5 |

A similar matrix of inversions must then be constructed:

| | | | | | | | | | | | |
|---|---|---|---|---|---|---|---|---|---|---|---|
| E♭ | E | A | B♭ | B | C | D | F | F♯ | G♯ | C♯ | G |
| E | F | B♭ | B | C | C♯ | D♯ | F♯ | G | A | D | G♯ |
| A | B♭ | E♭ | E | F | F♯ | G♯ | B | C | D | G | C♯ |
| B♭ | B | E | etc. | | | | | | | | |

And again the matrix is converted into order numbers from P-0:

| 1 | 7 | 3 | 10 | 12 | 9 | 2 | 11 | 6 | 4 | 8 | 5 |
|---|---|---|---|---|---|---|---|---|---|---|---|
| 7 | 11 | 10 | 12 | 9 | 8 | 1 | 6 | 5 | 3 | 2 | 4 |
| 3 | 10 | 1 | 7 | 11 | 6 | 4 | 12 | 9 | 2 | 5 | 8 |
| 10 | 12 | 7 | 11 | 6 | 5 | 3 | 9 | 8 | 1 | 4 | 2 |
| 12 | 9 | 11 | 6 | 5 | 4 | 10 | 8 | 2 | 7 | 3 | 1 |
| 9 | 8 | 6 | 5 | 4 | 3 | 12 | 2 | 1 | 11 | 10 | 7 |
| 2 | 1 | 4 | 3 | 10 | 12 | 8 | 7 | 11 | 5 | 9 | 6 |
| 11 | 6 | 12 | 9 | 8 | 2 | 7 | 5 | 4 | 10 | 1 | 3 |
| 6 | 5 | 9 | 8 | 2 | 1 | 11 | 4 | 3 | 12 | 7 | 10 |
| 4 | 3 | 2 | 1 | 7 | 11 | 5 | 10 | 12 | 8 | 6 | 9 |
| 8 | 2 | 5 | 4 | 3 | 10 | 9 | 1 | 7 | 6 | 12 | 11 |
| 5 | 4 | 8 | 2 | 1 | 7 | 6 | 3 | 10 | 9 | 11 | 12 |

*Structures Ia* is a work for two pianos, and the two pianos between them state all 48 forms of the row: Piano I states the twelve P forms and the twelve RI forms, and Piano II states the twelve I forms and the twelve R forms. The transposition levels for the row forms are selected by using the order numbers in the two matrices. For example, the twelve P forms in Piano I are governed by the first row of the inversion matrix (1,7,3, etc.); thus, the prime beginning with order number 1 would be first, the prime beginning with order number 7 would be second, and so on. (Note that these are not the same as P-1 and P-7.) In Example 13–2, Piano I states the prime beginning with order number 1, while Piano II states the inversion beginning with order number 1.

EXAMPLE 13–2   Boulez: *Structures 1a* (1952), mm. 1–7   *(Copyright 1955 by Universal Edition (London) Ltd., London. Copyright renewed. All rights reserved. Used by permission of European American Music Distributors Corporation, sole U.S. and Canadian agent for Universal Edition (London) Ltd., London.)*

The duration of each note is also dictated by the two matrices. All twelve rows of each matrix are worked through both forwards and backwards to provide durations for the 576 notes in the piece (12 notes $\times$ 48 row forms). The order numbers are used as multiples of 32nd-notes, so that the order number 1 represents one 32nd-note, 2 represents a sixteenth-note, 3 a dotted sixteenth-note, and so on. The duration series in Example 13–2 are:

| Piano I: | 12 | 11 | 9 | 10 | 3 | 6 | 7 | 1 | 2 | 8 | 4 | 5 |
|---|---|---|---|---|---|---|---|---|---|---|---|---|
| Piano II: | 5 | 8 | 6 | 4 | 3 | 9 | 2 | 1 | 7 | 11 | 10 | 12 |

If you compare these duration series with the number matrices, you will see that Piano I is taken from the last row of the I matrix, whereas Piano II is taken from the last row of the P matrix, both in retrograde order. Boulez's rhythmic structure, with 48 rhythmic patterns, is obviously more complicated than Babbitt's, with only four.

Dynamics and articulation are serialized by making a list of twelve dynamic levels ( *pppp* to *ffff* ) and ten "modes of attack." A single dynamic level and a single articulation are used with each row form, the particular one to be used being again dictated by the number matrices. In this case, instead of rows, diagonals of the matrices are used, some for the dynamics and others for articulation. Because the order numbers 4 and 10 do not appear in the articulation diagonals, the fourth and tenth modes of attack are not needed. In Example 13–2, Piano I uses the twelfth dynamic level and the twelfth mode of attack, while Piano II uses the fifth dynamic level and the fifth mode of attack.

Once all of these procedures were established, the actual notation of the composition could begin; however, by now there were few decisions left to be made. One of them was the choice of time signatures, which do not seem to follow any particular pattern; another was the choice of register. Octave register appears to be controlled only to the extent that a pitch class occurring in two row forms simultaneously must be used in the same register.

## LUIGI NONO: IL CANTO SOSPESO (1956), II

The pitch material of this composition derives from a series that is usually characterized as a "wedge" row (Example 13–3a); it can also be viewed as a hexachord followed by its retrograde at the tritone (Example 13–3b). In view of the structure of the duration set, the second interpretation is probably more appropriate. Only P-9 is used in this movement.

**EXAMPLE 13–3**   Series from Nono's *Il canto sospeso*

The duration set is a palindrome[1] based upon a Fibonacci series. This series, discussed in Chapter 7 in connection with musical form and the golden mean (see p. 152), is an infinite one in which each number (after the first two) is the sum of the previous two numbers:

1    2    3    5    8    13    21    34    etc.

Nono uses the first six numbers and their retrograde for his duration set:

1    2    3    5    8    13    13    8    5    3    2    1

In mm. 108–42 of this movement (the movement begins with m. 108), these values are distributed as needed among four rhythmic strands. Each strand uses its assigned values as multiples of some basic duration:

> Strand A: eighth-note
>
> Strand B: triplet eighth-note
>
> Strand C: sixteenth-note
>
> Strand D: quintuplet sixteenth-note

All four strands begin simultaneously and proceed at their own rates without pause, except that the four strands are distributed among eight voice parts, which allows the singers to breathe. Example 13–4, which shows the first presentation of the rhythmic series, may help to clarify how this works. All four strands start simultaneously at the beginning of the excerpt, with the first four durational values—1, 2, 3, and 5—distributed from the top down. As the duration of each strand is exhausted, the next durational value is assigned to it: 8 for Strand A; 13 for Strands B and C; 8, 5, and 3 for Strand D; 2 for Strand C; and 1 for Strand D.

**EXAMPLE 13–4**   Nono: *Il canto sospeso*, II, mm. 108–10 (rhythm only)   *(© Ars Viva Verlag 1957. Copyright renewed. All rights reserved. Used by permission of European American Music Distributors Corporation, sole U.S. and Canadian agent for Ars Viva Verlag.)*

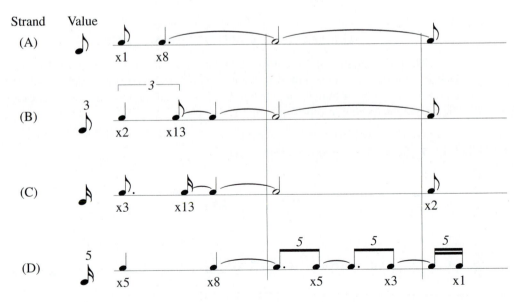

Pitch classes from P-9 are also distributed in order among the four strands as needed. In Example 13–4, Strand A would get order numbers 1 and 5, B would receive 2 and 6, C would receive 3, 7, and 11, and D would use 4, 8, 9, 10, and 12.

In the score, Example 13–4 appears as in Example 13–5. The strands are distributed as follows:

Strand A: Alto 2

Strand B: Soprano 2–Basso 1

Strand C: Soprano 1–Soprano 1 + Tenor 2–Tenor 2

Strand D: Alto 1–Basso 2–Soprano 1

The first note in m. 11, Basso 2, is evidently an error and should be a sixteenth-note quintuplet.[2]

EXAMPLE 13–5  Nono: *Il canto sospeso,* II, mm. 108–10

Because the pitch and duration sets are of equal length, if the composition were continued in this manner, each member of the row would always be assigned to the same number from the duration series. To avoid this, the duration set is rotated for each statement of the row:

| Statement 1: | 1 | 2 | 3 | 5 | 8 | 13 | 13 | 8 | 5 | 3 | 2 | 1 |
|---|---|---|---|---|---|---|---|---|---|---|---|---|
| Statement 2: | 2 | 3 | 5 | 8 | 13 | 13 | 8 | 5 | 3 | 2 | 1 | 1 |
| Statement 3: | 3 | 5 | 8 | 13 | 13 | 8 | 5 | 3 | 2 | 1 | 1 | 2 |

etc.

In the coda (mm. 142–57) each strand presents the entire duration series independently. The entrances are staggered, with Strand A beginning, followed by Strands B, C, and D. This allows all four strands to reach their maximum level of activity simultaneously for the climax of the movement in m. 150.

## INTEGRAL SERIALISM IN PERSPECTIVE

The three works that have been surveyed here demonstrate just three of many possible approaches to integral serialism. None of them serialize register or timbre, but all three serialize rhythm, and it is interesting to compare them in that regard. Babbitt's rhythmic series is apparently not derived from his pitch series at all, which might seem a weakness since there is no single organizing force at work. There is a connection between Nono's pitch series and his rhythmic series, in that both are symmetrically designed, but there is not a direct one-to-one correspondence between the two. Boulez probably comes closest to the ideal of having a pitch series control all elements of a work, but the listener could never recognize the relationship between a pitch series and a duration series derived from *order numbers* of transpositions and transposed inversions of the pitch series.

Babbitt later devised other methods that linked the durations more closely with the original pitch series. One method derives the duration set from the original row by numbering the notes chromatically, using the first note as 0:

| G | B♭ | F♯ | B | G♯ | A | E♭ | F | C | E | D | C♯ |
|---|---|---|---|---|---|---|---|---|---|---|---|
| 0 | 3 | 11 | 4 | 1 | 2 | 8 | 10 | 5 | 9 | 7 | 6 |

By substituting 12 for the 0 that begins the row, a durational set is established. The numbers in the set can serve as multiples of any constant value. In Example 13–6 the constant value is the eighth-note.

**EXAMPLE 13-6**  A Durational Series

Alternatively, the same series can be interpreted as **time points** within a measure. That is, the series 0, 3, 11, 4, etc., can be interpreted as the 0th eighth-note in a measure, the third eighth-note in a measure, the eleventh eighth-note in a measure, the fourth eighth-note in a measure, and so on, as in Example 13–7. The twelve eighth-notes in each measure are numbered 0 through 11 instead of 1 through 12, in order to correspond with the range of values in the duration series.

EXAMPLE 13–7    A Time-Point Series

The durations in Example 13–7 closely reflect the intervals between the adjacent notes of the series. To illustrate this, count the number of ascending half-steps between each note and the next one:

P-0:  G   B♭   F♯   B   G♯   A   E♭   F   C   E   D   C♯   (G)
         3    8    5   9    1   6    2   7   4   10   11   (6)

These numbers, it turns out, are the same as the durations in Example 13–7. That is, the first note is three eighth-notes in duration, the second is eight eighth-notes, and so on.

Although Examples 13–6 and 13–7 were derived from the same pitch series, each is unique, and each could be subjected to transposition, inversion, and retrograde operations.

The composers of integral serialism faced a number of problems, not the least of which was the resistance of performers who found that the difficulty of the music outweighed its rewards. Imagine the problems experienced by performers of the Boulez and Nono examples in this chapter, and you will understand their concern. Also discouraging was the lack of enthusiasm on the part of the musical public. The compositional method was ultimately irrelevant to the listener, since none of the relationships were audible. In fact, some of the most tightly controlled works give the listener the impression that they are completely random and disorganized (*Structures Ia* is a good example of this).

## OTHER ASPECTS OF SERIALISM

Our two chapters on serialism have not by any means exhausted the subject. A really thorough discussion of this topic (and one is sorely needed) would require many chapters. We should not leave the subject, however, without briefly mentioning a few other aspects of serialism.

Although most serial works use a pitch series of twelve pitch classes, there are some that use more or fewer than twelve. Stravinsky used the following four-note set in *Three Songs from William Shakespeare* (1953):

    B      G      A      B♭

and this five-note row in his *In Memoriam Dylan Thomas* (1954):

    E      E♭     C     C♯D

Berio used a thirteen-note set in *Nones* (1954). Notice that this set is symmetrical around its central note, A:

C   E♭   B   A♭   F   E   A   D   C♯   B♭   G   E♭   F♯

And Example 6–12 (p. 129), while not taken from a strictly serial composition, does employ a sixteen-note pitch series.

    Rotation of sets or of portions of sets is another possibility that composers have explored. Stravinsky used two methods of hexachordal rotation for *Abraham and Isaac* (1963).[3] In the first, the pitch classes are rotated in a circular fashion, right to left:

| | | | | | |
|---|---|---|---|---|---|
| G | G♯ | A♯ | C | C♯ | A |
| G♯ | A♯ | C | C♯ | A | G |
| A♯ | C | C♯ | A | G | G♯ |
| C | C♯ | A | G | G♯ | A♯ |
| C♯ | A | G | G♯ | A♯ | C |
| A | G | G♯ | A♯ | C | C♯ |

The second method of rotation works just like the first, but all are transposed to begin with the same note:

| | | | | | |
|---|---|---|---|---|---|
| G | G♯ | A♯ | C | C♯ | A |
| G | A | B | C | G♯ | F♯ |
| G | A | A♯ | F♯ | E | F |
| G | G♯ | E | D | D♯ | F |
| G | D♯ | C♯ | D | E | F♯ |
| G | F | F♯ | G♯ | A♯ | B |

Less-systematic reordering of rows also occurs. George Rochberg's *Twelve Bagatelles* (1952) uses a single row in only a few transpositions, but the row is frequently reordered. Example 13–8 employs the following row forms:

| | | | | | | | | | | | | |
|---|---|---|---|---|---|---|---|---|---|---|---|---|
| RI-8: | B | C | F | D | F♯ | B♭ | E | E♭ | A | C♯ | G | A♭ |
| I-8: | A♭ | G | C♯ | A | E♭ | E | B♭ | F♯ | D | F | C | B |
| | 1 | 2 | 3 | 4 | 5 | 6 | 7 | 8 | 9 | 10 | 11 | 12 |

**EXAMPLE 13-8** *Rochberg: Twelve Bagatelles (1952), No. 8, mm. 1–8.* *(© 1955 Theodore Presser Company. Used by permission of the publisher.)*

Whereas the rows in mm. 1–4 are presented in the correct order, those in mm. 5–8 are not; the final RI-8 is particularly reordered. Rochberg's purpose may have been to emphasize two particular arrangements of an [0,1,6] set type, labeled here as "a" and "b."

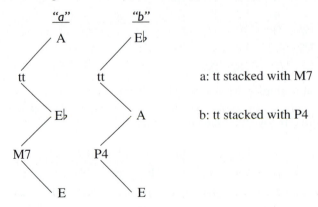

a: tt stacked with M7

b: tt stacked with P4

Occurrences of these two arrangements (or their inversions) are shown in the example. Notice particularly how many of them occur in mm. 5–8, where the rows are reordered.

Serialism has also been employed in electronic and microtonal music, an example of the latter being Ben Johnston's String Quartet No. 2 (1964).

## MUSIC AFTER SERIALISM

For the most part, serialism as a movement, as a compositional aesthetic, died out in the 1960s, but that is not to say that serial music is no longer being written. Instead, serial techniques have joined all of the other techniques, from free atonality to pitch centricity to traditional harmony, that composers have at their command. It is not uncommon, for example, to find a twelve-tone theme supported by pitch-centric, nonserial harmonies.

There are several reasons for the decline of serialism, especially integral serialism, as a movement. One is the insistence upon originality that robbed the twentieth century of any chance of developing a "style" in the way that there are Baroque and Classical styles. Also, the demands that integral serialism made on listener and performer proved intolerable to both. In the words of one writer and composer who was active throughout this period:

> And so integral serialism quickly reached an impasse, through its own limitations and the burdens it laid on performers. But its importance, in both aesthetic and historical contexts, must not be denied, for it forged a completely new musical language, as different from anything that had gone before (except Webern) as chalk from cheese, and paved the way to a new, more spontaneous music which is still the most potent means of emotive expression today.[4]

The same writer goes on to summarize the movement from free atonality in the early 1900s to serialism in the 1920s, then to integral serialism in the 1950s, and finally back to free atonality in the 1960s: "The cycle was then complete and serialism had come and gone, but leaving decisive and lasting traces of its sojourn."[5]

---

### SUMMARY

Integral serialism refers to the precompositional control not only of pitch, as in classical serialism, but of other elements of a composition as well. Rhythm, dynamics, articulation, register, row form, and timbre have all been subjected to precompositional ordering. In some cases these orderings are independent of each other, but often the composer attempts to relate all of the musical materials to a single series.

Other aspects of serialism discussed in this chapter included the use of tone rows with fewer or more than twelve pitch classes, the use of rotation, and the reordering of rows.

Though serialism has declined as a compositional technique, its influence on later styles has been substantial.

## NOTES

1. A palindrome is a structure that reads the same backwards as it does forwards. Examples are the word "noon" and Messiaen's nonretrogradable rhythms (see p. 128).

2. There are apparently at least two other errors, in mm. 125 and 135, both being occasions when the last note of the row is articulated slightly after the first note of the next statement. The second of these makes little difference, but "correcting" m. 125 significantly alters mm. 125–42.

3. George Perle and Paul Lansky, "Twelve-Note Composition," in Stanley Sadie, ed., *The New Grove Dictionary of Music and Musicians.*

4. Reginald Smith Brindle, *The New Music*, p. 52.

5. Ibid., p. 53.

## EXERCISES

### Part A: Fundamentals

1. Suppose that P-2 of some row begins on D and ends on B♭. Fill in the missing information below.

|     | Row form | First note | Last note |
|-----|----------|------------|-----------|
| (a) | P-2      | D          | B♭        |
| (b) | P-___    | ___        | A♭        |
| (c) | R-2      | ___        | ___       |
| (d) | R-___    | ___        | F         |
| (e) | I-2      | ___        | ___       |
| (f) | I-___    | C          | ___       |
| (g) | RI-2     | ___        | ___       |
| (h) | RI-___   | E♭         | ___       |

2. Identify any rows discussed in this chapter that are all-interval rows.
3. Identify any rows discussed in this chapter that are derived sets, and explain your answer.
4. Is combinatoriality employed in Example 13–1? Explain how you can tell that it is or is not.
5. Same question for Example 13–2.

## Part B: Analysis

1. Boulez: *Structures Ia* (1982), mm. 8–15. This excerpt is a continuation of Example 13–2. When doing the following exercises, consider both excerpts, as well as the discussion of *Structures Ia* in the text.

   (a) Identify the P forms in Piano I, and explain how they are derived from the matrices.

   (b) Do the same for the I forms in Piano II.

   (c) Study the durations used in Piano I, and explain how they are derived from the matrices. A rest should be counted as part of the duration of the note that precedes it.

   (d) Do the same for Piano II.

   (e) Try to determine what the dynamic "scale" must be, if 1 = *pppp* and 12 = *ffff*. Hint: Boulez inserts *quasi p* between *p* and *mp* and *quasi f* between *mf* and *f*.

   (f) Use the dynamic scale to determine which matrix diagonals are being used for Piano I and Piano II. Note that the dynamics in Example 13–B–1 count twice for each piano because they apply to two row forms.

**Boulez: Structures 1a (1952), mm. 8–15.** *(Copyright 1955 by Universal Edition (London) Ltd., London. Copyright renewed. All rights reserved. Used by permission of European American Music Distributors Corporation, sole U.S. and Canadian agent for Universal Edition (London) Ltd., London.)*

2. Analyze Stravinsky's use of his five-note row in the "Dirge-Canons (Prelude)" from *In Memoriam Dylan Thomas* (discussed on p. 277). In addition to labeling the row forms, comment on the relative consonance and dissonance of the vertical sonorities used.

## Part C: Composition

1. Compose an excerpt that will be similar to Nono's *Il canto sospeso* (discussed earlier). Instead of four strands use three—eighth-note, triplet eighth-note, and sixteenth-note—or choose three durations of your own. Notate each strand on a separate staff. Use Nono's pitch set, but instead of using Nono's twelve-element duration series, use this eleven-element series: 1, 2, 3, 5, 8, 13, 8, 5, 3, 2,1. Continue through at least three statements of the durational series (33 notes). If possible, this should be composed for instruments in your class. Make the rhythms as easy to read as you can, and include an analysis.

## FURTHER READING

ANTOKOLETZ, ELLIOTT. *Twentieth-Century Music*. See Chapter 15, Total Serialization in Europe, and pp. 387–396.

BRINDLE, REGINALD SMITH. *The New Music*. See Chapter 5, Integral Serialism, and Chapter 6, Numbers.

———. *Serial Composition*. See Chapter 14, Permutations and Other Variants of a Series, and the section titled "Integral Serialism" in Chapter 15.

DALLIN, LEON. *Techniques of Twentieth Century Composition*. See Chapter 15, Total Organization.

GRIFFITHS, PAUL. *Modern Music and After*. See "Europe 2: Total Organization, 1949–1954" and pp. 59–69.

———. "Serialism," in Stanley Sadie, ed., *The New Grove Dictionary of Music and Musicians*.

LESTER, JOEL. *Analytic Approaches to Twentieth-Century Music*. See Chapter 15, Other Aspects of Serialism, and pp. 277–285.

MORGAN, ROBERT P. *Twentieth-Century Music*. See Chapter 16, Integral Serialism.

SIMMS, BRYAN R. *Music of the Twentieth Century*. See pp. 84–90, 108–112, 348–352.

STRAUS, JOSEPH N. *Introduction to Post-Tonal Theory*. See pp. 235–245.

WITTLICH, GARY. "Sets and Ordering Procedures in Twentieth-Century Music," in Wittlich, ed., *Aspects of Twentieth-Century Music*. See pp. 430–444.

# ──── FOURTEEN ────

# The Roles of Chance
# and Choice
# in Twentieth-Century
# Music

## INTRODUCTION

There has been a general tendency in Western music to restrict the performer's options ever more closely, and at the same time an increasing dedication to honoring the composer's intentions at the expense of the performer's creativity. Compare Bach's *Well-Tempered Clavier* (1722, 1742), which lacks any indications of tempo, dynamics, or articulation, with Debussy's Preludes (1910, 1913), which are full of detailed and descriptive instructions, and compare them both with the examples of integral serialism in which every note has its own dynamic marking and articulation. Though elements of chance are present in any live musical performance (after all, there is always the possibility of a mistake), the emphasis has usually been on more control, not on improvisation.

Nevertheless, an important force in music in the second half of the twentieth century has moved in just the opposite direction, toward less control by the composer and more creative responsibility for the performer. As we shall see, this new responsibility can range from making an insignificant decision to shaping all aspects of the piece. In either case, the composer deliberately leaves something unspecified, up to chance or to the whim of the performer. Two terms used for music of this sort are **indeterminacy** and **aleatory.** Though some authors attempt to make a distinction between these two terms, we will not do so in this text.

A less significant but related movement has made use of chance in the compositional process itself. If it is a good thing for the composer to be less involved in the way a piece is to be performed, then it might follow that the composer should also be less involved in the way that it is composed, and this can be accomplished by introducing elements of chance into the compositional process.

These two approaches—chance in composition and choice in performance—form the two related branches of **experimental music,** a term that is appropriate for any music in which the final product is deliberately kept beyond the control of the composer.

## CHANCE IN COMPOSITION

In order to allow chance to play a part in composition, the composer must decide what aspects of the work are to be decided by chance and what the range of probabilities of each aspect should be. For example, we could compose a piece for piano without dynamics and then apply the dynamics randomly by flipping coins or rolling dice. We would still have to decide on the range of the dynamics (perhaps *ppp* to *fff*) and how often they were to change. In general, however, composers who make use of chance apply it much more broadly than this.

The most influential composer to make extensive use of chance in composition was an American, John Cage, who was mentioned in Chapter 8 in connection with Oriental philosophy (see p. 172). In a number of his chance compositions, Cage made use of procedures drawn from the *I-Ching*, a Chinese treatise on probabilities, making each decision by tossing a coin six times and looking up the result on a table of "hexagrams" that represent symbolically the 64 possible outcomes (that is, 2 to the 6th power) for six coin tosses.

*Imaginary Landscapes No. 4* (1951) provides an early example of Cage's use of chance and an example of his originality as well. Presumably Cage decided without the help of chance the instrumentation of this piece (twelve radios) and the number of performers (two for each radio). The *I-Ching* was employed to help determine the changing dynamic levels and frequencies to which each radio would be set. All of this is notated on a twelve-stave score employing both traditional musical symbols and numbers. Even though the score is precisely notated, chance has a role in the performance as well, because the signals that the radios pick up are unpredictable and will vary with each performance. The *I-Ching* was also used by Cage for *Williams Mix* (see pp. 154 and 247), as well as in other works.

Composers have employed other random decision-making techniques as well, of course. Cage used imperfections in paper to determine the placement of notes in *Music for Piano* (1952–56) and astronomical maps for *Atlas Eclipticalis* (1962). The arias for his opera *Europera 1* (1987) are selected by the nineteen singers from any out-of-copyright operas, although the singers do not know until the last minute whether or when they will actually get to sing. The orchestra parts are photocopies of instrumental parts selected at random by the composer, also from out-of-copyright operas. The parts may be distributed to the players at random. Perhaps the most outlandish use of chance is *The Thousand Symphonies* (1968) by Dick Higgins, in which the "score" was produced by firing a machine gun at manuscript paper.

Computers have been used to some extent in chance composition, since they can be programmed to produce an apparently random series of numbers within a specified range and to use those numbers in decision-making processes. The speed of a computer makes practical the use of much more complex probabilistic procedures. Conditional probabilities, for example, can vary according to one or more conditions that have been decided on previously. As a very simple example, suppose we want to generate a melody that will conform to the following rules:

1. Use only the notes C, E, and G.
2. Allow no repeated notes.
3. Use fewer G's than C's or E's.
4. Distribute the C's and E's evenly.

The following table would tend to produce such a melody, although we still must specify its length and the first note. To use the table, find the most recent note on the left border. Then use the percentages shown in that row to generate some note on the top border. For instance, if C is the most recent note generated, then the next note will probably be E (75%) but might be G (25%).

|   | *C* | *E* | *G* |
|---|---|---|---|
| G | 50% | 50% | 0% |
| E | 75% | 0% | 25% |
| C | 0% | 75% | 25% |

Conditional probabilities can be nested to any depth, with the result that the selection of a particular event may depend upon the results of the last several decisions.

Lejaren Hiller is a composer whose name is often associated with computer composition.[1] Together with Leonard Isaacson, he composed the first serious computer piece, the *Illiac Suite for String Quartet*, in 1957. Though the *Illiac Suite* was somewhat tentative creatively, the *Computer Cantata* (1963), by Hiller and Robert Baker, is a more substantial composition and explores conditional probabilities systematically. Other composers associated with this technique include Iannis Xenakis, who calls his computer music "stochastic music," Larry Austin, whose *Canadian Coastlines* (1981) is a complex eight-part canon for instruments and tape, and Barry Vercoe, whose *Synapse for Viola and Computer-Synthesized Tape* is a serial work in which many of the details were decided by a computer.

Computers have also been used for many years in an attempt to create new music in the style of some composer of the past, such studies typically concentrating either upon the compositional process or upon how a musical style is defined. Important work in the latter area has been done in recent years by the composer David Cope.

## CHOICE IN PERFORMANCE

Aleatory in performance can range all the way from the most insignificant detail to the entire shape of the piece. On the one hand are works in which the indeterminate elements may be so unimportant that any two performances of the piece will be very similar; on the other hand are pieces that are totally improvised and will vary greatly from one performance to the next. The elements of composition that may be left up to the performer include the following:

Medium (instrumentation)

Expression (dynamics, etc.)

Duration (rhythm and tempo)

Pitch

Form

In practice, these categories often appear in combination, but it will be useful to discuss them briefly individually, after which we will consider some examples from the literature.

Leaving the performing medium unspecified is not a practice unique to the twentieth century—Bach's *Art of Fugue* (1750) is a famous eighteenth-century example—but it is a practice that had been largely abandoned for some time. Nevertheless, a number of twentieth-century works leave open either the performing medium or the number of performers, or both.

Expression, including everything from dynamics and articulation to the most subtle nuance, has been of increasing concern to most composers. Even from Mozart to Beethoven we see development in this area, and much more from Beethoven to Debussy. However, composers interested in allowing the performer to have more freedom frequently omit expression marks, although the usual practice is not to do so unless other aspects of the piece are also indeterminate.

Indeterminacy in duration can be handled in a number of ways. Tempos can be "as fast as possible" or "as slow as possible." Rhythm can be left open by providing noteheads on the staff while leaving the durations completely up to the performer. The composer can exercise more control by the use of **proportional notation**, in which the spacing of the notes on the page indicates their approximate durations, as in Example 6–9 (p. 125).

A simple example of pitch indeterminacy is the instruction "as high as possible." More extended examples often show the general contour, while leaving the precise pitches up to the performer. An instance of this was encountered in Example 6–10 on p. 126. Here the flutes are given apparently random contours to follow repetitively for eighteen seconds, after which all are to begin at a fairly low pitch and work their way upward. A composer may choose not to provide even a contour, in which case the choice of pitch and register is entirely up to the performer.

The usual method of leaving the form of a work unspecified, short of total improvisation, is to allow the performer or conductor to choose the order in which the sections of a piece will be performed, how often they will be performed, and even whether they will be performed at all. This approach to form is sometimes called **open form** or **mobile form.**

Free improvisation, where nothing is specified, can be exhilarating for the performer, but it never seemed to catch on and was largely a phenomenon of the 1970s. More structured improvisation has had followers since at least the 1960s, and it is still flourishing under the guidance of composer-performers like John Zorn.

## SOME EXAMPLES OF PERFORMER INDETERMINACY

Stockhausen's *Piano Piece XI (Klavierstück XI)* (1956) was one of the first European works to employ open form. The score, a single page roughly 21 × 37 inches, consists of nineteen precisely notated segments of varying lengths, the proportions being governed by a Fibonacci series.[2] The segments are played in any order, and the performer is instructed to choose the order randomly without intentionally linking one to another. If a segment is played a second time, instructions in parentheses such as *8va* may allow some variation. When a segment is "arrived at for the third time," the piece is over, even though some segments may not have been played at all. Each segment is followed by symbols that specify tempo, dynamics, and mode of attack, and these are to be applied to the *next* segment in each case (the performer chooses the tempo, dynamics, and mode of attack for the first segment that is performed).

Cornelius Cardew's *Octet '61 for Jasper Johns* (1961) is a free-form composition "not necessarily for piano." The score consists of sixty "signs" that are to be interpreted cyclically—that is, sign 60 is followed by sign 1. The performer may begin anywhere and end anywhere, and the signs may be taken in reverse order if desired. An additional wild-card sign is provided for use "anywhere and as often as desired." The first six signs are shown in Example 14–1. Notice that sign 1 includes the Arabic numerals 6 and 7, sign 3 contains 3 and 5, and sign 6 contains 1, 6, and 7. Cardew provides hints for interpreting some of the symbols used in the signs, but the instructions emphasize creativity and interpretation rather than conformity. As an illustration of one of the many ways of interpreting signs 1–6, Cardew provides the illustration seen in Example 14–2. His key to the illustration follows the example.

**EXAMPLE 14–1**   Cardew: *Octet '61 for Jasper Johns* (1961), signs 1–6    *(Used by permission of C. F. Peters Corporation, on behalf of Hinrichsen Edition, Ltd., London. © 1962 by Hinrichsen Edition, Ltd.)*

**EXAMPLE 14–2**  Cardew: *Octet '61 for Jasper Johns* (1961), illustration and key from instructions to score  *(Used by permission of C. F. Peters Corporation, on behalf of Hinrichsen Edition, Ltd., London. © 1962 by Hinrichsen Edition, Ltd.)*

1.  Seven taken literally as a configuration in musical space. Six Cs, one added to each of the first six signs.

2.  Add E flats.

3.  Three As. Five A flats. Three sustained notes *forte:* the others *piano* or *pianissimo.* Five-note cluster-type chord.

4.  Two chords *piano* following the dot-dash rhythm of the Gs in 3.

5.  Slide from E down towards B.

6.  Six different registers for D (colour pitch). Seven described as in 1. One described as subsequent cluster. One C at given pitch—longer duration.

Stockhausen's *Piano Piece X (Klavierstück X)* (1961) calls for a tempo "as fast as possible." Macro-durations are indicated above the staff, as in Example 14–3. Here the durations above the staff are a quarter-note, a double whole-note tied to an eighth-note, an eighth-note, and so on. The pitches on the staff are to be played within the given duration, with ascending and descending beams indicating *accelerando* and *ritardando*. The long slurs that join some stems (for instance, the F♯4–G4 in the right hand near the beginning) call for the first note to be sustained until the second one is reached. The visual attractiveness of *Piano Piece X* is part of its appeal, and the same is true of many works composed in the second half of the century. Perhaps more than in any other period, it is helpful for the contemporary composer to be competent at drafting or in the use of notational software.

# Klavierstück X

Karlheinz Stockhausen

290

Morton Feldman's *The Straits of Magellan* (1962), for seven instruments, is a good example of controlled ensemble improvisation. Each box in Example 14–4 represents a unit of the basic tempo, M.M. 88. An empty box stands for silence. The other boxes are to be realized by improvisation, except that the symbol in each box restricts what the performer can do:

> *Arabic numeral:* Play that many notes in succession, except for the pianist, who should play them as a chord.
>
> *Roman numeral:* Play that many notes as a chord.
>
> *F:* Flutter-tongue one tone.
>
> *T:* Double-tongue one tone.
>
> *Diamond:* Play as a harmonic.

The dynamics are specified as "very low throughout," and "all sounds are to be played with a minimum of attack."

**EXAMPLE 14–4**    Feldman: *The Straits of Magellan* (1962), first 20 boxes on p. 1
(© 1962 by C. F. Peters Corporation. Used by permission.)

The third movement of Lukas Foss's *Baroque Variations* (1967) is titled "On a Bach Prelude (Phorion)" and is based on the Prelude to Bach's Partita in E Major for solo violin (an example of quotation music—see Chapter 8). This orchestral work requires a number of choices on the part of both the conductor and the performers. For example, at rehearsal no. 2 in the score, a section that "should last circa 2 minutes," the conductor chooses from four groups of instrumentalists, cuing first one, then another, with only general instructions in the score concerning which groups to favor and which to neglect. At 3, five soloists play passages they have selected independently from the "Bach sheet" provided with the score, while at 5 the woodwinds are provided with noteheads and the instruction to "place anywhere within bar, unevenly. Vary placement." Similar techniques are used throughout the movement, with nearly all of the pitch material being derived from the Bach work.

Foss's *Thirteen Ways of Looking at a Blackbird* (1978) uses a number of interesting techniques, including tape delay and pitch indeterminacy. The tenth song begins with a 30-second improvised duet for flute and percussion, the percussionist playing on the strings of a piano with tape-covered triangle beaters. Example 14–5 shows the composer's instructions for this duet along with a sample beginning. Note especially the instruction to "Use all twelve notes." The effect desired here, as in most improvisations, is one of free atonality, not serialism, and certainly not diatonicism.

EXAMPLE 14–5    Foss: *Thirteen Ways of Looking at a Blackbird* (1978), X, instructions and first system    *(Copyright © 1979 by Pembroke Music Co., Inc. Reprinted by permission.)*

The single movement of Witold Lutoslawski's Symphony No. 3 (1983) contains a number of *ad libitum* passages, most of them involving a kind of uncontrolled imitation. In Example 14–6 the conductor provides cues at nine points (see the arrows above the score) but otherwise does not conduct. The winds play their repeated patterns at a fast tempo, essentially in an uncoordinated fashion, until the conductor cues a change of pattern (the last arrow) or begins a conducted section. Notice that each group (piccolo/flutes, oboes, and horns) has its own pitch material and that the patterns within each choir are somewhat similar, resulting in uncontrolled imitation within each group. (In this excerpt, all of the instruments except the piccolo sound as written, and an accidental applies only to the note it precedes.) Other composers have sought simpler solutions to this problem. Einojuhani Rautavaara in his Symphony No. 5 (1985) uses a performance direction of "independently," while John Corigliano in his Symphony No. 1 specifies "nonaligned," both of which result in a similar kind of uncontrolled imitation.

EXAMPLE 14–6   Lutoslawski: Symphony No. 3 (1903), pp. 1–2 (winds only)

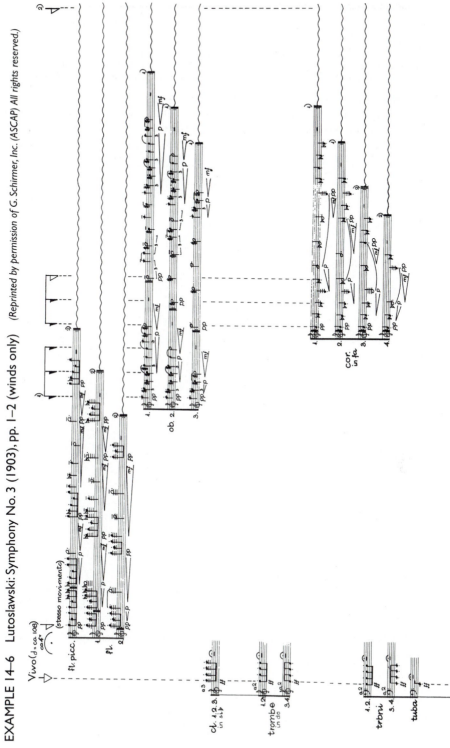

## GRAPHIC SCORES AND TEXT SCORES

A graphic score is one in which conventional musical notation has been abandoned in favor of geometric shapes and designs that suggest more or less clearly how the music is to be performed. The Feldman excerpt (Example 14–4) is an example of one approach to graphic notation. Whereas Feldman provides fairly specific guidance for his performers, Martin Bartlett provides much less for the unspecified ensemble that is to perform the second movement of *Lines from Chuang-Tzu* (1973). In this movement, shown in its entirety in Example 14–7, dynamics are indicated by the size of the dots. Nothing else is specified.

EXAMPLE 14–7   Bartlett: *Lines from Chuang-Tzu* (1973), II   *(Reprinted from SOURCE: Music of the Avant Garde, Issue 11, 1972, with permission from Composer/Performer Edition, 2109 Woodbrook, Denton, TX 76205.)*

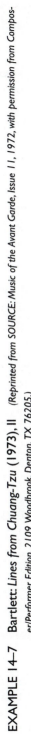

Even less information is given by Robin Mortimore for *Very Circular Pieces* (1970). In the movement shown in Example 14–8, "Repeat" is the only performance instruction.

EXAMPLE 14–8   Mortimore: *Very Circular Pieces* (1970), "Circular Piece"   *(Reprinted from SOURCE: Music of the Avant Garde, Issue 10, 1971, with permission from Composer/Performer Edition, 2109 Woodbrook, Denton, TX 76205.)*

A text score is one that consists only of words. The text usually provides instructions for an improvisation, but it may do little more than set a mood. Three examples will suffice as models. Christian Wolff's "Play," from the *Prose Collection* (1969), is fairly specific in its instructions. The beginning is shown in Example 14–9.

EXAMPLE 14–9   Wolff: *Prose Collection*, "Play," first forty-six words   *(Copyright © G. Schirmer, Inc. (ASCAP) International copyright secured. All rights reserved. Used by permission.)*

Play, make sounds, in short bursts,
Clear in outline for the most part;
quiet; two or three times more towards
as loud as possible, but as soon as you
cannot hear yourself or another player
stop directly. Allow various spaces
between playing (2, 5 seconds, indefinite). . . .

The second example, Stockhausen's *For Times to Come* (1970) (Example 14–10), is a composition for an unspecified ensemble, and it illustrates what Stockhausen calls "intuitive music."

EXAMPLE 14–10   Stockhausen: *For Times to Come* (1970), "Waves"   *(Reprinted with permission of Stockhausen-Verlag, 5067 Kuerten, West Germany.)*

Overtake the others
Hold the lead
Allow yourself to be overtaken
Less often

The third example, Stephen Montague's *Quintet* (1978), instructs the performer to record four interpretations of "a famous work" on the four tracks of a tape. The tape is then to be played while the musician performs live yet another interpretation, so that the audience hears the five versions simultaneously, each with its own tempos, dynamics, and so forth.

## MUSIC ON THE FRINGE

In the 1960s and 1970s especially, a number of composers wrote pieces that seem to many musicians to push the limits of what can be called "music." Traditional definitions of music often include references to organized sound and to the expression of ideas and emotions, but some works challenge these notions. One example is the last movement of Dick Higgins's *Constellations for the Theater (Number X)* (1965), a text score given in its entirety as Example 14–11.

EXAMPLE 14–11   Higgins: *Constellations for the Theatre (Number X)* (1965),"A Winter Carol"   *From Constellations and Contributions by Dick Higgins. (Copyright © 1961 by Richard C. Higgins. All rights reserved. Reprinted by permission.)*

> Any number of people may perform this composition. They do so by agreeing in advance on a duration for the composition, then by going out to listen in the falling snow.

This is not the only work to concentrate the attention of the audience on the natural sounds that exist in the environment. Pauline Oliveros's *Bonn Feier* (1976) is an environmental theater piece that uses an entire city or university as its performance stage. All of the normal activities that take place in the environment are part of the performance, but there are also a large number of specialized performers—actors, groups of musicians, picketers carrying blank signs, and so on. In addition, there are a number of "costumed guardians" who stand near the sources of everyday environmental sounds (motors, practice rooms, traffic) and point them out to people who pass by. The piece ends with a "final ritual" in which the performers move in a circle around a bonfire chanting "Feier" (the German word for a celebration or festival) "until each person can no longer participate."[3]

A famous work that often outrages audiences new to it is Cage's 4'33" (1952), for any instrument or combination of instruments. It consists of three movements, each of which consists only of the direction "Tacet," the durations of the three movements adding up to 4'33". While usually performed at the piano, it can be effective as an ensemble piece as well.

Other works seem at first to be hopelessly absurd, but the underlying purpose may still be serious. A movement of Mortimore's *Very Circular Pieces* (1970) contains the performance instruction "Play until 2000 A.D." What are we to do with this? Does it mean the piece is not to be performed at all? Or were we to keep it in our minds until the year 2000? Or was the purpose to encourage us to meditate on the coming millennium? And what about Paul Ignace's *Symphonie Fantastique No. 2*, a duplication of the Berlioz work sprung upon an unsuspecting concert audience, many of whom had heard the Berlioz the previous night? Is the purpose here humor, surprise, or, as the composer suggests, to get people to listen to the music in a new way?[4]

The list of musics "on the fringe" goes on and on. There is, for example, "biofeedback music," in which the performers control the sounds by means of changing the alpha-wave output from their brains. More sinister is a category that David Cope calls "danger music."[5] Some of it suggests self-directed violence, as in Takehisa Kosugi's *Music for a Revolution*, which begins, "Scoop out one of your eyes five years from now,"[6] while others, such as Philip Corner's *One Antipersonnel-Type CBU Bomb Will Be Thrown into the Audience*, are more threatening to the audience.

Lively accounts of these and other "fringe" movements can be found in the books by Cope and Michael Nyman listed at the end of this chapter.

### SUMMARY

Experimental music, in which the composer consciously abdicates control over the compositional process or the performance, or both, has been an important element of music in the second half of the twentieth century. Chance in composition has involved the use of a number of decision-making techniques, including the *I-Ching*, while the computer has made practicable aleatoric compositions that are much more complex. The element of chance (or, from the performer's viewpoint, choice) has been even more influential in the performance of music than in composition. The improvised portions of a score may be insignificant, or improvisation may be the major element of interest in the work. New notations have been devised for indeterminate music, including proportional and graphic notation; text scores dispense with notation entirely. Finally, a number of "fringe" movements have ranged from the absurd to the violent, calling into question our notion of what music really is.

### NOTES

1. Do not make the all-too-common error of confusing computer sound synthesis (see Chapter 12) with computer composition. Either or both may be employed in a particular composition.
2. Robin Maconie, *The Works of Karlheinz Stockhausen*, p. 101.
3. Oliveros, *Bonn Feier*.
4. Cope, *New Directions in Music*, pp. 166–167.
5. Cope, *New Directions*, pp. 168–171.
6. Michael Nyman, *Experimental Music*, p. 68.

### EXERCISES

#### Part A: Analysis

1. Study the pitch material in each of the three choirs in Example 14–6, remembering that the score is written at concert pitch and that an accidental applies only to the note it precedes.

   (a) What is similar about the pitch material in the three choirs?

(b) Analyze the pitch-class set types found in each choir.

(c) Do the pitch classes used in the winds complete an aggregate?

(d) How does the pitch material in the three choirs relate to the E's that open the movement?

2. Look up the word "music" in at least two dictionaries, and copy out the main (first) definitions. (Use standard dictionaries—"music" is not defined in *The New Harvard Dictionary of Music.*) Then relate those definitions to the kinds of works discussed in this chapter. Do some of the works lie outside the definitions, and if so, should the definitions be changed? Are the definitions even too restrictive for more conservative twentieth-century music? Can you suggest a better definition for "music," or a term for the kinds of pieces that you feel are not really music?

## Part B: Composition and Performance

1. Compose and rehearse an improvisatory piece for ensemble. Try to restrict the choices of the performers so that the piece will have the same basic shape each time it is performed. Explain how your controls will satisfy the assignment. Then perform it twice for the class.

2. Compose a graphic score to be performed by a soloist (unspecified medium), with few instructions. Explain (to your instructor) how you decided on the arrangement of the graphic symbols and how they might be interpreted. Have it performed by a volunteer from your class.

3. Compose a short piece for some instrument in your class in which some of the compositional decisions are made by random choice (flipping coins, etc.), and explain how you composed it. Make two versions of the piece, and have both performed for the class.

## FURTHER READING

ANTOKOLETZ, ELLIOTT. *Twentieth-Century Music.* See pp. 474–497.

BATEMAN, WAYNE. *Introduction to Computer Music.* See Chapter 11, Composition with the Computer.

BRINDLE, REGINALD SMITH. *The New Music.* See Chapter 8, Indeterminacy, Chance, and Aleatory Music; Chapter 9, Improvisation–Graphic Scores–Text Scores; and Chapter 12, Cage and Other Americans.

CHILDS, BARNEY. "Indeterminacy," in John Vinton, ed., *Dictionary of Contemporary Music.*

COPE, DAVID H. *Computers and Musical Style.*

———. *Experiments in Musical Intelligence.*

———. *New Directions in Music.* See Chapter 5, Indeterminacy; Chapter 6, Experimentalism; and Chapter 10, Automated Music.

DALLIN, LEON. *Techniques of Twentieth Century Composition.* See Chapter 18, Indeterminate Procedures.

DODGE, CHARLES, AND THOMAS A. JERSE. *Computer Music*. See Chapter 8, Composition with Computers.

GRIFFITHS, PAUL. "Aleatory," in Stanley Sadie, ed., *The New Grove Dictionary of Music and Musicians*.

————. *Techniques of the Contemporary Composer*. See Chapter 14, Indeterminancy, and Chapter 17, Algorithmic Composition.

HEUSSENSTAMM, GEORGE. *The Norton Manual of Music Notation*.

KARKOSCHKA, ERHARD. *Notation in New Music*.

KOSTELANETZ, RICHARD, ed. *John Cage*.

MORGAN, ROBERT P. *Twentieth-Century Music*. See Chapter 17, Indeterminacy.

NYMAN, MICHAEL. *Experimental Music*. See Chapter 3, Inauguration 1950–60: Feldman, Brown, Wolff, Cage; Chapter 4, Seeing, Hearing: Flexus; Chapter 5, Electronic Systems; and Chapter 6, Indeterminacy 1960–70: Ichiyanagi, Ashley, Wolff, Cardew, Scratch Orchestra.

READ, GARDNER. *Modern Rhythmic Notation*.

SIMMS, BRYAN. *Music of the Twentieth Century*. See Chapter 13, Indeterminacy.

STONE, KURT. *Music Notation in the Twentieth Century*.

WILLIAMS, J. KENT. *Theories and Analyses of Twentieth-Century Music*. See Chapter 16, Chance and Indeterminacy.

# FIFTEEN

# Minimalism and Beyond

## INTRODUCTION

This chapter is concerned with minimalism and with other trends that came to the fore even later. These later trends are known by an array of labels such as postminimalism, the new romanticism, the new tonality, totalism eclecticism, and polystylistics. All of these categories, which are for the most part fuzzily defined and overlapping, share at least one characteristic with each other as well as with minimalism: to some extent, at least, the music that they represent is pitch-centric and occasionally even tonal in the traditional sense of the term.

## MINIMALISM

**Minimal music,** also called **process music, phase music, pulse music, systemic music,** and **repetitive music,** may have had its roots in some of the works that Cage, Wolff, and Feldman composed in the 1950s, but the first important example of what has become known as minimalism was Terry Riley's *In C* (1964). This composition, still well known today, exemplifies most of the characteristics of the minimalist style, and we will discuss it in some detail.

*In C* is a composition of unspecified duration to be performed by an unspecified ensemble. The score consists of 53 figures—most of them quite short—that are to be performed in order. Each motive is repeated as often as the individual performer desires, except that the performer has an obligation to contribute to the overall ensemble effect. This means that the performers more or less randomly follow each other through the score, sometimes leading the rest of the ensemble, at other times lagging behind, so that several motives may be heard simultaneously, even though gradual progress is being made toward ending the piece. This process, sometimes called **phasing,** resembles that of a traditional canon, which is why *In C* was discussed in Chapter 7 under the heading "Canon and Fugue" (see p. 151).

The pitch material of the figures is extremely limited, very different from the complex motivic material of the avant-garde composers of the same period. They begin by establishing C major (see figures 1–2 in Example 15–1). A half-cadence on the dominant is reached at figure 15 (see figures 14–15), followed by an E minor section in figures 18–28 (see figure 22). After a return to C in 29–34 (see figure 29), a tonally ambiguous climax is reached at 35 (see figure 35). The remainder of the piece seems to return to C for a while but ends in G minor (see figures 52–53). Superimposed over this modulating canon is a constant pulse, or ostinato, provided by a pianist playing the two highest C's on the instrument in steady eighth-notes.

In all, the work employs only nine of the twelve pitch classes, and the nine are introduced gradually:

| Figure | New Pitch Class |
|---|---|
| 1 | C, E |
| 2 | F |
| 4 | G |
| 9 | B |
| 14 | F♯ |
| 22 | A |
| 35 | B♭ |
| 45 | D |

**EXAMPLE 15–1**    Riley: *In C* (1964), Figures 1, 2, 14, 15, 22, 29, 35, 52, 53

*(Used by permission of the composer.)*

Because it occurs so rarely, the introduction of a new pitch class, or of a new register, becomes a major event in the piece. Even without mentally cataloguing the pitch material used up to that point, the listener is immediately affected, even shocked, by the appearance of a previously unheard pitch.

Many of the characteristics of minimalism have been encountered in our discussion of *In C*. These characteristics would include the following:

Restricted pitch and rhythm materials
Tonal (or neotonal) language
Diatonicism
Use of repetition
Phasing
Drones or ostinatos
Steady pulse
Static harmony
Indeterminacy
Long duration

Many of these aspects are also found in some kinds of Eastern music, as is the meditative quality characteristic of many minimalist works. Riley, Steve Reich, and Philip Glass, the three Americans most closely associated with minimalism, all studied Eastern music, Glass's study of the improvisations of Ravi Shankar being especially important to the development of his mature style.[1]

Reich's *Come Out* (1966) was mentioned in Chapter 12 in reference to the tape loops that were used to construct the piece (see p. 247). *Come Out* concentrates on the phasing aspect of minimalism, taking it much further than *In C* does, and it incidentally illustrates the interest that some twentieth-century composers have had in mixing their music with politics. In this case, a victim of police violence during the 1964 Harlem riots wanted to prove that he was injured so that he would be taken to the hospital. He explains, "I had to, like, open the bruise up and let some of the bruise blood come out to show them." The words "come out to show them" were transferred to two loops and played simultaneously, but since no two tape players operate at precisely the same speed, the words move gradually out of phase. A recording of that process was in turn converted into two loops, and so on, building up the texture of the work to a dense and complex level.[2]

Notice that the phasing process in *Come Out* is different from that used in *In C*, because in *Come Out* the part that takes the lead keeps it and pulls ever farther ahead of the follower. Reich used the same approach for live performers in *Piano Phase* (1967). In this work the two pianists repeat in unison the pattern seen in Example 15–2, but soon Piano II increases the tempo slightly until the two instruments are one sixteenth-note apart. This process is repeated until Piano II completes the "loop" and rejoins Piano I in unison.

Gradually moving out of phase as in *Piano Phase* is difficult for performers to accomplish. Reich employs a simpler solution in *Clapping Music* (1972). Here the two performers clap the first measure in unison twelve times. They then move on to the second measure, in which the pattern in the Clap 2 part has been shifted one eighth-note to the left. After twelve times through this measure, the performers move on to the next, where Clap 2 is shifted one more eighth-note, and so on, until they are once more in unison.

A variation on the phasing technique was introduced by Reich in *Drumming* (1971) and *Six Pianos* (1973) (rescored as *Six Marimbas* in 1986). *Six Pianos* begins with four of the pianists playing a repeated rhythmic pattern in unison (rhythmic unison, not pitch unison). The two "out-of-phase" pianists, in unison with each other, gradually introduce a rhythmic pattern that, when completed, turns out to be the same as the original one, but two beats out of phase with it. Similar techniques are used in Reich's *Sextet* (1985). An important difference between this technique and the earlier phase pieces is that in this case the relationship between the two out-of-phase parts does not change through time.

Reich's *New York Counterpoint* (1985) makes extensive use of pulsing and various kinds of phasing. It is written for eleven clarinets, but ten of the clarinet parts are usually prerecorded by a single clarinetist, who then plays the "Live Cl." part along with the tape. The first movement begins with several minutes of pulsing chords, all diatonic to A♭ major, with the various parts fading in and out. Melodic patterns later appear that are phased as in Example 15–3. The three parts here are in a strict rhythmic canon, but the pitch material, while identical, is slightly reordered in each part. Similar techniques are used throughout the composition. Comparable works are *Vermont Counterpoint* (1982) and *Electric Counterpoint* (1987) for flute and guitar, respectively.

Another more recent work by Reich, *Different Trains* (1988), recalls his interest in the recorded human voice in *Come Out*, discussed earlier in this chapter. Here, though, the recorded voice is not looped but instead provides the basic motivic material for the string quartet that plays along with the taped voices and train sounds.

Though phasing is important in many of Reich's pieces, this is not true of all minimalist music.[3] Frederic Rzewski's *Coming Together* (1972), for example, another work with political overtones, is for a narrator accompanied by a single musical line, so phasing is impossible. Glass's *Strung Out* (1967) is for a single amplified violin, which begins by stating the central motive of the piece, seen in Example 15–4. Like *In C*, it gradually introduces pitches, in this case all diatonic to C major, until the climax of the piece is reached about 10'30" into the performance, after which the entire piece is repeated. Though the gradual introduction of pitches is important, the listener's attention is also drawn to the variation of the original motive, as well as to the two startling changes of bow technique (at about 2'50" and 6'25").

**EXAMPLE 15–4**  Glass: *Strung Out* (1967), opening five notes  *(Copyright © 1976 by Dunvagen Music Publishers, Inc. All rights reserved. Reprinted by Permission of G. Schirmer, Inc.)*

Nor is phasing a factor in Glass's ensemble works. Instead, the focus is on repetition, pulse, and triadic harmony. His music is insistently tonal, with harmonic progressions that range from banal to surprising. An example on the banal side is *Modern Love Waltz* (1977), where the harmony alternates throughout between an A major triad or an A dominant 7th chord and a B♭ dominant 7th chord.

Glass's *Wichita Vortex Sutra* (1988) consists of 136 measures, almost all of them repeated, in the key of F major. This lack of tonal variety is tiresome to some, but obviously not to all. The excerpt in Example 15–5 is typical of the work.

**EXAMPLE 15–5**  Glass: *Wichita Vortex Sutra* (1988), mm. 35–37  *(Copyright © 1988 by Dunvagen Music Publishers, Inc. International copyright secured. All rights reserved. Reprinted by Permission of G. Schirmer, Inc. (ASCAP))*

The usual approach that Glass takes in his more recent music is to establish a tempo through a pulsating background chord, over which various accompanimental figurations are laid. Changes of harmony follow, without disturbing the pulse or the accompanimental figures. After some time, an abrupt shift of tonal center, while maintaining the original pulse, announces a new section with new accompanimental figures. Melody in the traditional sense is absent. Glass frequently uses a singer in his works, but the vocalist usually has no text and instead is treated as an instrument.

Glass has achieved substantial popular success, enabling him to embark on larger projects. These include the operas *Einstein on the Beach* (1975), *Satyagraha* (1980), *The Photographer* (1983), *the CIVIL warS* (1984) and *Akhnaten* (1985), and the movie scores for *Koyaanisqatsi* (1982), *Kundun* (1997), and *Naqoyqatsi* (2002), among others, as well as six symphonies and collaborations with various dance companies.

**EXAMPLE 15–6**  Adams: *Short Ride on a Fast Machine* (1986), mm. 1–4.  *(Copyright 1986 by Hendon Music, Inc., a Boosey & Hawkes Company. Reprinted by permission.)*

John Adams's *Short Ride on a Fast Machine* (1986) is a good (and exhilarating) example of minimalism. Example 15–6 illustrates a primary motive of the piece, a motive that is heard unchanged throughout much of the work. Notice that the two clarinet parts (which sound a minor third lower) are phased one eighth-note apart. Although the tonal center of the work is clearly D Mixolydian, it contains a good deal of chromaticism, including the final cadence: ♭II–♭V–I. The use of nondiatonic pitch material is one characteristic that distinguishes Adams's minimalist style from that of most other minimalists. In *The Wound Dresser* (1988), for example, the first nineteen measures consist of a single nondiatonic [014589] pitch-class set that unfolds mostly in triadic patterns. The other six pitch classes enter rather rapidly after that, completing the aggregate (all twelve pitch classes) by m. 27.

Morton Feldman is a composer who is often credited with providing the model for the minimalist movement, although little of his music is truly minimalist as defined in this chapter. However, *Piano and String Quartet* (1985) and *For Samuel Beckett* (1987) are good examples of late minimalism. Both feature slowly changing textures and pitch material and much repetition, but not of the insistent, pulsating variety that led some critics of minimalism to refer to it as "wallpaper music."

Minimalism began to lose its appeal in the 1980s, and most composers have moved on to other things or have at least branched out. For example, while several of the best known minimalist works were composed by John Adams, including *Shaker Loops* (1978) and *Nixon in China* (1987), there is very little even remotely minimalist about Adams's Violin Concerto (1993), and, in fact, much of it is atonal. On the other hand, his minimalist background is much more apparent in *Hoodoo Zephyr*, which dates from the same year, especially in the track titled "Bump." The term **postminimalism** is often used in connection with works that have a minimalist underpinning but that have a more complex surface and in which the compositional process is less transparent than in the minimalist works of the 1960s and 1970s.

The influence of the minimalists has been considerable. In the United States this can be seen in the music of Laurie Anderson, a "performance artist" whose work lies somewhere between the traditionally popular and traditionally serious, and in rock music in groups such as Tirez Tirez. In Europe, minimalism has had an influence on the music of a large number of composers and experimental rock groups.[4] Unfortunately, the student of this music will find that much of it is available only in recorded form, although scores are gradually becoming more available.

## BEYOND MINIMALISM

The music of the last two decades of the twentieth century and the first decade of the twenty-first presents a dizzying array of compositional approaches and techniques, and this is reflected in the titles of the final chapters of two books on contemporary music: David Cope's *Techniques of the Contemporary Composer*, which ends with a chapter titled "Decategorization," and Paul Griffiths's *Modern Music and After*, which ends with a nearly ninety-page discussion called "Strings and Knots." Of course, twentieth-century music has always been a study in contrasts, and that is one thing that makes the study of it so fascinating—and sometimes frustrating. It was a century in which very disparate composers such as Rachmaninoff (1873–1943) and Webern (1883–1945) could come out of Europe and one in which Copland (1900–1990) and Cage (1912–1992) were produced in the United States. What is different about the period we are talking about is that so many composers feel free to work in a number of styles, often combining contrasting compositional approaches—tonality and atonality, for example—within the same work and even within the same movement. This is what is referred to by terms like totalism, eclecticism, and polistylistics that were mentioned in the introduction to this chapter. You will encounter many instances of eclecticism in the works discussed later.

In Chapter 8 we discussed the use of musical quotations in twentieth-century music, especially in music composed in the mid-1960s and later. In most cases these fragments were quoted out of context, superimposed on an atonal, avant-garde background, or swallowed up in a collage of other quotations in a stream-of-consciousness style. Another movement, which paralleled and grew out of quotation music, involved the return of triadic harmony in a style that is sometimes called neoromanticism, or the new tonality. This is related as well to neotonality, a term that was introduced in Chapter 5 for music, tertian or not, that establishes a tonal center through nontraditional means. As we shall see, the more recent music we are examining here tends to be much more consonant and much more reminiscent of earlier music.

In the music of George Rochberg, quotation technique led eventually to a "real and personal rapprochement with the past"[5] in the form of a traditional tonal style with a distinctive Romantic flavor. His first neoromantic work was the String Quartet No. 3 (1972). The beginning of the first movement is devoted to the kind of dissonant and disjunct figure that one might expect at the outset of an atonal work (Example 15–7).

**EXAMPLE 15–7**   Rochberg: String Quartet No. 3 (1972), I, m. 1   *(Copyright © 1973, 1976 by Galaxy Music Corp., New York. Used with permission.)*

A more lyrical, yet still dissonant, figure interrupts at m. 27, but the dissonant opening motive returns in m. 40. Another lyrical section, related to the one at m. 27, begins at m. 64 and contains elements of polytonality and the whole-tone scale. This leads to the passage shown in Example 15–8. In that excerpt, at m. 87 a B major triad appears beneath the whole-tone/polytonal material. This is followed in mm. 90–102 by a conventional harmonic progression in the key of B major, although we are reminded from time to time of the whole-tone/bitonal material. This B major progression, though not a quotation, is handled in a manner that strongly suggests nineteenth-century music, yet it seems somehow to have a beauty and meaning that it would not possess if it appeared in a nineteenth-century composition. Its purity and the directness of its communication are striking when they are juxtaposed against the typically dissonant and symmetrical twentieth-century structures.[6]

EXAMPLE 15–8   Rochberg: String Quartet No. 3 (1972), I, mm. 81–102   *(Copyright © 1973, 1976 by Galaxy Music Corp., New York. Used with permission.)*

Not all of Rochberg's music since 1972 is neoromantic (his String Quartet No. 7 [1979], for example, is not at all in that style), but much of it is. Often Rochberg will include both tonal and atonal movements in the same work, rather than mixing the two together in a single movement as in Example 15–8. The first movement of his String Quartet No. 6 (1978) is atonal, but the second movement is a tonal scherzo and trio, and the third is a set of continuous variations on the tune from Pachelbel's Canon in D. Every movement but the fourth in his String Quartet No. 5 (1978) is in the neoromantic style; the third movement is a scherzo and trio in a familiar nineteenth-century idiom (see Example 15–9), although the careful observer might quibble with a few details, such as the parallel 5ths in m. 6.

EXAMPLE 15–9    Rochberg: String Quartet No. 5 (1978), III, mm. 1–8

While most tonal music composed in the last part of the twentieth century either contrasted tonal elements with atonal ones or in some other way made its posttonal orientation apparent, some works, like Keith Jarrett's *Bridge of Light* (1990), sound largely nineteenth-century in origin.

Though Rochberg is the composer whose name is most closely associated with neoromanticism in the United States, he is certainly not the only representative of the style. The series of works composed by David Del Tredici on Lewis Carroll's Alice stories are an important example. Some of the music of Frederic Rzewski might be considered neo-romantic, although the motivation in his case often seems to be political instead of musical, an example being his piano variations on *The People United Will Never Be Defeated!* (1975). Well-known Europeans associated with neoromanticism or the new tonality include Arvo Pärt, Krzysztof Penderecki, Alfred Schnittke, and John Tavener.

Composers in the late twentieth century found that they were again free to take advantage of the expressive power of the triad, even in an atonal context. An early use of triadic materials is Schnittke's Violin Sonata No. 2 ("quasi una Sonata") (1968), an atonal work that is introduced by a loud, widely spaced G minor triad that reappears frequently in this one-movement work. The effect is reminiscent of the beginning of Stravinsky's *Symphony of Psalms* (see p. 232). Einojuhani Rautavaara's Symphony No. 5 (1986), also an atonal work, begins with a progression that takes nearly three minutes to unfold: C–e♭–d–F♯. (Notice the two doubly-chromatic mediants.) Each chord begins softly, builds in intensity, and then explodes in a dissonance from which the next sonority gradually emerges.

John Tavener's *Celtic Requiem* (1969) is an extraordinary collage of materials from nursery rhymes to noise over an ever-present E♭ major triad. His *The Protecting Veil* (1987) is pitch-centric throughout; in fact the first four minutes of the work are entirely diatonic in F major, although traditional tonal progressions are not used, and the first movement ends over a C♯m7 chord. The work does end in F major.

Tavener and others occasionally reach back historically for techniques that even predate tonality. Examples include mensuration canons in Pärt's *Festina Lente* (1988) and Tavener's *The Protecting Veil*. In Example 15–10, the parallel fifths between the Solo Cello and Cello I evoke medieval organum, but the dissonances created by the real inversion in Cello II are obviously from a later century.

EXAMPLE 15–10    Tavener: *The Protecting Veil* (1987), first 2 measures after J

Penderecki's Symphony No. 2 (1980), though chromatic, is clearly in F♯ minor. The beginning of this work, shown in Example 15–11, seems to suggest that key, but it soon shifts to F minor. Especially striking and Romantic in flavor is the progression B minor–F minor in mm. 6–7.

**EXAMPLE 15–11**    Penderecki: Symphony No. 2 (1980), mm. 1–8

Pärt's *Fratres* (1977), a work that exists in several versions, is based upon a Phrygian scale on A with a raised third (C♯), which gives the work a wonderful major/minor quality. (In one version the scale is on G.) It is "tonal" throughout, as are his later works.

Triadic harmony in the new tonality may or may not conform to traditional tonal progressions. For instance, the nine triads in Example 15–12 contain only one fifth-related progression, the B♭ to E♭ from the second chord to the third one.

EXAMPLE 15–12    Schnittke: Piano Sonata No. 1 (1988), page 4

Example 15–13 is from a pitch-centric song that begins and ends in F and in which the harmonic language is largely tertian. Notice the conventional bass line at the beginning of the excerpt (F–G–A♭–B♭–C), although the chords above it are not simple triads.

EXAMPLE 15–13   Libby Larsen: *Sonnets from the Portuguese*, "I thought once how Theocritus had sung" (1991), mm. 7–11   *(© 1998, Oxford University Press.)*

Compositions in the new tonality do not, as a rule, adhere to the large-scale tonal relationships found in tonal music of earlier centuries. For example, each of the three movements of Gavin Bryars's *By the Var* (1987) begins in G♯ minor, but the piece ends in C major. Another example is Pärt's *Berlin Mass* (1992), which has the following tonal structure:

| | |
|---|---|
| Kyrie | G Aeolian |
| Gloria | G Aeolian/Minor |
| First Alleluia | G Major |
| Second Alleluia | E Aeolian |
| Veni Sancte Spiritus | E Aeolian |
| Credo | E Major |
| Sanctus | C♯ Aeolian |
| Agnus Dei | C♯ Aeolian–E Major |

Just as extraordinary, in traditional terms, as the relationship between the beginning and ending keys is the fact that, with the exception of the last movement, none of the movements contain modulations or even significant tonicizations of other keys.

## SUMMARY AND CONCLUSION

While the postserial avant-garde tradition has not died out, it has certainly met with serious opposition in the forms of indeterminacy, minimalism, and neoromanticism. Indeterminacy, the subject of Chapter 14, was a reaction against the total control that is the basis for integral serialism. Minimalism opposes the atonal ideals of the incessant recycling of pitch material, of constant variation, and, of course, of atonality itself. Neoromanticism does these things, too, but it represents also a complicated relationship between today's composer (and listener) and the music of the past.

And so twentieth-century music continues into the twenty-first century as it has always been—a maddening but fascinating collage of approaches and materials, a period without a style. It may be, of course, that the differences among composers and techniques that seem so blatant to us now will appear to be only matters of detail to later generations and that the music of the twentieth century will have a characteristic "sound" that will be easily identified, much as the sound of Haydn and Mozart represents a certain portion of the eighteenth century. But those who struggle to understand twentieth-century music are generally more impressed by its contrasts than by its consistencies.

One can't help but wonder about Brahms, who died in 1897 (when this writer's grandparents were teenagers): What would he think of what has happened to music, and could he have predicted in 1897 what music might be like in our time? Surely none of us can imagine what music will be like at the end of the twenty-first century, when the grandchildren of today's college students will themselves be grandparents, and the newest of today's music will represent a bygone era. It is enough, perhaps, if we can greet each turn in the musical road with an open mind, a receptive ear, and a sense of what has come before.

## NOTES

1. John Rockwell, *All American Music*, p. 111.

2. Barry Schrader, *Introduction to Electro-Acoustic Music*, pp. 19–20.

3. Some writers prefer to treat phase music as a separate category from minimalism, since minimalist music does not always employ phasing, but they share many of the same characteristics and are often created by the same composers.

4. A representative list is given in Wim Mertens, *American Minimal Music*, p. 11, to which might be added the names of Simon Bainbridge (British) and Wolfgang Rihm (German).

5. Rochberg, in the liner notes for Nonesuch album H-71283, *George Rochberg: String Quartet No. 3*.

6. An analysis of the first one hundred measures of this movement appears in Jay Reese, "Rochberg the Progressive."

## EXERCISES

### Part A: Analysis

1. Listen to a recording of Riley's *In C* (1964). Excerpts from this work are given in Example 15–1. Try to notate the other figures that make up the work.
2. Listen to a recording of Glass's *Strung Out* (1967). The opening is given in Example 15–4. Using a watch with a second hand, identify the introduction of new pitches (not pitch classes) as well as other significant events in the piece, such as changes in articulation. The piece is played twice without pause on the only available recording.
3. Analyze the harmonies and nonchord tones of the B major progression in Example 15–8.
4. Do the same for Example 15–9 (entire excerpt). You will find two chords that are almost traditional augmented-6th chords, but not quite.
5. Number the chords in Example 15–12, and label them according to root and type. Next, label any chromatic mediant progressions as "<cm>" and any doubly chromatic mediant progressions as "<dcm>." Analyze the other root relationships. Are there any repeated or sequenced progressions involving these chords?
6. Analyze the harmonies and nonchord tones in Example 15–13, being sure to take the vocal line into consideration. Identify the root and quality of the tertian chords in mm. 7, 8, 9 and 11. The nontertian chord in m. 10 will require a different approach.
7. Listen to the entire third movement of Rochberg's String Quartet No. 5. Diagram the form. Identify as many tonal areas and important cadences as you can (the movement begins in A minor).
8. Listen to the entire third movement of Rochberg's String Quartet No. 6. Write down the two lines that constitute the four-measure theme (the key is D major). Then try to follow the theme through the subsequent variations. After several variations (how many?), the theme is augmented into an eight-measure form for one variation—this happens again later. In other variations, the original lines of the theme are almost totally obscured, but the basic four-bar structure is still audible in most cases. Rochberg occasionally ends a variation on I instead of V, and in two variations he inverts the descending contour of the original melody. Try to identify and characterize each variation.

### Part B: Composition

1. Compose *In F*, an imitation of Riley's *In C*, for instruments and/or vocalists in your class. See the discussion of *In C* in the text.
2. Compose a phase piece in imitation of Reich's *Clapping Music* for some combination of performers in your class. See the discussion of this work in the text.
3. Try to compose a neoromantic excerpt in imitation of the first movement of Rochberg's String Quartet No. 3. This is a difficult assignment, because the tonal music should not sound silly or mawkish when it enters. Write this for some combination of performers in your class.

## FURTHER READING

COPE, DAVID H. *Techniques of the Contemporary Composer*. See Chapter 21, Decategorization.

GANN, KYLE. *American Music in the Twentieth Century*. See Chapter 8, Minimalism, and Chapter 13, Totalism and the 1990s.

GRIFFITHS, PAUL. *Modern Music and After*. See "Minimalism and Melody," pp. 209–244, and "Strings and Knots," pp. 239–327.

MERTENS, WIM. *American Minimal Music*.

MORGAN, ROBERT P. *Twentieth-Century Music*. See Chapter 20, A Return to Simplicity: Minimalism and the New Tonality.

NYMAN, MICHAEL. *Experimental Music*. See Chapter 7, Minimal Music, Determinacy, and the New Tonality.

REESE, JAY. "Rochberg the Progressive."

SCHWARZ, K. ROBERT. "Steve Reich: Music as a Gradual Process."

SIMMS, BRYAN R. *Music of the Twentieth Century*. See Chapter 16, Recent Music in Europe and America.

WILLIAMS, J. KENT. *Theories and Analyses of Twentieth-Century Music*. See Chapter 17, Minimalism.

# Appendix

**Prime Forms, Forte Labels, and Interval-Class Vectors**

The tables below contain all of the possible prime forms (set classes) that contain three to nine pitch classes. Column 1 displays the prime form of the set class (the letter "T" is used, if necessary, to stand for the number 10). Column 2 contains the Forte label for the set class—that is, the name that Allen Forte gave to the set in *The Structure of Atonal Music*, which is the label that is used in all of the current literature. Column 3 contains the interval-class vector of the set class. The next three columns contain the same information, in reverse order, for the **complement** of that set. The complement of any set of pitch classes includes all of the remaining pitch classes out of the total of twelve. For example, the complement of the black keys of the piano would be the white keys of the piano.

The set classes are arranged numerically by prime form in order to make it easier to find the Forte labels and the interval-class vectors. Forte's original tables arranged the sets by interval-class vector, which explains why the Forte labels seem to be out of order in some cases.

| TRICHORDS | | | | NONACHORDS | |
|---|---|---|---|---|---|
| [012] | 3–1 | <210000> | <876663> | 9–1 | [012345678] |
| [013] | 3–2 | <111000> | <777663> | 9–2 | [012345679] |
| [014] | 3–3 | <101100> | <767763> | 9–3 | [012345689] |

*(continued)*

| TRICHORDS | | | | | NONACHORDS |
|---|---|---|---|---|---|
| [015] | 3–4 | <100110> | <766773> | 9–4 | [012345789] |
| [016] | 3–5 | <100011> | <766674> | 9–5 | [012346789] |
| [024] | 3–6 | <020100> | <686763> | 9–6 | [01234568T] |
| [025] | 3–7 | <011010> | <677673> | 9–7 | [01234578T] |
| [026] | 3–8 | <010101> | <676764> | 9–8 | [01234678T] |
| [027] | 3–9 | <010020> | <676683> | 9–9 | [01235678T] |
| [036] | 3–10 | <002001> | <668664> | 9–10 | [01234679T] |
| [037] | 3–11 | <001110> | <667773> | 9–11 | [01235679T] |
| [048] | 3–12 | <000300> | <666963> | 9–12 | [01245689T] |

| TETRACHORDS | | | | | OCTACHORDS |
|---|---|---|---|---|---|
| [0123] | 4–1 | <321000> | <765442> | 8–1 | [01234567] |
| [0124] | 4–2 | <221100> | <665542> | 8–2 | [01234568] |
| [0125] | 4–4 | <211110> | <655552> | 8–4 | [01234578] |
| [0126] | 4–5 | <210111> | <654553> | 8–5 | [01234678] |
| [0127] | 4–6 | <210021> | <654463> | 8–6 | [01235678] |
| [0134] | 4–3 | <212100> | <656542> | 8–3 | [01234569] |
| [0135] | 4–11 | <121110> | <565552> | 8–11 | [01234579] |
| [0136] | 4–13 | <112011> | <556453> | 8–13 | [01234679] |
| [0137] | 4–Z29 | <111111> | <555553> | 8–Z29 | [01235679] |
| [0145] | 4–7 | <201210> | <645652> | 8–7 | [01234589] |
| [0146] | 4–Z15 | <111111> | <555553> | 8–Z15 | [01234689] |
| [0147] | 4–18 | <102111> | <546553> | 8–18 | [01235689] |
| [0148] | 4–19 | <101310> | <545752> | 8–19 | [01245689] |
| [0156] | 4–8 | <200121> | <644563> | 8–8 | [01234789] |
| [0157] | 4–16 | <110121> | <554563> | 8–16 | [01235789] |
| [0158] | 4–20 | <101220> | <545662> | 8–20 | [01245789] |
| [0167] | 4–9 | <200022> | <644464> | 8–9 | [01236789] |
| [0235] | 4–10 | <122010> | <566452> | 8–10 | [02345679] |
| [0236] | 4–12 | <112101> | <556543> | 8–12 | [01345679] |
| [0237] | 4–14 | <111120> | <555562> | 8–14 | [01245679] |
| [0246] | 4–21 | <030201> | <474643> | 8–21 | [0123468T] |
| [0247] | 4–22 | <021120> | <465562> | 8–22 | [0123568T] |
| [0248] | 4–24 | <020301> | <464743> | 8–24 | [0124568T] |
| [0257] | 4–23 | <021030> | <465472> | 8–23 | [0123578T] |
| [0258] | 4–27 | <012111> | <456553> | 8–27 | [0124578T] |
| [0268] | 4–25 | <020202> | <464644> | 8–25 | [0124678T] |
| [0347] | 4–17 | <102210> | <546652> | 8–17 | [01345689] |
| [0358] | 4–26 | <012120> | <456562> | 8–26 | [0134578T] |
| [0369] | 4–28 | <004002> | <448444> | 8–28 | [0134679T] |

| PENTACHORDS | | | | SEPTACHORDS | |
|---|---|---|---|---|---|
| [01234] | 5–1 | <432100> | <654321> | 7–1 | [0123456] |
| [01235] | 5–2 | <332110> | <554331> | 7–2 | [0123457] |
| [01236] | 5–4 | <322111> | <544332> | 7–4 | [0123467] |
| [01237] | 5–5 | <321121> | <543342> | 7–5 | [0123567] |
| [01245] | 5–3 | <322210> | <544431> | 7–3 | [0123458] |
| [01246] | 5–9 | <231211> | <453432> | 7–9 | [0123468] |
| [01247] | 5–Z36 | <222121> | <444342> | 7–Z36 | [0123568] |
| [01248] | 5–13 | <221311> | <443532> | 7 | 13 [0124568] |
| [01256] | 5–6 | <311221> | <533442> | 7–6 | [0123478] |
| [01257] | 5–14 | <221131> | <443352> | 7–14 | [0123578] |
| [01258] | 5–Z38 | <212221> | <434442> | 7–Z38 | [0124578] |
| [01267] | 5–7 | <310132> | <532353> | 7–7 | [0123678] |
| [01268] | 5–15 | <220222> | <442443> | 7–15 | [0124678] |
| [01346] | 5–10 | <223111> | <445332> | 7–10 | [0123469] |
| [01347] | 5–16 | <213211> | <435432> | 7–16 | [0123569] |
| [01348] | 5–Z17 | <212320> | <434541> | 7–Z17 | [0124569] |
| [01356] | 5–Z12 | <222121> | <444342> | 7–Z12 | [0123479] |
| [01357] | 5–24 | <131221> | <353442> | 7–24 | [0123579] |
| [01358] | 5–27 | <122230> | <344451> | 7–27 | [0124579] |
| [01367] | 5–19 | <212122> | <434343> | 7–19 | [0123679] |
| [01368] | 5–29 | <122131> | <344352> | 7–29 | [0124679] |
| [01369] | 5–31 | <114112> | <336333> | 7–31 | [0134679] |
| [01457] | 5–Z18 | <212221> | <434442> | 7–Z18 | [0145679] |
| [01458] | 5–21 | <202420> | <424641> | 7–21 | [0124589] |
| [01468] | 5–30 | <121321> | <343542> | 7–30 | [0124689] |
| [01469] | 5–32 | <113221> | <335442> | 7–32 | [0134689] |
| [01478] | 5–22 | <202321> | <424542> | 7–22 | [0125689] |
| [01568] | 5–20 | <211231> | <433452> | 7–20 | [0125679] |
| [02346] | 5–8 | <232201> | <454422> | 7–8 | [0234568] |
| [02347] | 5–11 | <222220> | <444441> | 7–11 | [0134568] |
| [02357] | 5–23 | <132130> | <354351> | 7–23 | [0234579] |
| [02358] | 5–25 | <123121> | <345342> | 7–25 | [0234679] |
| [02368] | 5–28 | <122212> | <344433> | 7–28 | [0135679] |
| [02458] | 5–26 | <122311> | <344532> | 7–26 | [0134579] |
| [02468] | 5–33 | <040402> | <262623> | 7–33 | [012468T] |
| [02469] | 5–34 | <032221> | <254442> | 7–34 | [013468T] |
| [02479] | 5–35 | <032140> | <254361> | 7–35 | [013568T] |
| [03458] | 5–Z37 | <212320> | <434541> | 7–Z37 | [0134578] |

## HEXACHORDS

In this table, Z-related sets are listed across from each other. Because Z-related sets by definition have the same interval-class vector, there is only one column of vectors.

| | | | | |
|---|---|---|---|---|
| [012345] | 6–1 | <543210> | | |
| [012346] | 6–2 | <443211> | | |
| [012347] | 6–Z36 | <433221> | 6–Z3 | [012356] |
| [012348] | 6–Z37 | <432321> | 6–Z4 | [012456] |
| [012357] | 6–9 | <342231> | | |
| [012358] | 6–Z40 | <333231> | 6–Z11 | [012457] |
| [012367] | 6–5 | <422232> | | |
| [012368] | 6–Z41 | <332232> | 6–Z12 | [012467] |
| [012369] | 6–Z42 | <324222> | 6–Z13 | [013467] |
| [012378] | 6–Z38 | <421242> | 6–Z6 | [012567] |
| [012458] | 6–15 | <323421> | | |
| [012468] | 6–22 | <241422> | | |
| [012469] | 6–Z46 | <233331> | 6–Z24 | [013468] |
| [012478] | 6–Z17 | <322332> | 6–Z43 | [012568] |
| [012479] | 6–Z47 | <233241> | 6–Z25 | [013568] |
| [012569] | 6–Z44 | <313431> | 6–Z19 | [013478] |
| [012578] | 6–18 | <322242> | | |
| [012579] | 6–Z48 | <232341> | 6–Z26 | [013578] |
| [012678] | 6–7 | <420243> | | |
| [013457] | 6–Z10 | <333321> | 6–Z39 | [023458] |
| [013458] | 6–14 | <323430> | | |
| [013469] | 6–27 | <225222> | | |
| [013479] | 6–Z49 | <224322> | 6–Z28 | [013569] |
| [013579] | 6–34 | <142422> | | |
| [013679] | 6–30 | <224223> | | |
| [023679] | 6–Z29 | <224232> | 6–Z50 | [014679] |
| [014568] | 6–16 | <322431> | | |
| [014579] | 6–31 | <223431> | | |
| [014589] | 6–20 | <303630> | | |
| [023457] | 6–8 | <343230> | | |
| [023468] | 6–21 | <242412> | | |
| [023469] | 6–Z45 | <234222> | 6–Z23 | [023568] |
| [023579] | 6–33 | <143241> | | |
| [024579] | 6–32 | <143250> | | |
| [02468T] | 6–35 | <060603> | | |

STRAUS, JOSEPH N., *Introduction to Post-Tonal Theory*, 3rd Edition, ©2005, pp. 261–264. Reprinted by permission of Pearson Education, Inc., Upper Saddle River, NJ.

# Bibliography

ALDWELL, EDWARD, AND CARL SCHACHTER. *Harmony and Voice Leading*. 2nd ed. New York: Harcourt Brace Jovanovich, 1989.

ANDERTON, CRAIG. *MIDI for Musicians*. New York: Amsco, 1986.

ANTOKOLETZ, ELLIOTT. *Twentieth-Century Music*. Englewood Cliffs, N.J.: Prentice Hall, 1992.

APPLETON, JOHN H., AND RONALD C. PERERA, EDS. *The Development and Practice of Electronic Music*. Englewood Cliffs, N.J.: Prentice Hall, 1975.

AUSTIN, WILLIAM W. *Music in the 20th Century*. New York: W. W. Norton, 1966.

BARTOLOZZI, BRUNO. *New Sounds for Woodwind*. Translated and edited by Reginald Smith Brindle. London: Oxford University Press, 1967.

BATEMAN, WAYNE. *Introduction to Computer Music*. New York: John Wiley, 1980.

BENWARD, BRUCE, AND MARILYN SAKER. *Music in Theory and Practice*. 7th ed. New York: McGraw-Hill, 2003.

BERRY, WALLACE. *Form in Music*. 2nd ed. Englewood Cliffs, N.J.: Prentice Hall, 1986.

———. *Structural Functions in Music*. Mineola, N.Y.: Dover, 1987.

BRINDLE, REGINALD SMITH. *Contemporary Percussion*. London: Oxford University Press, 1970.

———. *Musical Composition*. London: Oxford University Press, 1986.

———. *The New Music*. London: Oxford University Press, 1975.

———. *Serial Composition*. London: Oxford University Press, 1966.

BUNGER, RICHARD. *The Well-Prepared Piano*. Colorado Springs: Colorado College Music Press, 1973.

CARR, IAN. *Miles Davis*. New York: William Morrow, 1982.

CHADABE, JOEL. *Electric Sound: The Past and Promise of Electronic Music*. Englewood Cliffs, N.J.: Prentice Hall, 1996.

CHOU, WEN-CHUNG. "Asian Concepts and Twentieth-Century Western Composers," *Musical Quarterly* 57:2 (April 1971), pp. 211–229.

COGAN, ROBERT. *New Images of Musical Sound*. Cambridge, Mass.: Harvard University Press, 1984.

COGAN, ROBERT, AND POZZI ESCOT. *Sonic Design*. Englewood Cliffs, N.J.: Prentice Hall, 1976.

COPE, DAVID H. *New Directions in Music*. 6th ed. Madison, Wisc. Brown & Benchmark, 1993

———. *Computers and Musical Style*. Madison, Wisc.: A-R Editions, 1991.

———. *Experiments in Musical Intelligence*. Madison, Wisc.: A-R Editions, 1996.

———. *Techniques of the Contemporary Composer*. New York: Schirmer Books, 1997

CRAFT, ROBERT. *Stravinsky: Chronicle of a Friendship, 1948–71*. New York: Alfred A. Knopf, 1972.

DALLIN, LEON. *Techniques of Twentieth Century Composition*. 3rd ed. Dubuque, Iowa: Wm. C. Brown, 1974.

DEMPSTER, STUART. *The Modern Trombone*. Berkeley: University of California Press, 1979.

DE STWOLINSKY, GAIL. *Form and Content in Instrumental Music*. Dubuque, Iowa: Wm. C. Brown, 1977.

DODGE, CHARLES, AND THOMAS A. JERSE. *Computer Music*. New York: Schirmer Books, 1985.

EMMERSON, SIMON, ED. *The Language of Electroacoustic Music*. Chur, Switzerland: Harwood Academic Publishers, 1987.

ERICKSON, ROBERT. *Sound Structure in Music*. Berkeley: University of California Press, 1975.

FINK, ROBERT, AND ROBERT RICCI. *The Language of Twentieth Century Music*. New York: Schirmer Books, 1975.

FORTE, ALLEN. *The Structure of Atonal Music*. New Haven, Conn.: Yale University Press, 1973.

GANN, KYLE. *American Music in the Twentieth Century*. New York: Schirmer Books, 1997.

———. *The Music of Conlon Nancarrow*. Cambridge: Cambridge University Press, 1995.

GARIÉPY, LOUISE, AND JEAN DÉCARIE. "A System of Notation for Electro-Acoustic Music: A Proposition." *Interface* 13:1 (March 1984), pp. 1–74.

GAULDIN, ROBERT. *Harmonic Practice in Tonal Music*. New York: W. W. Norton, 1997

GRIFFITHS, PAUL. *Modern Music and After*. Oxford: Oxford University Press, 1995.

GRIMES, EV. "Ev Grimes Interviews John Cage." *Music Educators Journal* 73:3 (November 1986), pp. 47–49ff.

GROUT, DONALD JAY. *A History of Western Music*. 3rd ed. New York: W. W. Norton, 1980.

HEISS, JOHN C. "Some Multiple-Sonorities for Flute, Oboe, Clarinet, and Bassoon." *Perspectives of New Music* 7:1 (Fall–Winter 1968), pp. 136–142.

HEUSSENSTAMM, GEORGE. *The Norton Manual of Music Notation*. New York: W. W. Norton, 1987.

HICKS, MICHAEL. "Text, Music, and Meaning in the Third Movement of Luciano Berio's *Sinfonia*." *Perspectives in New Music* 20 (1981–1982), pp. 199–224.

HINDEMITH, PAUL. *Craft of Musical Composition*. London: Schott, 1968.

HOWAT, ROY. "Bartók, Lendvai, and the Principle of Proportional Analysis." *Music Analysis* 2:1 (March 1983), pp. 69–95.

HOWE, HUBERT S. *Electronic Music Synthesis*. New York: W. W. Norton, 1975.

HOWELL, THOMAS. *The Avant-Garde Flute*. Berkeley: University of California Press, 1974.

KARKOSCHKA, ERHARD. *Notation in New Music*. Translated by Ruth Koenig. New York: Praeger, 1972.

KENNAN, KENT, AND DONALD GRANTHAM. *The Technique of Orchestration*. 6th ed. Englewood Cliffs, N.J.: Prentice Hall, 2002.

KOSTELANETZ, RICHARD, ED. *John Cage*. New York: Praeger, 1970.

KOSTKA, STEFAN, AND DOROTHY PAYNE. *Tonal Harmony with an Introduction to Twentieth-Century Music*. 5th ed. New York: McGraw-Hill, 2004.

KRAMER, JONATHAN D. "The Fibonacci Series in Twentieth Century Music." *Journal of Music Theory* 17:1 (Spring 1973), pp. 111–148.

———. "Moment Form in Twentieth Century Music." *Musical Quarterly* 64:2 (April 1978), pp. 177–194.

KŘENEK, ERNST. *Studies in Counterpoint*. New York: G. Schirmer, 1940.

LENDVAI, ERNÖ. *Béla Bartók: An Analysis of His Music*. London: Kahn & Averill, 1971.

LESTER, JOEL. *Analytic Approaches to Twentieth-Century Music*. New York: W. W. Norton, 1989.

MACONIE, ROBIN. *The Works of Karlheinz Stockhausen*. London: Oxford University Press, 1976.

MAEGAARD, JAN. "A Study in the Chronology of Op. 23–26 by Arnold Schoenberg." *Dansk aarbog for musikforskning* (1962), pp. 93–115.

MANNING, PETER. *Electronic and Computer Music*. 2nd ed. Oxford: Clarendon Press, 1993.

MERTENS, WIM. *American Minimal Music*. New York: Alexander Broude, 1983.

MESSIAEN, OLIVIER. *The Technique of My Musical Language*. Paris: Alphonse Leduc, 1944.

MORGAN, ROBERT P. *Twentieth-Century Music*. New York: W. W. Norton, 1991.

NYMAN, MICHAEL. *Experimental Music*. New York: Schirmer Books, 1974.

OSMOND-SMITH, DAVID. *Playing on Words*. London: Royal Music Association, 1985.

PARTCH, HARRY. *Genesis of a Music*. 2nd ed. New York: Da Capo, 1974.

PELLMAN, SAMUEL. *An Introduction to the Creation of Electroacoustic Music.* Belmont, Calif.: Wadsworth, 1994.

PERLE, GEORGE. *Serial Composition and Atonality.* 5th ed. Berkeley: University of California Press, 1981.

PERSICHETTI, VINCENT. *Twentieth-Century Harmony.* New York: W. W. Norton, 1961.

PISTON, WALTER. *Harmony.* 5th ed. Revised by Mark DeVoto. New York: W. W. Norton, 1987.

PRESSING, JEFF. *Synthesizer Performance and Real-Time Techniques.* Madison, Wisc.: A-R Editions, 1992.

PROCTOR, GREGORY. "Technical Bases of Nineteenth-Century Chromatic Harmony: A Study in Chromaticism." Ph.D. Diss., Princeton University, 1978.

RAHN, JOHN. *Basic Atonal Theory.* New York: Longman, 1980.

RANDEL, DON ED. *The New Harvard Dictionary of Music.* Cambridge, Mass.: Belknap Press, 1986.

READ, GARDNER. *Contemporary Instrumental Techniques.* New York: Schirmer Books, 1976.

———. *Modern Rhythmic Notation.* Bloomington: Indiana University Press, 1978.

REESE, JAY. "Rochberg the Progressive." *Perspectives of New Music* 19 (1980–81), pp. 394–407.

REID, SARAH. "Tonality's Changing Role: A Survey of Non-Concentric Instrumental Works of the Nineteenth Century." Ph.D. Diss., University of Texas, 1980.

RINGO, JAMES. "The Lure of the Orient." *American Composers Alliance Bulletin* 7:2 (1958), pp. 8–12.

ROADS, CURTIS. *The Computer Music Tutorial.* Cambridge, Mass.: MIT Press, 1996.

ROCKWELL, JOHN. *All American Music.* New York: Alfred A. Knopf, 1983.

SADIE, STANLEY, ED. *The New Grove Dictionary of Music and Musicians.* 2nd ed. London: Oxford University Press, 2001.

SALZEDO, CARLOS. *Modern Study of the Harp.* New York: G. Schirmer, 1921.

SAMSON, JIM. *Music in Transition.* New York: W. W. Norton, 1977.

SCHAEFFER, PIERRE. *Traité des objets musicaux.* Paris: Éditions du Seuil, 1966.

SCHMALFELDT, JANET. *Berg's Wozzeck.* New Haven, Conn.: Yale University Press, 1983.

SCHOENBERG, ARNOLD. *Style and Idea.* Berkeley: University of California Press, 1984.

SCHRADER, BARRY. *Introduction to Electro-Acoustic Music.* Englewood Cliffs, N.J.: Prentice Hall, 1982.

SCHWARTZ, ELLIOTT. *Electronic Music: A Listener's Guide.* New York: Praeger, 1975.

SCHWARZ, K. ROBERT. "Steve Reich: Music as a Gradual Process." *Perspectives of New Music* 19 (1980–81), pp. 373–392; 20 (1981–82), pp. 225–286.

SIMMS, BRYAN R. *Music of the Twentieth Century.* New York: Schirmer Books, 1986.

SLAWSON, WAYNE. *Sound Color.* Berkeley: University of California Press, 1985.

SMITHER, HOWARD E. "The Rhythmic Analysis of Twentieth-Century Music." *Journal of Music Theory* 8:1 (Spring 1964), pp. 54–88.

STEINKE, GREG A. *Bridge to 20th-Century Music*, rev. ed. Needham Heights, Mass.: Allyn & Bacon, 1999.

STONE, KURT. *Music Notation in the Twentieth Century*. New York: W. W. Norton, 1980.

STRAUS, JOSEPH N. *Introduction to Post-Tonal Theory*. 3rd ed. Englewood Cliffs, N.J.: Prentice Hall, 2005.

STRAVINSKY, IGOR. *Poetics of Music*. Cambridge, Mass.: Harvard University Press, 1947.

TURETZKY, BERTRAM. *The Contemporary Contrabass*. Berkeley: University of California Press, 1974.

VAN DEN TOORN, PIETER C. *The Music of Igor Stravinsky*. New Haven, Conn.: Yale University Press, 1983.

VINCENT, JOHN. *The Diatonic Modes in Modern Music*. New York: Mills Music, 1951.

VINTON, JOHN, ED. *Dictionary of Contemporary Music*. New York: E. P. Dutton, 1974.

WEBERN, ANTON. *The Path to the New Music*. Edited by Willi Reich, translated by Leo Black. Bryn Mawr, Pa.: Theodore Presser, 1963.

WILLIAMS, J. KENT. *Theories and Analyses of Twentieth-Century Music*. Fort Worth, Tex.: Harcourt Brace, 1997.

WINOLD, ALLEN. *Harmony: Patterns and Principles*. Englewood Cliffs, N.J.: Prentice Hall, 1986.

WISHART, TREVOR. *On Sonic Art*, rev. ed. Amsterdam: Harwood Academic Publishers, 1996.

WITTLICH, GARY, ED. *Aspects of Twentieth-Century Music*. Englewood Cliffs, N.J.: Prentice Hall, 1975.

WUORINEN, CHARLES. *Simple Composition*. New York: Longman, 1979.

YASSER, JOSEPH. *A Theory of Evolving Tonality*. New York: American Library of Musicology, 1932.

# Index